Europe and the Decline of Spain

EARLY MODERN EUROPE TODAY

Editor: Professor J. H. Shennan

Europe and the Decline of Spain

A Study of the Spanish System, 1580–1720

R. A. STRADLING
Lecturer in History, University College, Cardiff

London
GEORGE ALLEN & UNWIN
Boston   Sydney

First published in 1981

GEORGE ALLEN & UNWIN LTD
40 Museum Street, London WC1A 1LU

© George Allen & Unwin (Publishers) Ltd, 1981

British Library Cataloguing in Publication Data

Stradling, R. A.
 Europe and the decline of Spain. – (Early
 modern Europe today)
 1. Spain – History
 I. Title   II. Series
 946′.05   DP66

ISBN 0-04-940061-4

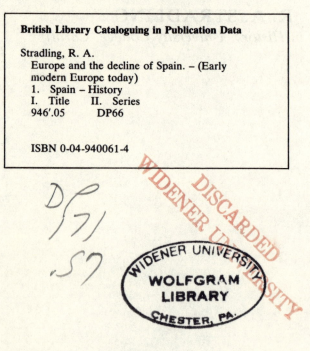

Set in 10 on 11 point Times by Inforum Limited, Portsmouth
and printed and bound in Great Britain by
William Clowes (Beccles) Limited, Beccles and London.

Early Modern Europe Today

In introducing a new historical series it is difficult not to begin by offering some justification for its appearance. Yet if we accept that history is ultimately unknowable in the sense that our perception of the past as distinct from the past itself is forever changing, then no apologia is required. That is certainly the premiss on which this series is posited. In the last several decades the changes have been particularly rapid, reflecting fundamental shifts in social and political attitudes, and informed by the growth of new related disciplines and by new approaches to the subject itself. The volumes contained within this series will seek to provide the present generation of students and readers with up-to-date history; with judgements and interpretations which will no doubt in turn form part of the synthesis of future scholarly revisions. Some of the books will concentrate on previously neglected or unconsidered material to reach conclusions likely to challenge conventional orthodoxies in more established areas of study; others will re-examine some of these conventional orthodoxies to discover whether, in the light of contemporary scholarly opinion, they retain their validity or require more or less drastic reassessment. Each in its own way, therefore, will seek to define and illumine some of the contours of early modern Europe, a coherent period at once remote from our own world yet crucial to an understanding of it. Each will combine considerable chronological range with thematic precision and each, finally, will be completed by a significant bibliographical chapter. It is hoped that this last, prominent feature, which will make the series especially distinctive, will be of value not only to readers curious to explore the particular topic further but also to those seeking information of a wide range of themes associated with it.

To my mother, and the memory of my father

The sea of faith
Was once, too, at the full, and round earth's shore
Lay like the folds of a bright girdle furl'd;
But now I only hear
Its melancholy, long, withdrawing roar

Dover Beach, Matthew Arnold

Acknowledgements

To write at all is never easy, but to research and write a topic in European history from a base in a provincial institution is a task requiring constant encouragement and co-operation. The constraints imposed by excesses of distance and responsibilities and shortages of time and money, have at least produced a degree of personal empathy (perhaps too much) with the problems of a politico-military system which perennially struggled with similar exigencies. My own were somewhat alleviated by an annual research grant from University College, Cardiff, and, at the critical 'conjuncture', by an award from the Twenty-Seven Foundation which enabled me to spend precious time in the archives of Spain and Belgium. Fieldwork apart, the routine business of information-gathering would have been impossible without the efficient service provided by the Inter-Library Loan section of the British Library, compensating as it does in large part for the difficulty of access to a copyright library. My studies in Brussels and Simancas were made more rewarding by the sympathetic assistance of two outstanding archivists, Dr Denise van der Veghde and Doña Adela de Vega.

My greatest intellectual debt is to Albert Lovett, whose intense dedication to our subject, profound knowledge of Habsburg Spain, and voracious curiosity about historical problems represent an example worthy of all imitation. From my earliest apprenticeship in historical research his selfless assistance has been unstinted. Gwyn Williams and John Elliott were generous with advice and support when the life of this book was in its earliest, and thus most vulnerable, stages. The experience of teaching an option course on the Spanish monarchy has continually helped to develop and crystallise ideas. Amongst my students, Kevin Littlewood, Mark Pierce and Jane Surtees, have left impressions on the argument. (The first of these was also good enough to examine much of a first draft.) Joe Shennan stoically performed his appointed task of critically appraising the typescript, which was ultimately prepared, with cool efficiency and patience, by Bina Thompson. The maps were prepared by Howard Mason. An unconventional type of obligation is present in the formal layout of the book. Most practising historians of a certain generation will recognise it as based upon Christopher Hill's peerless study of *The Century of*

Revolution (1961), which justly dominated the seventeenth-century syllabus for so many years. I hope that the pattern of the central chapters will make the contents less difficult of digestion as to the whole and of reference as to the parts. It certainly made the book less difficult to write. Finally, my wife agreed to run a one-parent family more often and for longer periods than is reasonable. The ignorance, errors and misconceptions which remain are entirely my own. So also are all translations from primary and secondary sources in Spanish, French and Italian.

Contents

List of Maps

The Problems and Their Available Data

Though many of its practitioners still cling to a contrary belief, the writing of history will never be the simple exercise in cybernetics that the heading to this introduction may imply. All the same, the phrase does suffice to convey a valid metaphor about the processes of an historian's mind (either subliminal or methodological) in the realisation of his chosen subject. Unlike the closed and finite nature of a mathematical problem, however, an historical topic is an open-ended phenomenon, a jigsaw in which many pieces have been lost, and others not yet even cut. In a sense it is more akin to modern physics, in which the principle of uncertainty has come to be accepted as fundamental. This opening bibliographical essay concerns itself with the main published materials (what are called in the trade 'the secondary sources') out of which grew the present book. It is an attempt to assemble, arrange and describe them for the benefit of those readers who – whether professionally or otherwise – might wish to consider further the issues raised. Of course, the attempt is somewhat invalid, or at least has no abstract validity. Historical knowledge is, inherently and ideally, not susceptible of the artificial division made here for a specific functional purpose. Like the first French Republic, it is 'one and indivisible'; naming of its parts ought not to obscure its necessary unity. Thus the particular descriptive taxonomy adopted below could be potentially misleading, unless the user recognises that many of the works categorised in one section would be equally at home in another, or in all. This caveat applies with special force to the material allocated to the initial section on 'Material Structures'.

Discussion of the various textbooks, monographs and scholarly articles is conducted with strict relevance to the content of this book, as explained in its title and subtitle. Despite one phrase used therein we are not directly concerned with the 'Decline of Spain' in the sense which has come into general use. That is to say, I have not sought to examine the internal socio-economic development of Castile and its dependencies. There is no attempt at an analysis of material infrastructures *per se*. Rather, such evidence has been considered as one component amongst others in the practical functioning of a European system of applied power. It is the internal dynamic and the external expression of Spanish politics – if you like the 'Decline of Spain' as a European problem – which seemed to be in need of reconsideration. It would be correct to regard this theme as a more 'traditional' one than that which has recently obsessed most specialists on Habsburg Spain. Furthermore, it is true that this latter interpretation of the phrase lies behind the mandatory excursions into the Spanish monarchy which remain an essential element of any lecture course or general textbook dealing with post-Reformation Europe. Such treatment, however, is often merely routine and marked with a narrow national perspective; it rarely conveys the convincing impression that Spanish power, pride and prejudice was a central, and largely common, experience of the political communities of early modern Europe. For this reason it is necessary to re-emphasise that the struggle and failure of Spain to maintain a position of hegemony was the most significant international phenomenon of the seventeenth century, having repercussions at almost every level of historical investigation. But, moreover, and more significantly, a considerable amount of postwar research on these levels, as well as directly upon the fabric of the Spanish system itself, has made possible and timely a new interpretative synthesis.

Whatever one's attitude to the still hotly debated theory of 'the general crisis of the seventeenth century' and its successive hypothetical mutations, few would deny that it has produced a vigorous, innovative and long-overdue renaissance of comparative work and thought. Shortly before the war, the American scholar R. B. Merriman (whose volumes on the rise of Spanish power are still greatly stimulating) made a fascinating, if ultimately unsuccessful, attempt to examine intellectual and political 'cross-currents' between the regions of Europe during the mid-century socio-political crisis (A1). Since then, the pursuit of underlying structures and patterns across political boundaries, however experimental in method and speculative in conclusion, has much enlarged the scope of historical explanation. Research of this type, encouraging the production of models and hypotheses, has happily cross-fertilised with the more insular investigation of internal issues within the nation-states. In France and the United Kingdom, above all, the problems of the seventeenth century have produced a greater amount of professional discussion than those of any other before our own. For the former, in particular, this has led to a complete overthrow of a long-dominant orthodoxy, insisting on *le grand siècle* as the era which witnessed the inexorable triumph of Bourbon absolutism and French European ascendancy. The internal weakness and continual crisis of the French state is now seen to be intimately related to the Thirty Years' War – an all-embracing internecine struggle to which the policy and aspirations of Spain were central. In the face of all this, even British historians are showing signs of adopting wider angles of approach and comparative techniques, as witness J. R. Jones's pioneering essay (A2). But, in any case, the difference between the two compendium volumes on the 'General Crisis', which gather together the most valuable contributions to the debate – and are little more than a decade apart – is sufficiently indicative of the greater willingness of historians, whatever their speciality, to take into account the broader panoramas (A3; A4).

The overall growth of a European perspective is thus a major justification for my present theme. Treatment of it would not have been possible, however, without a great rekindling of interest in Habsburg Spain which has taken place since the late 1950s, when the outstanding work of Garrett Mattingly, Domínguez Ortiz and John Elliott was first published, and which has tended to centre on the administrative makeup, management and functioning of the Spanish system. Of course, many areas of this subject remain obscure and unattended – the period following the fall of Olivares, particularly, is still a dark age of almost unrelieved ignorance, representing a lacuna of information which is unequalled in the historiography of any major European nation. Partly for this reason, the present study could not have taken shape without considerable use of primary documentary sources along with some other, less accessible material, both printed and in manuscript. Such sources are given a separate referential sequence throughout the text, and are listed and described in a concluding appendix.

(A1) R. B. Merriman, *Six Contemporaneous Revolutions* (1938).
(A2) J. R. Jones, *Britain and Europe in the Seventeenth Century* (1966).
(A3) T. Aston (ed.), *Crisis in Europe, 1560–1660* (1965).
(A4) G. Parker and L. Smith (eds), *The General Crisis of the Seventeenth Century* (1978).

Material Structures

Despite the many reservations about the *directness and immediacy* of the relationship which are made in the present study, it cannot be questioned that the state of Spain's economy was of fundamental importance to her political survival over the 'long period' it covers. Because of its basic and pervasive influence, therefore, our considerations must begin at this level. Speaking of the economic decline of Spain, in his seminal interpretation published nearly twenty years ago, J. H. Elliott concluded that 'there are always the same cards, however we shuffle them' (B1). The cards have become limp and greasy with use, but the game continues, and its name is Patience. Debate and controversy over the nature of internal decline and its various features is today raging with undiminished energy. This is by no means un-healthy nor unproductive. It can now be seen that Spain's economic malaise was on the whole no different *in character* to that of other European countries, but that, for unique structural reasons, it began earlier, was more intense, and lasted longer. The reader should be aware, on the other hand, that recent investigation suggests no actual collapse of economic enterprise at least until the middle of the century; a proposition which does represent an interesting corrective to the assumptions at present obtaining. A recent reinterpretation of the theme, in part inspired by these tentative indications, is put forward by Henry Kamen (B2), and impinges nodally upon the main concerns we are dealing with. In general terms, however, it is doubtful that an overall synthesis in English of the work of postwar economic historians will be available for many years to come. In the meantime, the book by Jaime Viçens Vives (B3), though it incorporates the views of many of his own pupils from the fields of Catalonia and Valencia, must be regarded as both provisional and incomplete, particularly as regards Castile. A more succinct and directly useful statement of Vives's conclusions, especially enlightening on Spanish commercial perfor-mance, can be found in essay form (B4).

Though many of his ideas and assumptions are now in need of careful modification, the work of the great American economist Earl J. Hamilton is still indispensable, particularly for its accumulation of statistics on silver imports and price levels, (B5; B6). Though monetar-ism seems to be making a comeback, Hamilton's analysis of Spain's problems according to the nostrums of classical economic theory is too schematic and inflexible. Nevertheless, the magisterial summary of his views contained in (B7), despite its fundamental flaw of treating Spain as a 'closed economy', somehow immune to European conditions and trends, is still the yardstick against which newer theories must be tested. Like Hamilton, Pierre Vilar and John Elliott see the reign of Philip III, location of the 'twenty-year crisis of Castile', as of critical importance in the failure of Spanish capitalistic and agricultural development. It seems to the present writer that Vilar's famous essay on Don Quixote, deriving more from the work of French literary structuralists such as Barthes than from the statistical methods of the Sorbonne historians, is a rather overrated piece, but the influence of its perceptions is undeniable (B8). Elliott himself has recently returned to the theme of 'the age of disillusion', as presented in the writings of the Castilian *arbitristas* (B9); and whatever one's reservations about the existence of a collective mentality of depression, it is certainly difficult to avoid the conclusion that this period of conjuncture – defeat, harvest failure, plague, debasement of the coinage and the expulsion of the Moriscos – was one of massive ferment in Castile's history. Elliott's earlier article (B1) remains central, not only for its comments upon the domestic crisis, but as the most stimulating and cogent introduction to seventeenth-century Spain in its European context. In its suggestive treatment of the delicate and complex relationship between Castile's physical resources and imperial commitments it is, in more than one sense, the starting point for the present study.

To go from this little gem to the limitless treasure trove of Fernand Braudel's great recreation of the Mediterranean (B10) may seem a dizzy step. But although the epic sweep of these volumes is an historical experience which no undergraduate – whatever his special interests – should ignore, the huge canvas is constructed with fastidious skill from a myriad pointillistic sections, each having its independent life and characteristics. Not all of Braudel's conclusions are acceptable, and some of his stylistic foibles can be irritating. But every writer on 'the long sixteenth century' (as he terms it) is deeply in Braudel's debt. It was he, above all, who drew our attention to the size and complexity of the Spanish monarchy and its undertakings, who introduced us to the inner workings of its apparatus as well as to the profound and immutable physical structures on which it rested. My own thoughts have derived constant shape and stimulus from the reading and re-reading of this peerless masterpiece.

Whilst Braudel's two volumes *can* be tackled as if they were more or less conventional in format, and are available in excellent translation, neither applies to the work of his compatriot, Pierre Chaunu. The collaboration of Chaunu and his wife, Huguette, on charting and synthesising the documentary record of Seville's trade with the New World was an enterprise of unprecedented scope, a labour from which experts will be able to derive assistance and guidance for generations to come. The series of ten volumes of data and interpretation which resulted was completed in 1960 (B11). By no means all the major implications of Chaunu's achievement have yet been even tentatively explored; and in its original form it is both inaccessible and daunting to the student. Thankfully, a one-volume reduction of the main outlines has recently become available (B12), which (though useful as it stands for its presentation of statistics) seems a prime candidate for rapid translation. In the meantime, an English audience has to make do with the authors' *compte-rendu* reprinted in a recent compendium (B13).

The question of historical demography is one which lies much closer to the heart of a study of the present type. The ability of the Spanish system to mobilise its population in the various departments of the war effort depended intimately upon the size and distribution of that population. Thanks to the painstaking work of historians from France and the UK, as well as Spain, we now have a fairly full and convincing picture of the main trends in population history in the seventeenth century, both as regards Castile and its major dependencies. In the former, at least until mid-century, the trend was one of substantial decline, accompanied by a shift of density to the south and other peripheral regions. Both these factors, stimulated as they were by recurrent subsistence crises, economic slumps and plague epidemics, consistently reduced the fighting power of the Spaniards. A similar process can be observed at work in the major alternative source of manpower to Castile, the kingdom of Naples. Despite recovery in the second half of the century, it is doubtful that either province had regained its population levels of 1590 (respectively about 6 and 2.5 million) by the end of the War of Succession. Though the fundamental importance of population history is now generally recognised, as far as the English reader is concerned Spain lags far behind the rest of western Europe. There exists an excellent short synthesis by Jorge Nadal, drawing upon his own research in Catalonia and that of Domínguez Ortiz from Castile, which would be supremely useful in translation (B14). Domínguez's conclusions on population and society in seventeenth-century Spain are contained in the first volume of his *Sociedad Española*, which appeared in 1963 (B15). For the time being, however, the student can refer with much profit (especially for comparative purposes) to a recent Pelican volume which provides a comprehensive introduction to existing data (B16).

Finally, two excellent general studies of early modern material structures deserve attention. The Fontana volume is the work of several competent hands, which manage (for the most part) stimulating short descriptions of European economic resources, institutions and trends (B17). Henry Kamen's ambitious survey of European social history is in some respects both flawed in accuracy and superficial in judgement, and a second edition is much needed (B18). Even as it stands, however, it is a considerable achievement, displaying a breadth of reading and originality in presentation unusual and refreshing in an English expert on the period. In the wealth of its information and the human concern of its treatment, this book has become indispensable for any serious approach to the seventeenth century.

(B1) J. H. Elliott, 'The decline of Spain', *Past and Present*, no. 20 (1961) (reprinted in A3, above, and elsewhere).

(B2) H. Kamen, 'The decline of Spain: an historical myth?' *Past and Present*, no. 81 (1978).

(B3) J. Viçens Vives, *An Economic History of Spain* (New York, 1959).

(B4) J. Viçens Vives, 'The decline of Spain in the seventeenth century', in C. Cipolla (ed.), *The Economic Decline of Empires* (1970).

(B5) E. J. Hamilton, *American Treasure and the Price Revolution in Spain, 1501–1650* (1934 and reprinted).

(B6) E. J. Hamilton, *War and Prices in Spain, 1651–1800* (1947).

(B7) E. J. Hamilton, 'The decline of Spain', *Economic History Review*, vol. 8 (1938), reprinted in E.M. Carus-Wilson (ed.), *Essays in Economic History*, Vol. 1 (1954).

(B8) P. Vilar, 'The age of Don Quixote', translated and reprinted in P. Earle (ed.), *Essays in Economic History, 1500–1800* (1974).

(B9) J. H. Elliott, 'Self-perception and decline in early seventeenth-century Spain', *Past and Present*, no. 74 (1977).

(B10) F. Braudel, *The Mediterranean and the Mediterranean World in the Age of Philip II*, 2 Vols (1972–4). This translation is based upon the second French edition of 1966, but has some important new material.

(B11) H. and P. Chaunu, *Séville et l'Atlantique, 1504–1650*, 8 Vols in 10 (Paris, 1955–60).

(B12) P. Chaunu, *Séville et l'Amerique 1500–1800* (Paris, 1978).

(B13) H. and P. Chaunu, 'The Atlantic economy and the world economy', translated and reprinted in Earle (see B8, above).

(B14) J. Nadal Oller, *La Población Española; siglos XVI a XX* (Barcelona, 1966).

(B15) A. Domínguez Ortiz. *La Sociedad Española en el siglo XVII*, 2 Vols (Madrid, 1963–9).

(B16) C. McEvedy and R. Jones, *Atlas of World Population History* (1978).

(B17) C. Cipolla (ed.), *The Fontana Economic History of Europe*, Vol. 2 (1974).

(B18) H. Kamen, *The Iron Century: Social Change in Europe, 1550–1660* (1971).

The European Context

Faced with the enormous aggregation of material which the incorporation of new techniques (amongst other things) has caused, the author of any modern survey of seventeenth-century Europe must experience difficulties in selecting and presenting information which are, in the last analysis, intractable. One reaction to this has been the resort to combined operations, both in fieldwork and in compilation of results, a tendency which (in the latter case, at least) began as early as Lord Acton's project for the 'Cambridge Modern History' before the nineteenth century was out. One has a natural sympathy with those confronted by such problems. Nevertheless, from the present point of view, it is essential that such a general textbook is concerned to integrate its treatment of the Spanish monarchy, and its struggle for hegemony, into the overall picture; and, equally important, that Spain's major adversaries in the Fifty Years' War – France and the United Provinces – are handled relevantly and fully. The issues dealt with here cannot be properly grasped without, as it were, this parallel supply of comparative information.

Of the two volumes of the 'New Cambridge Modern History' which deal with this period, the first, edited by the late J. P. Cooper, is by far the more valuable (C1). Both in his stimulating introduction and his purposeful chapter on sea power, Professor Cooper constantly illustrates how Spain occupied and maintained a central position. These brilliant contributions deserve much wider circulation. Ironically, the specifically 'Spanish' chapters are less impressive. J. H. Elliott's, on 'The Spanish Peninsula', was written ten years before the volume (the last to be published) actually appeared, and by then had been completely superseded by his other published work. H. R. Trevor-Roper's essay on 'Spain and Europe' is at once irritating and extremely useful. Irritating because of its characteristic *obiter dicta*, embodying as they do a hopelessly old-fashioned Whig polemic; useful, because of its superb assertiveness and *élan*, rare qualities which add spice to any seminar discussion. And yet, despite its apparent obsolescence, it is notable that the Regius Professor's view of the Spanish system as a Jesuitical plot against the liberties and consciences of Europeans is one that is very closely approached, from a diametrically opposite 'ideological' direction, by that of J. V. Polisensky (C3). The fact that conservative writers like Trevor-Roper and Roland Mousnier (doyen of French seventeenth-century specialists) can agree substantially in terms of basic attitudes with Marxists like Polisensky and Vilar, speaks volumes both of the pervasive effect of Madrid's polity and the traditional, insular, survival of the prejudices to which it gave rise. Returning to our brief: F. L. Carsten's volume in the Cambridge series, though containing Juan Reglà's valuable introduction to later Habsburg Spain, is of limited general usefulness, dealing with the peninsula in time-honoured fashion purely as the object of French war and diplomacy (C2).

The appearance in the 1960s of the first volumes in the 'Fontana History of Europe' series elevated the standards of English-language textbooks to a sensible degree. The student of this period is fortunate in having at his disposal three fine volumes under this imprint which between them cover most of it in exemplary fashion. All three writers are aware – as any post-Braudel student ought to be – that the established apparatus and policy-commitment of Castilian imperialism possessed its own inherent logic, distinct from (though not unrelated to) the specifically domestic crisis. Elliott's book displays a firm and lucid command of international politics in the reign of Philip II (C4). Geoffrey Parker's recent contribution offers a splendidly controlled narrative of the Thirty Years' War, providing a sure and informed guide through its various phases. Though Spanish policy rightly is kept near the centre of attention, the book's construction sometimes impedes clear or profound discussion of the issues at stake (C5). John Stoye's *Europe Unfolding* is wholly admirable in its approach to a relatively neglected period, and incorporates stimulating and analytical comment on Spain's predicament in the crucial mid-century decades (C6).

Another honourable exception to the normal run of textbooks is represented by H. G. Koenigsberger's volume, which is a collection under one cover of three extended essays originally published separately (C7). It is extremely penetrating – indeed indispensable – on Philip II, whilst on Philip IV and the Thirty Years' War, if more superficial, it is equally vigorous in interpretation. Also basically interpretive is the present writer's suggested revision of prevailing assumptions about Spain's performance as a European power, containing the nuclei which are (hopefully) developed in the following pages (C8). Almost inevitably, however, the outstanding work of analysis and reappraisal which has appeared since the war remains untranslated from the French. I refer to Pierre Chaunu's exciting and masterly examination of *La Civilisation de l'Europe Classique*, which covers what might be called 'the long seventeenth century' (*c*. 1620 to *c*. 1760). Its insights into the power, culture and society of *ancien régime* Europe are staggering; it is packed with statistical information, superbly illustrated, and instinct with penetration and perception (C9).

(C1) J. P. Cooper (ed.), *The Decline of Spain and the Thirty Years' War*, *1609–1659*, Vol. 4 of 'New Cambridge Modern History' (1970).
(C2) F. L. Carsten (ed.), *The Ascendancy of France, 1648–1688*, Vol. 5 of 'New Cambridge Modern History' (1961).
(C3) J. V. Polisensky, *The Thirty Years' War* (1974).
(C4) J. H. Elliott, *Europe Divided 1559–1598* (1968).
(C5) G. Parker, *Europe in Crisis, 1598–1648* (1979).
(C6) J. Stoye, *Europe Unfolding, 1648–1688* (1969).
(C7) H. G. Koenigsberger, *The Habsburgs and Europe, 1516–1660* (1971).
(C8) R. A. Stradling, 'Seventeenth-century Spain: decline or survival?', *European Studies Review*, vol. 9 (1979).
(C9) P. Chaunu, *La Civilisation de l'Europe Classique* (Paris, 1966).

Early Modern Spain

The present situation as regards professional investigation into the history of metropolitan Spain in the Habsburg era is healthier than ever before. The old establishment – in which dilettante aristocrats and serving officers, leavened by the odd politician, priest or retired civil servant, dominated historical studies – has now largely broken down. Especially since 1975, the process by which university departments have taken up their proper role in this respect has naturally accelerated. The previous covert 'conditioning' of the subject as regards research and teaching areas has been abandoned. Though this augurs well for the future, Spain is still for the time being the Cinderella of Europe. Neither in quantity nor quality does the amount of published work available to the student even begin to compare with the postwar corpus in the historiography of France, England or the Netherlands. Even in the rendering of its present account, Spanish history has had to rely to an inordinate extent upon the contribution of foreign experts. Nor has pursuit of the subject been galvanised, as elsewhere, by regular outbreaks of strenuous controversy. Whether prevailing conditions in Spanish politics has been *mainly* responsible for this stagnation is not certain; after all, the situation in the case of Italy is, if anything, even worse, despite its vastly different postwar history.

Given the relative poverty of secondary materials, it may be considered paradoxical that a number of textbooks are available to the English reader which are admirable by any standards, and which, in some important respects, tend to complement rather than compete with each other. J. H. Elliott's account of *Imperial Spain* has deservedly become established (D1). Its urbane and lucid presentation of political and religious characteristics is well-nigh definitive, as is the firm delineation of imperial administration. All in all, it is a monument to the continuing traditions and strengths of British scholarship. The criticism that Elliott's relative inattention to the socio-economic infrastructure tends to detract from the book's value is, it seems to me, only partially valid. Considering the general state of knowledge at the time of writing, his information is both full and sound, particularly on the first half of the period covered. A more serious reservation lies in Elliott's exiguous treatment of the later Habsburgs. This deficiency was expressly tackled by J. Lynch in the preparation of his two-volume survey, which also devotes much space to the economic and social record of the seventeenth century (D2). This second volume is partly vitiated by its obsession with a questionable thesis concerning the relationship between the two spheres of the Hispanic world; 'the story of the seventeenth century [is] not the waning of the Hispanic world, but the recession of Spain within that world'. This apart, Professor Lynch's discussion of the major international issues is informative and perceptive. He is alive to the iron constitution of the Spanish body politic, a quality which actually helped to prolong its death-throes, and his book is exceptionally good in assessing the effects of the 'fifty years' war' upon the peninsula. As already implied, his treatment of the later Habsburg period is the fullest and most intelligent to hand in any language. Its value is, moreover, further enhanced by detailed scholarly references which direct the reader to the main sources of published work on its subject. Shortly after the appearance of Lynch's second volume, the distinguished Madrid historian Antonio

Domínguez Ortiz – none of whose many and varied contributions had previously been accessible to the non-Spanish reader – offered a new and invigorating synthesis (D3). Though it stops short at 1659, two-thirds of its content is devoted to what is nowadays termed 'structural analysis', comprising the most detailed and valuable summary yet to be made available in English. Somewhat more old-fashioned, no doubt, in current estimation, but still to my mind fresh and imaginative, is the approach of M. Deforneaux, which operates within the context of 'culture and society' (D4). This draws upon, and liberally quotes from, the surviving documentation of the Habsburg era which lies outside the official world of the state papers; the unparalleled body of imaginative prose, social and moral disquisitions, correspondence and memoirs – in short the rich effusion of a print- and publicity-conscious people. Finally, all students of Spanish history (of whatever period) ought to be familiar with the most inspired and cogent introduction to the subject happily translated from its author's contribution to the renowned French series 'Que Sais-Je? (D5).

(D1) J. H. Elliott, *Imperial Spain, 1469–1719* (1963 and reprinted).
(D2) J. Lynch, *Spain under the Habsburgs*, Vol. 1: *Empire and Absolutism, 1516–98* (1964); Vol. 2: *Spain and America, 1598–1700* (1969).
(D3) A. Domínguez Ortiz, *The Golden Age of Spain, 1516–1659* (1971).
(D4) M. Deforneaux, *Daily Life in Spain in the Golden Age* (1970).
(D5) P. Vilar, *Spain: A Brief History* (1967 and reprinted).

Aspects of the Spanish System

Since Braudel's *Mediterranean*, first published in 1949, opened up so many new and previously unsuspected areas of exploration, there has been a steady augmentation of our knowledge of both the static and dynamic elements of Spanish imperialism. Broadly speaking, there has been an interesting division of labour along characteristic national lines. French or French-trained specialists have worked on its material aspects – population, commerce, banking and finance. British researchers have, by and large, concentrated on administrative and institutional areas. The American school has (until recently) specialised in politics and diplomacy. Native historians, led by the figures of Antonio Domínguez Ortiz, and Jaime Viçens Vives, have during the last generation moved rapidly towards greater self-sufficiency, so to speak. Though it is doubtless proper that their involvement should have become less essential, Habsburg Spain has traditionally and aptly been, more than any other subject, the domain of the historical international brigades. And this did not begin with the consuming passions of the 1930s themselves. Prescott pointed out more than a century ago, for example, that 'English writers have done more for the illustration of Spanish history than for that of any other, except their own'.

(1) *Policies and People*

Rumours of the death of political history, reputedly withering under the scathing contempt of the Parisian radicals, have thankfully been much exaggerated. In particular, its most maligned branch, the study of international diplomacy (once the pampered plant of any syllabus), has been saved from atrophy by the inspiration of one man, the American scholar Garrett Mattingly. Though gifted *par excellence* with powers of narrative, Mattingly was also a deeply reflective thinker, capable of making nonsense of fashionable claims about the triteness and superficiality of 'the history of events'. His *Renaissance Diplomacy* is at once a profound analysis of institutional evolution and a contribution to the history of ideas (E1). The book's many insights and perspectives derive at base from Mattingly's unrivalled knowledge of the Spanish diplomatic network, the personalities who staffed it and the principles which informed it. It remains essential reading for those in search of a firmer grasp of the development of the European state system from the shattered unity of mediaeval Christendom, and especially the complex and ambiguous central role played by the Spanish monarchy. It would be idle to pretend that Mattingly's pupils inherited all his talents. For example, C. H. Carter's monograph on the diplomacy of Philip III is little more than a series of intricate spy stories which, though absorbing in their interrelationship, cast only a glimmer of light upon the inner workings of policy (E2). The efforts of Carter, Loomie and De Lamar Jensen, examples of which are collected in the Mattingly *Festschrift*, help, it is true, to build up a picture of the enormous scale and variety of Madrid's diplomatic involvement in the politics of Europe (E3). But Carter's own study of one of its greatest executants, the celebrated Count of Gondomar (prelude to a long-awaited biography), is disappointing, and adds little to his mentor's earlier portrait (E4).

Nevertheless, the study of international relations as expressed through the medium of diplomacy has become much more than the mere description of the political games of a privileged caste. Its intimate relationship to a variety of vested interests, its sensitivity to change, and its dependence on a complex machinery of policy-making are all factors illustrated, for example, in B. Chudoba's investigation of the Spanish Habsburgs' contacts with their central European cousins (E5). Chudoba's outline has since been much amplified by the work of Polisensky (above, C3), the late Peter Brightwell, and M. Fraga Iribarne (E6). These scholars have considerably extended our knowledge of the origins of the Thirty Years' War, and the key involvement of Madrid in the affairs of 'Germany' during its earlier phases; an involvement attested, not just by the vast (and still comparatively untapped) body of official papers in the Spanish state archives at Simancas, but by collections of primary material in Czechoslovakia, Austria and Bavaria.

The mainsprings of policy were all the same at Madrid, a prerogative firmly reasserted from the beginning of the ministry of Philip IV's chief adviser, the Count-Duke of Olivares. Since the appearance in 1963 of J. H. Elliott's magisterial monograph (E7) our whole approach to the rule of the much-maligned Don Gaspar de Guzmán has been revolutionised, a development dealt with in its historiographical context below (pp. 85–88). This superb book is, of course, much more than a study of policy. It provides, *inter alia*, the most rigorous regional analysis for the Spanish peninsula in this critical period that exists in any language. In its treatment of a locality's reactions to the pressures of war it is a vital contribution to our knowledge of the European crisis. Yet the author never loses sight of the central concern of his theme (as expressed in the subtitle); his research constantly and dramatically illustrates the steadily escalating problems of the Madrid government in the years leading up to 1640. It still constitutes the only direct examination of Olivares's policy deployed on a larger canvas. Unfortunately, it has not led to an increase in scholarly interest in this great and fascinating figure commensurate with his stature, or that of Elliott's book, not to mention the unflagging obsession with Richelieu and (lately) Mazarin. Elliott himself has subsequently filled out various aspects of the count-duke's political rationale in two stimulating and tantalising essays (E8 and E9). But pending the completion of Elliott's own full-scale career biography, the standard study of Olivares's 'life and times' remains that of Gregorio Marañón (E10), characteristically rich in personal detail and psychological speculation, but poverty-stricken in political interpretation. Despite its many frustrations, however, the fact merits mention that a condensed version of this book is available in a cheap edition which could be tackled by anyone with an A-level reading knowledge of Spanish (E11).

For all the dynamic influence of Olivares upon the events of the 1620s, it has now been firmly established that he had no part in the original decision to renew the struggle against the United Provinces in 1621. This fateful development has now been thoroughly examined by Dr Brightwell, whose formulation of the phrase 'the Spanish system' the present author has so promiscuously expropriated (E12). Much new and useful information concerning the policy-decisions and disagreements of Olivares's first (and superficially triumphant) years of direction is contained in Ródenas Vilar's monograph, which selects a rather arbitrary chronological slice (E13); whilst the disastrous final years dominate the terribly unstructured, but still essential, cogitations of Cánovas del Castillo (E14). Despite its obscurities of style and presentation, Cánovas's work, the fruit of a lifetime's study, yet seems to me fundamentally sound at the purely political level. Moreover, it still provides the basis for any treatment of policy in the hugely neglected second half of Philip IV's long reign. A recent overview of the whole reign has some solid merits, particularly in devoting space to the Italian dimension in its narrative treatment of the monarchy's fifty years' war against its European rivals (E15). But, despite the use of certain French documentary sources ignored by other specialists, it succeeds in casting very little new light upon the ministry of Olivares's putative successor, Don Luis de Haro. Some evidence for an interpretation of the Haro period and the policies of the 1650s and 1660s is considered in an article by the present writer, who has also dealt with a vital area of Madrid's concern (the problematic Anglo-Portuguese connection) during the gloomy final stages of struggle for great-power status (E16 and E17).

The strictly (not to say crudely) materialistic interpretation of Spain's struggle and defeat in the crucible of Flanders, put forward above all by Pierre Chaunu, must, despite its exclusive accent on monocausality, be considered in any overall assessment (E18). For Chaunu, both the formulation of policy in Madrid, and the fate of its execution in war, derived intimately and ultimately from the fluctuating cycles of Atlantic trade and imports of silver. A more fertile and less schematic reading of the dependence of policy on the Atlantic connection, representing a valuable primary corrective to Chaunu, is advanced in J. H. Elliott's ingenious article, which concentrates mainly on the Olivares period (E19).

As for the reign of Carlos II, here the curtain descends almost completely. Maura's two-volume chronicle, in all essentials the same as an account first published forty years earlier, still holds this obscured stage (E20). Theatrical allusions are well-nigh irresistible on this baroque subject, if only because Maura's descriptive vignettes of the *dramatis personae* of the Caroline court are reminiscent of many versions of its contemporary English equivalent. None of the latter can claim, however, to have provided the basis for a West End flop, virtually the only distinction of a shameless English digest of Maura produced, apparently, by a nonentity (E21). Considerably more acute and revealing than Maura on the policy dilemmas of the period – though this, lamentably, is not saying very much – is one of several valuable contributions to Spanish history by the German scholar, Ludwig Pfandl (E22). Of an altogether different order of distinction there are J. Maravall's thought-provoking essays upon an earlier phase of that now-resurgent phenomenon, Castilian nationalism. They provide a tentative examination of those insular and isolationist attitudes, cutting right across the normal assumptions of policy, which sprang to the surface in the last years of the last Habsburg (E23). It should be pointed out, too, that many of the studies discussed in the following subsection contain, as an integral element, discussions and interpretations of policy, above all in the Olivares period.

(E1) G. Mattingly, *Renaissance Diplomacy* (1955 and reprinted).
(E2) C. H. Carter, *The Secret Diplomacy of the Habsburgs, 1598–1625* (1964).
(E3) C. H. Carter (ed.), *From the Renaissance to the Counter-Reformation. Essays in Honour of Garrett Mattingly* (1966).
(E4) C. H. Carter, 'Gondomar: Ambassador to James I', *Historical Journal*, vol. 7 (1964).
(E5) B. Chudoba, *Spain and the Empire, 1519–1643* (1952).
(E6) M. Fraga Iribarne, *Don Diego de Saavedra y Fajardo y la Diplomacía de su Época* (Madrid, 1955).
(E7) J. H. Elliott, *The Revolt of the Catalans: A Study in the Decline of Spain (1598–1640)* (1963).
(E8) J. H. Elliott, 'The statecraft of Olivares', in idem and H. G. Koenigsberger (eds), *The Diversity of History* (1970).
(E9) J. H. Elliott, *El Conde-Duque de Olivares y la Herencia de Felipe II* (Valladolid, 1977).
(E10) G. Marañón, *El Conde-Duque de Olivares: la Pasión de Mandar* (3rd edn, Madrid, 1952).
(E11) G. Marañón, *El Conde-Duque de Olivares* (Austral edn, Madrid, 1969).
(E12) P. Brightwell, 'The Spanish system and the Twelve Years' Truce', *English Historical Review*, vol. 89 (1974).
(E13) R. Ródenas Vilar, *La Política Europea de España durante la Guerra de Treinta Años, 1624–30* (Madrid, 1967).
(E14) A. Cánovas del Castillo, *Estudios sobre el Reinado de Felipe IV*, 2 Vols (Madrid, 1888–9).
(E15) M. Devèze, *L'Espagne de Phillipe IV (1621—65)*, 2 Vols (Paris, 1970–1).
(E16) R. Stradling, 'A Spanish statesman of appeasement: Medina de las Torres and Spanish policy, 1639–70', *Historical Journal*, vol. 19 (1976).
(E17) R. Stradling, 'Spanish conspiracy in England, 1661–63', *English Historical Review*, vol. 87 (1972).
(E18) P. Chaunu, 'Séville et la "Belgique", 1555–1648', *Revue du Nord*, vol. 42 (1960).
(E19) J. H. Elliott, 'América y el problema de la decadencia española', *Anuario de Estudios Americanos*, vol. 28 (1971).
(E20) Gabriel, duque de Maura, *Vida y Reinado de Carlos II*, 2 Vols (Madrid, 1954).
(E21) J. Nada, *Carlos the Bewitched* (1962).

(E22) L. Pfandl, *Carlos II*, trans. M. Galiano (Madrid, 1947).
(E23) J. Maravall, *La Oposición Política bajo las Austrias* (Madrid, 1974).

(2) *The System at War*

In the course of the last decade, the exceptional industry of Geoffrey Parker, both as researcher and writer, has brought to our attention a plethora of previously hidden details concerning the military functioning of Spanish power. It is remarkable, when one considers that the examination of this aspect of their imperial past has always been an obsession of traditional Spanish historians, how much of the iceberg had remained submerged until the publication of Parker's work upon the army of Flanders (F1). The value of the book is enhanced by the fact that its absorbing analysis of army organisation – command, composition, supply, transport, ancillary services and internal sociology – is set firmly into the context of the chronological phases of the whole 'eighty years' war' in the Low Countries, and the policy dynamic which lay behind it. Moreover, it reveals, as rarely before, the intensity and scale of Castile's spiritual and material commitment to a successful ultimate settlement. Inevitably, given the range of relevant topics, some are only lightly touched upon; and the author's grasp of the period of renewed war in Flanders (after 1621) is less impressive than that displayed for the sixteenth century. But Dr Parker himself has subsequently remedied several shortcomings (if such they are) in a series of scholarly articles, now usefully collected in one volume (F2). The essays range from the most detailed and esoteric kind of 'extended footnote', to examples which involve the use of the widest of wide-angled lenses. Of particular interest are 'Why did the Dutch Revolt last so long?', 'The Dutch Revolt and the polarisation of international politics', and, notably, its author's original contribution to *Past and Present*, 'Spain, her enemies, and the Revolt of the Netherlands'. The first two of these deploy material especially concerned with what is often called the 'Dutch period' of the Thirty Years' War (1621–31).

Also included in the above collection is the intriguing exercise in 'counter-factual' history, 'If the Armada had landed'. Utterly heretical though its technique may be to many, there is no denying that it helps to highlight many aspects of reality – just as an outstanding work of imaginative 'fiction' often does. What is underlined in this instance is the sheer hitting power, weight and mobility of Spain's forces. The strengths and weaknesses of the instruments of war available to Madrid, as epitomised in the Invincible Armada, have been vividly and dramatically illustrated by the exploits of the marine archaeologists, upon whose expert work Dr Parker has drawn (F3; F4). This invaluable new area of investigation has meant little less than the establishment of a fresh body of evidence, of a kind which is increasingly coming to complement and cross-fertilise with the documentary sources. It happens also, by way of bonus, to be one of intrinsic challenge and excitement, both for practitioner and reader. Although much of this research was unavailable to Mattingly in the preparation of his marvellous book (F5), he nevertheless anticipated many of its conclusions; both in general, such as the astonishing complex of problems confronted and overcome, and the relative efficiency of Spanish planning in large-scale amphibious operations, and in particular, such as the individual courage and expertise of the commanders, above all the naval officers. *The Defeat of the Spanish Armada* is one of very few works of history which, whilst based upon profound scholarship and embodying brilliant reinterpretation, have yet (deservedly) become popular classics.

As suggested above, the armada of 1588 is an epitome of the Spanish system, both 'pure' and 'applied'. The work of both Mattingly and Parker has pointed up the necessary element of interdependence (in terms of strategic thinking) and liaison (in terms of tactical operations) between the terrestrial and maritime aspects of Spain's war effort. The persistence of these considerations is the subject of a recent Spanish monograph (F6) which provides, in many ways, the maritime equivalent to Parker's *Army of Flanders*. It concentrates upon the second phase of Spain's war against the Dutch – so often subsumed in general treatment of the Thirty Years' War – utilising a mass of material from the Spanish archives to construct a convincing picture of the amazing resilience and resourcefulness of the naval establishment during a period when Castile's military strength, especially its maritime aspect, is usually written off. Whilst this major contribution remains untranslated, the English student can approach its subject via a series of recent articles (F7; F8; F9). The first of these offers a tantalising glimpse of the solid practical services that English sources (official and otherwise) provided to the Spaniards on the 'western approaches' to the Low Countries; the second considers Madrid's maritime-economic campaign against the Dutch; and the third attempts to question the legendary status of the battles of the Downs and Rocroi as definitive in terms of the military failure of Spain. The message of reappraisal has now, it is gratifying to note, reached the domain of the 'pure' military historian, as witness a new and thorough examination of the whole 'eighty years' war' in the Netherlands (F10).

The picture is unfortunately much less complete for Spain's other important theatres of war. Some light is incidentally thrown upon the central European aspect by J.V. Polisensky's latest compilation, which is in essence a bibliographical and statistical appendix to his earlier study (F11; C3, above). (Of course, some new material exists, more or less inaccessibly, in Czech and German periodicals.) As for the vortex of internecine peninsular war into which Castile's energies were sucked in the mid-century decades, the only reliable modern study is that of Sanabre on the Catalan struggle (F12). A later peninsular war is described succinctly, yet with some necessary detail, by H. Kamen in the book noted in the following subsection (G6, below). Surprisingly there is no recent general account of the most significant war of all, the purely Franco-Spanish conflict of 1635–59; less surprising is the total neglect of the wars in Italy, at least from the Spanish point of view.

(F1)   G. Parker, *The Army of Flanders and the Spanish Road: The Logistics of Spanish Victory and Defeat, 1567–1659* (1972 and reprinted).
(F2)   G. Parker, *Spain and the Netherlands, 1559–1659: Ten Studies* (1979).
(F3)   C. Martin, *Full Fathom Five: Wrecks of the Spanish Armada* (1975).
(F4)   R. Sténuit, *Treasures of the Armada* (1972).
(F5)   G. Mattingly, *The Defeat of the Spanish Armada* (1959 and reprinted).
(F6)   J. Alcalá-Zamora, *España, Flandes, y el Mar del Norte, 1618–39* (Barcelona, 1975).
(F7)   H. Taylor, 'Trade, Neutrality, and the English Road, 1630–48', *Economic History Review*, 2nd series, vol. 25 (1972).
(F8)   J. Israel, 'A conflict of empires: Spain and the Netherlands, 1618–1648', *Past and Present*, no. 76 (1977).
(F9)   R. Stradling, 'Catastrophe and recovery: the defeat of Spain, 1639–43', *History*, vol. 64 (1979).
(F10)   C. Duffy, *Siege Warfare: The Fortress in the Early Modern World 1494–1660* (1979).
(F11)   J. V. Polisensky, *War and Society in Europe, 1618–48* (1978).
(F12)   J. Sanabre, *La Acción de Francia en Cataluña en la pugna por la hegemonía de Europa, 1640–1659* (Barcelona, 1956).

(3) *Administration, Central and Provincial*

Although the theme of 'government', in the central sense of the consultative and executive apparatus at Madrid, receives excellent coverage in the textbooks by Elliott and Domínguez Ortiz noted above (D1; D3), a distinct absence of specialist studies is apparent. Nevertheless, a huge gap has been filled by Dr Thompson's painstaking and often perceptive examination of the vast 'underworld' of officialdom and capitalism which laboured, never entirely harmoniously, to produce, organise and direct the men and materials of war (G1). Focusing upon the concerns of the Council of War within the peninsula, the book nevertheless provides a wealth of detail of relevance to the Spanish war effort in general, emanating from years of research in regional as well as central repositories. Its author is, perhaps understandably, less sanguine than some current commentators (myself included) on the question of Spain's great-power survival. In particular, the book cites many examples of the malfunctioning of the internal machinery, doubtless archaic and convoluted as it in many ways was, under the appalling strain of Philip II's escalating war policy. But it also catalogues the ceaseless and unremitting struggle of Spanish government against corruption, inefficiency and insufficiency – a veritable war within a war in which success did not always elude them.

The later period of Philip II's management of the Spanish monarchy, and especially the workings of his secretariat and the ministers and councils they serviced, is illuminated by A. W. Lovett's career study of the greatest of Antonio Pérez's successors, Mateo Vázquez (G2). For the early reign of Philip III, we have the rather densely argued article by P. Williams; which, however, is a preview of a full-scale study of the Habsburg conciliar system which promises to be both revelatory and definitive (G3). With the exception of Olivares (and even that, as we have seen, is a partial one) none of the grand *validos*, or chief ministers, of the seventeenth-century Habsburgs has proved grand enough to justify a major biography; a consummation which, had they guessed it, would have considerably upset Lerma and Don Juan José, if not Don Luis de Haro. F. T. Valiente's approach to the *valimiento* as an institution of government is occasionally informative, though in its attempt to pose as a comprehensive monograph instead of an extended essay it often falls into tendentiousness (G4). It remains, however, the only worthwhile book on Lerma and Haro as politicians, pending the (perhaps impossible) study of them as statesmen.

On a different plane altogether there is the masterly work of Domínguez Ortiz on the public finance of the reign of Philip IV (G5). Casting a powerful light upon almost every aspect of government and policy, and particularly searching in the field of money- and credit-supply for the desperate needs of imperial defence, this is a truly seminal book. As will be obvious to the informed reader, my debt to Henry Kamen's pioneering and wideranging work on the early Bourbon period (G6) is equally great. Like Domínguez, Dr Kamen has performed an essential yet enormous task in tackling the intractable records of a confused and neglected subject. The result is that boon for the student, a detailed yet lucid analysis of administration and finance which, at the same time, provides useful summaries of the political background. Many of the book's concerns also have the extra advantage of casting a backward glance at the later Habsburg period, which considerably adds to its value, given the current dire condition of the reign of Carlos II – a situation, by the way, which Dr Kamen himself is currently set upon improving.

Despite the inarguably dominant role of Castile within its structure, the present study none the less attempts to consider the Spanish monarchy as an entity. Such an undertaking, though still fraught with problems of source material, has been made much more viable than it was only a decade ago. Largely responsible for this is the growth in what (for want of a better word) may be termed 'regional' history. Since Elliott's *Revolt of the Catalans* showed the way for Spain, other major dependencies of the crown have been examined against the background of their relationship with Madrid and its imperial dilemmas. The ambiguous 'constitutional' relationship between Madrid and Brussels, for example, has been explored by C. H. Carter (G7) and by G. Parker and H. de Schepper (reprinted in F2, above). Both conclude that the independence of the 'Belgian' Archdukes (1598–1621) was limited and conditional; but that Brussels did in practice enjoy a reciprocal political contact with Madrid that was not, on the whole, reproduced elsewhere. It is true that, perhaps until the mid-1620s individual viceroys (like Feria in Milan and Osuna in Naples) could and did influence and/or ignore the policy of the central government. But the relative autonomy of Flanders persisted even into the period of the Olivares 'dictatorship', during the sole rule of Isabella (1621–33) and that of her successor, Don Fernando (1635–41). Madrid's usually tactful handling of Flemish susceptibilities did much to strengthen the Spanish Netherlands as a bulwark of the system. The frustrations of this development for their 'kith and kin' in the north can still be detected in the standard account, which flies in the face of 'the edict of history' by treating the Low Countries as a single entity (G8). Geyl's own version of the counter-factual method nevertheless offers an essential different perspective.

The most recent of provincial studies is J. Casey's on Valencia, 'the loyal kingdom' crippled by the expulsion of the Moriscos in 1609 (G9). Since Dr Casey's theme tends to lack a focal point of crisis like 1640 (the Valencian establishment actually co-operated in the expulsion campaign) his material inevitably arranges itself in a manner which tends to lack general interest and relevance to the main themes of the present book. (Moreover there is still nothing worthy of note on the important subject of the Portuguese revolt.) Much more directly comparable to Elliott's work on Catalonia is R. Villari's brilliant account of Naples under the Spanish viceroys (G10). This is the most comprehensive treatment to date of an extra-peninsular province during the crucial era of war and revolution. It gives a superb and well-documented account of the fiscal exploitation of the Regno after 1618, and its tracing of the development of Naples' great socio-political crisis in the 1640s is of tremendous value. Several of the themes broached by Villari are currently under investigation by Italian specialists; the crass neglect of their own seventeenth-century history by Italian scholars will shortly be a thing of the past. In this connection, Domenico Sella's new study of the Milanese, though it appeared too late for my use, must be noted (G11). In the absence of any general modern work in English on the Italian peninsula, the reader must fall back upon H. M. Vernon's sentimental and convoluted account of political and military events (G12), supplemented in particular areas by D. Mack Smith (G13, a delightful volume), and the detailed studies of H. G. Koenigsberger, on Spanish Sicily (G14; G15).

(G1) I. A. A. Thompson, *War and Government in Habsburg Spain, 1580–1620* (1976).

(G2) A. W. Lovett, *Philip II and Mateo Vázquez de Leca: The Government of Spain, 1572–92* (Geneva, 1977).

(G3) P. Williams, 'Philip III and the restoration of Spanish government, 1598–1603', *English Historical Review*, vol. 88 (1973).

(G4) F. T. Valiente, *Los Validos en la Monarquía Española del siglo XVII* (Madrid, 1963).

(G5) A. Domínguez Ortiz, *Política y Hacienda de Felipe IV* (Madrid, 1960).

(G6) H. Kamen, *The War of Succession in Spain, 1700–1715* (1969).

(G7) C. H. Carter, 'Belgian "autonomy" under the archdukes', *Journal of Modern History*, vol. 36 (1964).

(G8) P. Geyl, *The Netherlands in the Seventeenth Century*, 2 Vols (1961–4).

(G9) J. Casey, *The Kingdom of Valencia in the Seventeenth Century* (1979).

(G10) R. Villari, *La Rivolta Antispagnola a Napoli, 1585–1647* (Bari, 1967).

(G11) D. Sella, *Crisis and Continuity: The Economy of Spanish Lombardy in the Seventeenth Century* (1979).

(G12) H. M. Vernon, *Italy from 1494 to 1790* (1909).

(G13) D. Mack Smith, *The History of Sicily, 800–1715* (1971).

(G14) H. G. Koenigsberger, *The Government of Sicily under Philip II* (1951).

(G15) H. G. Koenigsberger, 'The revolt of Palermo, 1647', reprinted in *Estates and Revolutions* (1971).

(4) Intellectual and Artistic Currents

Now that the traditional thesis of the 'Scientific Revolution of the Seventeenth Century' is under attack, Spain's undoubted lack of contribution to it somehow assumes less importance. Moreover, it has never *quite* been realised that in the school of Salamanca, Castile can claim to have nurtured the minds which brought into being the social sciences, by inventing the 'dismal science' of economics. A useful layman's introduction to the thought of this helpless species, just as subject to public ridicule in the land and time of their origin as they are everywhere today, is contained in a recent survey (H1).

The Spain of this period was also at the centre of the ferment of thought and expression that we now call 'the baroque movement'. Amongst other things, the baroque embodied an intense and pervasive propaganda weapon for the monarchy's political prejudices and spiritual values. José Maravall's profound interpretation places Philip IV and his court firmly at the apex of this phenomenon (H2). Some idea of the relationship between thought and action can be grasped through H. Trevor-Roper's more limited and conventional – though still suggestive – approach to the world of Peter Paul Rubens (H3). Rubens was the quintessential baroque painter, an overt (though not uncritical) advocate of the aspirations of Habsburg Catholicism. These very tendencies have encouraged both deprecation and ignorance of the baroque by art historians and historians of ideas in this country. The 'opposing camp' is, however, inadequately dealt with, and awaits its general interpreter (see, however, C9 above). A recent study of the Black Legend, for example, is limited, superficial, and extremely mundane in approach (H4). H. G. Koenigsberger has attempted an intriguing assessment of the continued cultural dynamic of Italy for long after the close of the 'classical' Renaissance (reprinted in G15 above), which studies the osmosis of energy from material to spiritual investment. Though it has some useful references to Spain and is neat in format P. Skrine's introduction to the baroque strikes me as somewhat old-fashioned and uninspired (H5). There is a good survey of the major schools of painting (H6); and an excellent study of the most original and influential of all baroque artefacts, the opera (H7). The various genres of Spanish Golden Age literature are comprehensively treated in P. Russell's valuable compendium (H8).

As an international force, spearheading universal attitudes (if not universalist ambitions), the Spanish monarchy made its impression upon the political thought of the period, a process thoroughly examined in a recent monograph (H9). More specific and less subtle types of propaganda – the war of words engaged by more or less talented hacks – receive attention in an older study by J. M. Jover (H10). This unusual and informative book concentrates on the French declaration of war against Spain in 1635 – a critical point, the writer cogently argues, in the reshaping of ideas away from assumptions of mediaeval Christendom towards a more nationally orientated world of loyalty and belief; the world of *raison d'état*, but something more. In Jover's view, 1635 – like 1898 – produced a new generation of politicians, whose residual illusions about the *Res Publica Christiana* had been finally shattered, a still poorly considered aspect of the failure of the Spanish system. Lastly, Professor Mousnier's searching study (H11) explores the fanatic world of competing ideologies, both religious and nationalist, centred on what was the most significant event of the early seventeenth century.

(H1)   M. Grice-Hutchinson, *Early Economic Thought in Spain, 1177–1740* (1978).
(H2)   J. Maravall, *La Cultura del Barroco* (Madrid, 1975).
(H3)   H. R. Trevor-Roper, *Princes and Artists: Patronage and Ideology at Four Habsburg Courts, 1517–1633* (1976).

(H4) W. Maltby, *The Black Legend in England: The Development of Anti-Spanish Sentiment, 1558–1660* (Durham, NC, 1971).

(H5) P. Skrine, *The Baroque: Literature and Culture in Seventeenth-Century Europe* (1978).

(H6) G. Bazin, *Baroque and Rococo* (1964).

(H7) M. Robinson, *Opera Before Mozart* (1966 and reprinted).

(H8) P. Russell (ed.), *A Companion to Spanish Studies* (1973).

(H9) L. Diez del Corral, *La Monarquía hispanica en el pensamiento político Europeo* (Madrid, 1975).

(H10) J. M. Jover, *1635: Historia de una polémica y semblanza de una generación* (Madrid, 1949).

(H11) R. Mousnier, *The Assassination of Henry IV. The Tyrannicide Problem and the Consolidation of the French Absolute Monarchy in the Early Seventeenth Century* (1973).

The Philippine
Empire and Europe 1580–1610

> Though it has great territories, great riches, and great power, it has also huge expenses, powerful enemies and many responsibilities, which oblige it every year, not only to spend what it gains, but even to run up a grand debt. (The monarchy according to an Italian observer, 1602)[1]

> An English spy in Madrid: 'Does Philip ever cease to work?'
> Philip II: 'I have written forty letters in my own hand this morning.' (From Alexander Korda's film *Fire Over England*, 1937)

Policy and Government

It would, perhaps, be an overstatement to say that King Philip II *created* the system of Spanish hegemony in Europe. Using the X-ray of hindsight, we can observe the embryo developing during the reign of the Emperor Charles V; the outline of its bone structure can be detected, maybe even some of its vital organs. But its successful birth, and the subsequent acquisition of strength, maturity and individuality, took place under the direction of the Prudent King. Philip II gave the Spanish system its peculiar cast and distinctness, and for historians, as much as his contemporaries, he came to symbolise its salient features.

His life as heir to the unique empire of Charles V coincided with the rise of Castile to a commanding position within it. Philip was born in the year that unpaid and undisciplined German soldiery – many of them heretics to boot – sacked Rome in the name of the king of Castile. In his teens he saw Spanish resources and troops become the spearhead of campaign, whether disastrously (as at Algiers in 1541) or triumphantly (as at Muhlberg six years later). Before he was thirty, in the Netherlands, he commanded an army of which the Castilian *tercios* were already the backbone. The circumstances of his father's abdication, in the mid-1550s, meant the inauguration of a new political entity, and one explicitly centred upon the kingdoms of Spain. It was separate from the Holy Roman Empire – which passed to Philip's uncle, Ferdinand and his family – but retained many significant links with it. Despite the frequent use here of the term 'the Spanish monarchy' to describe them collectively, it only slowly (and never completely) came to supplant others utilised for the Spanish Habsburg dominions. And though, under the leadership of Castile, it was more or less unitary *in action*, no more than the empire of Charles V could it ever be a *community*. Indeed, unless perhaps for a small group during the rule of Olivares, there are few indications that many of its denizens ever nurtured such an aspiration.

At Philip's accession to its thrones and titles in 1556, the Spanish monarchy was already firmly committed to a pan-European political strategy. Apart from its wide geographical dispersal, which necessitated the presence of Spanish administrators from Brussels to Brindisi, of Spanish troops and galleys from Ostend to Otranto, the later policy of Charles V had involved it inextricably in the affairs of those flourishing states which fringed the English Channel and the North Sea. One result, for example, was that Philip found himself king of England, Wales and Ireland, because of his marriage to the half-Spanish queen, Mary Tudor. Even when this bizarre arrangement suddenly ceased, the equally sudden and unexpected collapse of France into near-anarchy at the outset of the new decade maintained Madrid's necessary interest in the world north of the Pyrenees. Indeed, within a very short space, the series of disparate but powerful protest movements against centralised, monarchical government, expertly orchestrated by extreme Calvinists, and welded together by religious fervour, spread from the Valois kingdom to Philip's own Low Countries provinces. The king was inalterably determined to resist illegal challenge to his prerogative, as he would a military threat to his patrimony. The latter threatened in the Mediterranean theatre rather than in Flanders, and in these same years the intensifying struggle against the Ottoman coincided with a bitter and bloody insurrection of the Spanish Moors (the Alpujarass rebellion, 1568). Nevertheless, and surprisingly, it was in the north not the south that the decisions and events of the 1560s led to a spiralling escalation of commitment that quickly came to seem infinite. For Philip's attitude to the Flemish dissidents inevitably involved him in a religious confrontation; and indeed, he was directly concerned to combat Protestantism wherever it seemed to lay the axe to his own authority, to threaten the viability of his monarchy. Given the geographical situation of the Low Countries at the crossroads of Europe, physically juxtaposed with major powers as well as being the gateway to heretic Germany, such a programme was bound to involve an increasing interest in these areas. This was the logic which, after twenty years of unremitting yet vain effort, eventually brought about the overt and massive military interventions in the affairs of both England and France. The decade 1585–95 was one of a 'reckless accumulation of commitments' (D2/I) without precedent in European politics.

The persistent image of Philip II is that of the all-powerful ruler of a global empire, paradoxically immured in his tiny office deep inside the Escorial Palace; and, as he grew older, becoming ever more an obstinate creature of sedentary routine. The portrait cannot be said to distort reality overmuch. The king genuinely loved outdoor pursuits – hunting, and, later, gardening, above all. But an overwhelming sense of duty, perhaps reinforced by the need for mortification of the flesh so appropriate to his monastic environment, chained him to his desk for long and punishing hours. Philip was also a prisoner of his immutable convictions on the level of policy. He (and therefore his monarchy) was condemned by his very existence as Most Catholic King to a life-sentence of war. His prior and unquestioning task was to defend in arms the interests of God and His Church, to a degree which was, quite simply, absolute. It was the essence of the contract between the Habsburg rulers and their maker and benefactor, that they would unceasingly advance His cause, just as He automatically protected theirs. Such an understanding can hardly be reckoned absurd or unreasonable. The organic relationship between spiritual sanction and temporal necessity was encapsulated in two words, *reputación* and *conservación*, frequently utilised by Spanish statesmen when describing the most fundamental mainsprings of policy (E9). They translate – roughly and respectively – as 'prestige' and 'security', but their actual meaning possessed a more metaphysical dimension. *Reputación* referred to the monarchy's spiritual (or, if you like, psychological) self-esteem, as well as to its external status amongst the other courts of Europe. Both these were dependent on the confessional impetus endowed by a religious mission, the maintenance of Catholic Christianity. *Conservación* was often used in the context of the so-called 'domino theory' of territorial strategy (see below p. 69–70), but it was closely associated, too, with the crown's transcendental duty to preserve the inheritance of which it was God's custodian. In terms of policy-making, therefore, spiritual and secular arguments were in the last analysis identical; which is why, in the normal run of things, the former appears in the surviving records as an implicit rather than an explicit element.

If things were predetermined thus, it might be asked, why were such arguments and such documents necessary at all? The distinction which should be drawn here is one which resembles that between strategy and tactics. Though the strategic objectives never varied, tactical approaches often differed considerably. Human law naturally interpreted and moderated the divine, as in the dominant theology of the Counter-Reformation. For example, Philip did not regard himself as bound to take action against heresy, however pernicious, occurring in areas clearly outside the boundaries of his legal responsibility (such as the Baltic kingdoms, or, more dramatically, the city of Geneva). (On the less clear-cut questions, the advice of an *ad hoc* committee of specialist clerics was sought.) At a more mundane level, the problem of available material resources was often relevant; confronting this was a matter for the king's conscience, and, in practice, was rarely seen as a sufficient excuse for inaction. In any case, the decision-making process could be as rational and wideranging as its higher *raison d'être* was (to our eyes) irrational and narrow. Philip II himself, it is true, allowed little delegation of ultimate responsibility. In his last years he was borne down by increasingly painful illness and a huge backlog of work. He formed a small Cabinet of professional advisers (the *Junta Grande*) which, by default rather than design, began to take decisions during Philip's sickness crises. Eventually, the king designated this cabal as a government for his son and heir. But, so long as he was sentient, Philip's was always the last word. The elaborate network of interlinked councils which formed the framework of central administration operated ceaselessly, amassing information (literally by the ton), processing, analysing and summarising it. But no council was ever allowed to encroach upon the king's sacred right to rule, in each as in all. More than any other of his race, Philip II's style of government was autocratic.

One must be much more careful, however, about terming it 'absolute'. Even within the borders of Castile a wide gap existed between the king's *de jure* authority and its *de facto* exercise. Severe limitations to his power were both legal and practical. He could levy neither troops nor taxes at will, whilst in many wilder regions of the kingdom his government was so remote as to be mythic. Indeed, some of the celebrated reforms of a century earlier, associated with the policies of Ferdinand and Isabella, were becoming ineffectual. The strains of war and the dreadful socio-economic crisis of the 1590s had led to a perceptible rise in vagrancy and organised banditry in the countryside, which posed a threat to public order and the functioning of government. The Supreme Inquisition, on which the crown depended for a whole range of administrative services, had increasingly drifted away from its control. Outside Castile such problems existed even more acutely, and were complicated by the morass of constitutional and customary traditions which inhibited royal power. These differed in nature and extent in every province of the monarchy. Just as in the case of his higher contract with a divine master, however, Philip honoured each mundane corpus of immemorial rights and privileges, always in spirit, and mostly to the letter. In 1585, when raising resources for the Invincible Armada, he desisted from exploiting the insurrection in Naples to impose a regime which would serve that end. Likewise, in 1591, when revolt provided opportunity and defence needs supreme reason, he refused to tamper with the *fueros* of Aragon in order to make that province more amenable to Madrid. On the contrary, Philip was actually surrendering influence in Castile's dependencies by the gradual alienation of royal property and jurisdiction in exchange for revenues which, in many cases, were expended on the upkeep of the provinces themselves. In short – possibly though not conclusively as a result of his miscalculations in the Netherlands in the 1560s – Philip II was the most constitutionally conscious of autocrats. One result of such sensibilities was that, since little demand for assistance was pressed outside it, the physical burden of the monarchy's wars fell almost exclusively upon Castile.

Though Philip's world empire was ruled by him alone, it was administered by a body of civil servants and senior officials which probably did not exceed 2,000 in number. Though indeed enormous by the standards of the time, this figure may be put into perspective by the fact that it is considerably less than that employed by the modern Welsh Office in the running of the tiny principality of which the writer is a native.

During the efflorescence of Castilian higher education in the sixteenth century, the universities had begun systematically to provide the trained personnel of an expanding imperial bureaucracy. For the most part, such men were possessed of superb technical equipment and broad humanist intellects. The graduates (*licenciados*) of Castile could be recruited into the central conciliar system as part of a permanent 'departmental staff'; or they might work in the office of some great royal secretary or minister who housed and fed them, and obtained their preferment; again, such men could leave Madrid to seek posts in royal justice or administration in the localities, or even in the Indies. From their ranks, the king chose his chief secretaries, a handful of able functionaries of effectively ministerial status, through whose hands passed the important affairs of the monarchy. The experience of such men was perhaps of a kind which could be called narrow. On the other hand, the royal councils and their subcommittees were themselves staffed by personnel of direct and varied experience of the wider world; not only by titled nobility (*títulos*) who had been viceroys, ambassadors, or army commanders, but also by gentlemen (*caballeros*) who were commissioned officers, explorers, judges, priests, and even by merchants and bankers, men of low (and often foreign) birth but great practical knowledge. Many who were called upon to serve or advise the councils were weather-beaten men of action, such as had sailed through shot and hurricane on the world's oceans, or at the head of a regiment of pikemen had withstood the charge of German *Landsknechte* or Turkish *sipahis*. Others were hard-bitten businessmen with interests and contacts all over Europe and beyond. It was this symbiosis of the book and the desk on the one hand, and the wide open horizons of empire on the other, which gave the administration of the Spanish system inventiveness and resilience, which imparted to it a dynamism quite at variance with the impression of torpor and routine so often conveyed in the textbooks.

The Philippine monarchy was not a single *imperium*. As already suggested, it was an unprecedented, and largely crude, agglomeration of many empires. To appreciate this, one has to consider the breathtaking record of the Castilian *conquistadores*. Within the century that elapsed before 1580, the following had been brought into some form of dependent association with Castile:

> The kingdom of Aragon within the peninsula and its (essentially Catalan) Mediterranean empire.
> The remaining independent Arab kingdoms of southern Spain.
> The major part of the Burgundian inheritance in the Low Countries, the Rhineland and eastern France.
> The huge land empires of the Aztecs in central America and the Incas in the subcontinent.
> The Philippine Islands, 5,000 miles across the Pacific from New Spain.
> Portugal and its vast global colonial and trading system in Africa, Brazil and the East Indies.

The Spanish monarchy was thus an empire of empires, in fact the greatest aggregation of peoples, jurisdiction and wealth that the world had ever seen. But with the tremendous power that derived from this process came also cumulative vulnerability. The effort needed to sustain such a vast construction would probably have been finally counter-productive in any case; but, naturally and understandably, it was the focus of resentment and fear on the part of other sovereign states. It was inevitable that such an all-embracing political entity should be in a permanent condition of war. In geopolitical, as well as confessional, terms, the destiny of the monarchy was therefore inescapable.

During Philip II's last decade, his empire for the first time came under pressure on all its major frontiers simultaneously. This mighty challenge to its power and influence was a foretaste of the total war which was to engulf the monarchy in the course of the next century. Most of Philip's defence problems stemmed from his early mishandling of the Flemish protest movement; now, a generation later, the organised and powerful Dutch rebel provinces held together the threads of a web of resistance to Spain, in which were woven the interests of England, France, Venice, and even the Ottoman empire. By the mid-1590s, common rumour and the exaggerated reports of spies told of specific articles of confederation between these geographically and culturally disparate blocs. Such an instrument of cohered collaboration

was actually beyond the scope of contemporary diplomacy. Nevertheless, the more modest and precarious agreements between Philip's
enemies, often covering the exchange of money, materials, soldiers
and other war services, was enough to fight him to a standstill. In its
campaigns to prevent the creation of an independent, Calvinist, Dutch
republic, and the assumption by a Calvinist of the French throne, the
Spanish system reached full maturity. The rapid sophistication of its
methods of political vigilance and military dynamism, involving as it
did the smooth and congruent functioning of communications, transfer
and transport, enabled Spain to fight this many-fronted war. To fight,
but not to win. Philip's failure to achieve his outstanding political
objectives by military action indeed amounted to defeat. In the
maritime theatres of the North Sea and the Atlantic, defeat, and its
consequent loss of position (though not as comprehensive or
definitive as often assumed) was especially clear. The demand upon the
resources of the army of Flanders in fighting campaigns in France and
Holland at the same time was too great, whilst the large guerrilla
operations in western and southern France, fought by native warlords
with Spanish assistance, were gradually extinguished. In the year of his
death, Philip felt obliged to abandon his commitment in France, and by
the Treaty of Vervins accepted the claims of Henry of Bourbon.

The withdrawal, however, was a tactical one, and represented no
relaxation of overall effort. On the contrary, the new king, Philip III,
took up the task with the vigour and enthusiasm of youth. A new and
more energetic attempt to reduce the English challenge was made by
direct intervention in Ireland, and an expeditionary force landed at
Kinsale. ('Whoever England wishes to gain, must in Ireland begin the
strain', a current saying ran in Madrid.) In these years, too, the tempo
of the war in Flanders was considerably increased, whilst a more
aggressive policy was conducted towards the Turks and their North
African satellites. The new king's keenness to cut a dash in the fields of
Mars, so often a feature of dynastic succession, does not seem to have
lasted long (G3), and he quickly transferred his affections to those of
Diana. Probably he was depressed by what, to say the least, was
indifferent success. The expedition to Ireland was a fiasco; the army of
Flanders was badly mauled in pitched battle with the Dutch at Nieuw-
poort (1600); an attempt on the great pirate capital of Algiers never
even reached its destination (1601). Though the humiliation of 1596,
when Spain's domestic defences were cruelly exposed by the English
sack of Cadiz, was not repeated, this was not an auspicious start to the
new reign and the new century. Despite the steady improvement in
fortunes which followed the appointment of Ambrogio Spínola to
command in Flanders, his élite army was crippled by mutiny in the
years after the highly expensive capture of Ostend (1604). Neverthe-

less, the settlement with England (1604) and the armistice in the Low Countries (1607, confirmed by Madrid as an articled truce for twelve years in 1609) were events influenced not only by the diminishing prospect of general victory, but also by the actual incidence of particular defeat. In both these negotiations, the political driving force came from Brussels. The Archdukes Albert and Isabella, respectively cousin and sister of Philip III, to whom upon their marriage in 1598, sovereignty in the Netherlands had been (conditionally) transferred, were strong advocates of peace. The reasons for Madrid's gradual inclination to their way of thinking were many and complex, financial considerations looming large amongst them. But so closely related and interdependent were the arguments used by the 'doves', that they are difficult to distinguish and discriminate and it is not intended to rehearse them at this point (but see below, pp. 38–42). One interesting element, however, does deserve comment: the extent of influence of strictly domestic pressures upon the decisions taken by Philip III and his chief minister, the Duke of Lerma.

The evidence would not seem to justify an interpretation of 'the era of peacemaking' which approximates to that currently being advanced for the formation of attitudes in international relations in the later modern period – the so-called 'primacy of domestic policy'. All the same, a tendency is apparent in this generation, which though never organised and falling far short of agitation, can be termed one of protest, especially in the normally complaisant context of Castilian politics. The rapid escalation of royal tax demands upon the kingdom in the years following the defeat of the Invincible, sparked off an outburst of public criticism of defence commitments. Dissent was voiced in the Cortes (assembly) of Castile in 1591, and grew in volume and incidence as living conditions slumped dramatically in the middle of the decade. (It is interesting that this was contemporaneous with similar events in the Parliaments of Elizabeth I.) The spirit of insular, chauvinist Castile, dormant for most of the century, can be detected in the speeches of the *procuradores* (delegates) to the Cortes. It was a feeling related to that of their forefathers who (during the revolt of the *Comuneros* of 1520) had violently opposed the superimposition of 'German' interests on those of the kingdom itself. Castile should attend to her own affairs and abandon her disastrous dabbling in those of northern Europe; this was the message of many commentators. If more taxes *must* be raised, complained one delegate, they should be spent on defending the villages of Murcia against the constant raids of the Moors who plundered and enslaved the king's subjects.

There must surely be some limit [added another] to the struggle against those distant heresies, for which we pay tribute, even of our bread. Our wars only suffice to make us poorer and our enemies richer. The protection of the Faith is the cause of the whole of Christendom; it is not for Castile alone to bear the cost. (E23)

Many observers took the opportunity of Philip II's death to place such arguments in writing before his successor, among them such intellectual luminaries as Barrientos, Narbona, Mariana and Valencia. The thrust of the more strictly economic diagnoses of the *arbitrista* school also was often against the debilitating incubus of imperial policy. As we have seen, they had little immediate effect. But their expression coincided with the severe crisis at the turn of the century, during which endemic famine in the countryside was succeeded by epidemic plague in the towns. Even if the king's council were not unduly swayed by the evidence for the exhaustion and suffering of the people after thirty years of continuous war, they could certainly see the force of the suggestion that Castile's resources should now be expended in areas closer to her own interests. Many critics had stressed the prior importance of the Mediterranean and Atlantic theatres, under severe threat from the activities of heretic and infidel pirate squadrons, to the economy and security of Castile.

At first, such criticism, however respectful and constructive, was not encouraged, and the Inquisition took swift action against men like Narbona and Mariana. But the alternative view of things which they represented was not without effect, and during the course of the reign this can be detected fermenting in the attitudes of the politicians in Madrid.

Policy and Resources

Philip II and his son were rulers of approximately 16 million European subjects. This immensely scattered and dispersed population almost certainly did not exceed that (so much more concentrated) of the kingdom of France. Moreover, Madrid's mastery over their destinies was – as we have seen – nowhere complete, above all in the crucial matter of mobilising them for war. In Castile itself, the crown could not force men to the colours at will. When a programme of conscription was undertaken, for the first time, in the 1590s, it was found that great numbers were legally protected against it, and that many others could escape the recruiting sergeant with relative ease and impunity. In Flanders (population 1½ million) and Spanish Italy (5 million), military service was on a volunteer basis, though in these provinces, as opposed to Portugal and the crown of Aragon, regular levies were in practice forthcoming.

The demographic trend throughout the sixteenth century had been slowly upwards, but precisely in this decade it was suddenly and tragically reversed. This watershed was reached by other regions of Europe around the same time, though nowhere as convulsively as in Castile. During the previous generation, Castile had become danger- ously dependent on food supplies from outside the peninsula, some sources of which (notably the Ukrainian grainlands) were distant and unpredictable. In the countryside, local dearth and economic disloca- tion had been in evidence long before the widespread harvest failures of the mid-1590s. The conditions of general war in western Europe, which hampered supply and forced up prices, aggravated the internal problems of sharp increases in taxation and inflation. By 1599, when a potent virus of bubonic plague arrived in Spain, successive years of malnutrition had reduced the physiological resistance of the unprivileged masses to a low ebb. For five years, the epidemic raged along an axis from north to south of Castile. The final aggregate death-toll of subsistence crisis and disease was 600,000, in a popu- lation of less than 6 million – literally a decimation. It was a body blow of incalculable political and economic consequences. As one writer remarked during a similar crisis of the 1640s, 'the power of kingdoms consists of population. Whoever possesses the most people, not whoever has the most kingdoms, is the greatest prince' (E6). A period of demographic decline in the monarchy had begun, which was to last (at least) until the 1660s – in other words throughout the period of desperate struggle to defend its European hegemony.

The overall military strength of Spain had probably risen to about 125,000 (three-quarters of them Castilians) by the accession of Philip III. Despite the population crisis, this figure decreased only slightly in the years before the Truce of Antwerp with the Dutch, and rep- resented a formidable establishment. In terms of both quantity and quality it was far superior to the combined forces of its enemies. The members of Spain's armed forces were, however, distributed across three continents and half-a-dozen seas. In Europe alone they gar- risoned the fortresses (*presidios*) of the African and Tuscan coasts; defended the peninsula itself; manned the naval expeditions of 1588–1602, and stood guard in the Duchy of Milan, training ground of the Spanish army. They occupied several strongpoints along the land routes from Italy to the Netherlands, and finally, conducted the main campaigns of the war effort in Flanders, where one-third of the total was concentrated.

If the Spanish system is envisaged as a huge industrial plant, then energy had to be supplied to its machinery, lubrication for their moving parts, raw materials for its production; and (since war was the most labour-intensive of industries) a labour force of manifold skills and experience had to be on hand. This vast enterprise was one which operated round-the-clock. Unlike its rivals (with the exception of the

Dutch), the Spanish armed services and all their supportive organs were permanent, and not demobilised during the winter months, or even during (nominal) peace. It was managed by the officials of the central government in Madrid and supervised by agencies responsible to them. Even the remoter American colonies, now under constant threat of attack, relied overwhelmingly on the Council of the Indies in Seville for the direct provision of military material and personnel. Not surprisingly, the apparatus conveys a regular impression of strain and disrepair. Resources were often insufficient or locally unavailable, tackling problems frequently improvised or simply confused. These troubles can easily be exaggerated, however. In some respects, the monarchy contained excellent natural and economic resources, nor was their exploitation and distribution in the hands of incompetent amateurs. Castile was well stocked with beasts of burden and transport, and, like Naples, possessed good supplies of wool. Milan was a centre of textile production, so that the provision of, for example, military clothing and ship sails was catered for. Northern Spain was the site of the most intensively worked iron deposits in Europe, and boasted a flourishing shipbuilding industry. Other regions of the peninsula contained war-related resources such as copper, sulphur and saltpetre. In short, though some key areas were already experiencing shortfalls, 'there was an abundance of strategic war materials' (G1). The crucial difficulties arose at the manufacturing stage in the armaments industries, and in the 1590s intense efforts were made to resolve them. Spanish industry was too small-scale and undeveloped (especially in terms of technology) to provide the mass-production levels and standardisation necessary for the defence needs of the crown. Only five ordnance factories of any consideration existed within Spain, and it was usual for at least two of these to be out of commission. A new plant set up in Vizcaya in 1596 worked at only half-capacity for the remainder of the war. Such failures were all the more significant because of the decline of Milan as a major armaments centre, especially after 1609. In the manufacture of weapons, indeed, the United Provinces and England already far outstripped Spain in efficiency of design and production, a fact which applied to small arms as well as artillery.

In consequence, a whole range of finished goods, and many important raw materials, had to be purchased in quantity by the crown from sources of foreign (indeed sometimes actually hostile) origin. Such transactions were increasing and extending to involve most regions of western Europe, so that the needs of the Spanish war-machine created a permanent traffic of investment, speculation, exchange and transport. They represented a continuous (if fluctuating) demand for goods and services in the general economic context of Europe, and had a significance for the overall performance of that economy. Every prominent capitalist, whatever his 'national' or confessional allegiance, fought for his share of the opportunities presented by Madrid's imperialism. Notwithstanding state regulations, despite the constant prohibitons and audits within the Hispanic world, foreign enterprise was woven into the fabric of the Spanish system, which indeed could not operate without it. Conversely, both within and without the monarchy, powerful vested interests derived benefit from its defence needs and policy.

Naturally, the degree of cohesion and control which the Madrid government could impose on such matters was considerably less than that which we would expect of a modern administration. In this sense, it may be conceded that to describe it as a 'system' is misleading. According to Dr Thompson, indeed, the reigns of Philip II and Philip III witnessed a gradual contraction of direct state involvement, a kind of pragmatic devolution of interest to private enterprise (G1). This process, described as the succession of *administración* (royal monopoly of production and supervision) by *asiento* (provision by private contract) is certainly to be detected in some respects, though it may be wondered to what extent the former was ever established, or even aimed at, by Habsburg government. The hegemony of interventionist principles and the 'public sector' was as yet an undreamed of philosophy, and in the Spanish context was permanently undercut, in any case, by the sheer scale and urgency of its businesses. Working materials had to be improvised and adapted to circumstances, even where it meant ignoring or infringing regulations. Even then, success was often unforthcoming and breakdowns in particular areas frequent – such failures may be described as *endemic*, but not *systemic*. In the same month in 1600, for example, the Council of State in Madrid dealt with desperate complaints from two of its commanders concerning the lack of supply. They stood in considerable contrast, since one was the Archduke Albert, titular ruler of Flanders and commander-in-chief of the main army, and the other was Don Juan de Velázquez, in charge of a small frontier garrison in Vizcaya, on the borders with France. In both cases, the troops were unpaid, ill-fed and ill-clothed, and terrible shortages existed in weapons and powder. Mutiny threatened, and the complainant could not be responsible, nor properly discharge his duty to the king in case of a military emergency. Though (in my opinion) such grievances were usually exaggerated as a matter of form, in anticipation of possible failure and dishonour, they do illustrate real structural problems. Of course, these deficiencies and inefficiencies existed in much worse case amongst Spain's rivals; but whereas the Spaniards did not succeed in improving their methods – things were much the same in 1600 as in 1560 or 1640 – other countries did, one feels, make sporadic progress. In different ways and at different tempi, the United Provinces, France and even England, struggled towards a kind of mercantilist autarky in which war experience was crucial and which increased the role and potency of government. One should not anticipate or overestimate this change, but it can hardly be questioned that, during the course of the 'long seventeenth century', Spain's enemies became better able to take advantage of her weaknesses. Fernand Braudel is guilty of more than a typical hyperbole when he claims that, with Philip II bogged down in the campaigns of the 1590s, 'the Dutch and the English were con-quering the world' (B10/I). But it does seem that for Spain there was no longer 'a favourable ratio between the amount of social energy available and the amount of space to be organised' – Mattingly's ingenious formula for success in the early modern world (E1).

If the subject of the mobilisation and exploitation of resources is ultimately a matter for relative and subjective judgement, so too is its essential corollary, prevailing economic conditions. At present it seems that the actual economic collapse – the productive extinction – of Spain and Italy may have been delayed for longer than previously assumed. Current research indicates that the location of the definitive economic crisis in the period 1590–1620 (one favoured for some time) may have to be modified. This, however, still leaves unsolved the important problem of the identification and description of the chronological phases of economic decadence. All the same, the work of the Chaunus (B11) has illustrated the extent of both the short- and long-term advantages which Spain derived from the Seville trade. There is increasing evidence that domestic manufacturing industries – mining, luxury goods, and the very important area of shipbuilding, survived the financial crisis of the turn of the century. Some experts feel that the crisis of the late 1620s was decisive here, others that not until 1650 or so can we safely speak of absolute decline, either in agrarian or manufacturing terms. In either case, its importance is less than central to my main theme. No more in the sustained effort needed to construct a world empire in the sixteenth century than in the prolonged struggle to maintain it in the seventeenth, did Spanish power rest on the basis of an expanding economy. Admittedly, periodic and localised booms attended the various stages in discovery of, and the organisation of trade with, the New World. But nothing remotely resembling an economic revolution (or what is nowadays referred to as a 'take-off') can be detected. Castile did not suddenly streak ahead of the rest of Europe in methods of production, technical innovation or economic forms; there was no spurt in science and technology, as in the England of the eighteenth century. The ineluct-able geophysical deficiencies of the peninsula, which so firmly limited its agricultural development, were no more in evidence in 1600 than in 1500 (though it may have been that medium-term climatic changes exacerbated their effect). Social attitudes and cultural factors were no more or less inimical to effective economic development, whether the 'turning point' came in 1570, 1620 or 1650. To concede, as one can hardly fail to do, that Spain's performance as a great power would have been better given a healthier economic outlook is not to attribute its failures to economic causes, for negative arguments cannot be made to support a positive conclusion. To the student of the Spanish monarchy in its international dimension, the question of its economic viability is circumstantial rather than substantial.

Since the war, by way of a gloss upon, or sophistication of, the 'monocausal' dominance of economic factors, the thesis has been advanced that the formulation and execution of defence policies depended in detail upon the crown's financial condition. To examine this question it is necessary to describe the fiscal machinery of the Spanish system and the situation of its 'exchequer', especially in relation to an appropriate 'case study', the important transition of defence policy in the early years of the seventeenth century. During the 1590s, the crown's revenues were running at a figure of about ten million ducats per annum. This was more than a threefold increase over the levels of the beginning of Philip II's reign, the result of rocketing silver imports and greatly increased (Castilian) taxation. In the quinquennium 1596–1600, more silver reached the royal coffers from the mines of the New World colonies than at any other time in their history. Nevertheless, the costs of war were escalating even more quickly. The Invincible Armada alone, for example, had cost a year's gross revenue. Expenditure on this scale necessitated the invention of a heavy new sales tax (the *millones*), and not long afterwards, monetary manipulation (through the issue of copper, or *vellón*, coinage). Though this greatly assisted the war effort, it only compounded the crown's strictly budgetary problems. From the gross revenue given above, a plethora of deductions had ostensibly to be made. The most burdensome of these was the servicing of the consolidated debt – that is to say, the annual payment of dividends on state bonds (*juros*) in which thousands of Castilians invested. In the decade in question, such payments totalled between 4 and 5 million ducats, and had reached 8 million by 1607; in other words, this commitment halved the crown's income 'at a stroke'. But even the remainder is not to be regarded as a true net figure, for Philip had many more recurrent expenses of a non-defence nature – hundreds, perhaps thousands, of pensions and gratuities to civil servants, veteran soldiers or their dependants, priests, artists, architects. The list seems endless. And even this by no means covers what might be regarded as court (or 'household') expenditure, which certainly exceeded 500,000 ducats a year under Philip II and increased substantially after his death. In accounting terms, it may be doubted whether the crown was solvent, even when its defence commitments are left to one side.

In practice, however, accounting and budgeting was never really attempted, for neither revenue nor expenditure could be estimated with any accuracy. In the case of the former, for example, neither taxation nor the short-term defence loans of the bankers (*asientos de dinero*) ever realised the sums agreed on. From most Castilian taxation returns, the (unpredictable) costs of collection and the profit of the tax-farmers was deductable whilst the receipt of *asiento* sums was reduced by charges for many services rendered by those involved in its transfer to the army (*adehalas*). As for expenditure, it is enough to remark that (obviously) the costs of war in any one year were completely unforseeable. It was the system of *asientos de dinero* which covered all these sins, held the royal finances together, and allowed the Spanish system to operate. At the same time, however, repayment of the high interest rates and capital to the bankers (*hombres de negocio*) was at once the king's greatest single expense *and* his prior commitment. In the year of Philip III's accession, his ordinary and extraordinary defence expenditure (taken together) was no less than 10 million ducats, equalling his total (theoretical) revenue. The huge gap was bridged by the bankers. It will be evident from this that the Spanish monarchy was a Micawberesque institution, operated on credit, or rather upon a crude and unreliable basis of deficit finance.

The urgent need to defray the interest charges upon defence loans meant that the crown's honouring of its other responsibilities was intermittent. In fact, the king was constantly obliged to renege (temporarily) on payments of a 'domestic' or non-military nature, although this did not always produce the desired result of enabling him to pay and supply his armies – especially not in this period. Such stratagems might reassure the bankers of the sincerity and solvency of the government, but their relationship with it depended overwhelmingly upon the annual silver receipts, by far the most negotiable security for its loans. The relationship could break down as a result of various events, usually occurring in combination. A slump in silver returns might prevent due repayment; a sudden military emergency might oblige the government to meet its costs directly, thus interrupting repayment, and representing the arbitrary diversion of security; the crown's demand for loans might exceed what its bankers were ready to advance. To some extent, all these factors were present in the years leading up to 1607, forcing Philip III in that year to utilise the *decreto y medio real* – not improperly rendered as a 'bankruptcy' by most historians. The *decreto* was the cancellation of interest on *asientos*, and the transfer of capital into *juros* at much lower rates of interest; which, in technical terms, means the conversion of a floating debt into a consolidated one. Care was usually taken to exempt the most powerful banking firms, whose continued collaboration could not be prejudiced, from the worst effects of the *decreto*. The financial resources thus made liquid could then be used for direct payments on urgent accounts. Following this, new contracts for loans were renegotiated (the *medio*) – a complex and often protracted process, but always the bankers (now perhaps differently constituted) would come round. Sometimes they would insist on the fixing of higher interest rates to insure themselves against the crown's unreliability. In point of fact, this unreliability can be easily exaggerated. The *decreto* of 1607 did, it is true, come only eleven years after an earlier one; but the normal incidence was about every twenty (at least until the later years of Philip IV) and rich profits accrued to the financiers in the intervals. The defaulting of governments was, after all, an occupational hazard which in the Spanish case was remarkable for its *infrequency*. Moreover, compared to investment in trade or (when it was available) land, the Madrid government remained highly competitive. In any case, for over a century European financiers – German, Italian, Portuguese, and even (indirectly) the Dutch – found the attractions of fine American silver, and the astronomical interest rates on *asientos*, too great to resist. Silver, of which Spain retained an effective monopoly, was by far the most negotiable commodity in the whole European economy.

In 1601–5 there was a serious (but temporary) drop in the level of silver, and this event has been seen as the classic instance of a financial emergency dictating policy-decisions (E18). The silver 'hiccough' helped to bring about a *decreto* in 1607, and (so the argument runs) was instrumental in the reluctant acceptance of the armistice and truce in the Low Countries. It must be conceded that the problem of money supply *did* almost certainly exert a more powerful influence on this occasion than hitherto; but this was mainly because the basis for continuing the war was in all other respects already regarded as weak. Financial criteria, therefore, may have argued in favour of retrenchment, but this is no reason for regarding them as the decisive, far less as the exclusive, consideration. Those who pleaded for peace were not (as one might expect) the officials of the Treasury in Madrid, but the soldiers on the spot. Indeed, whilst Albert and Spínola were crying 'back!' it was precisely the *Consejo de Hacienda* which most vociferously shouted 'forward!'. Moreover, there was no mutiny amongst the bankers to put beside that of the army of Flanders; and by 1609, when it was finally agreed to confirm the armistice, the silver situation had righted itself and Atlantic trade returns had substantially recovered. The indication is that by this time the majority opinion amongst those with some experience of the northern wars, and who had a say in policy-making, was that even an infinite supply of silver would not guarantee victory.

The 'conjuncture' of this period was, moreover, much more complex than a simple crisis of silver receipts and cash-flow calculations. We have already touched upon one of its aspects, the growth of 'domestic' pressure upon policy-making. These were associated with the emergence of another vital consideration, the growing potential threat from France. During the first decade of the century, Spanish envoys and agents kept Madrid informed about the rising tide of Henry IV's impatience, the increase in French diplomatic activity and military preparations. Given Spain's weaknesses at so many points along the various frontiers with the Bourbon kingdom, a settlement with the United Provinces might act as a suitable deterrent to French belligerence. Any potential challenge from this source had to be regarded with the utmost gravity, the more so when it coincided with serious danger in the Mediterranean, from the Barbary states of north Africa. The single pirate state of Algiers, for example, posed a threat which could not be disregarded. At the height of its power in precisely this epoch, its huge fleet of over 100 units actually outnumbered the Spanish naval establishment. Consequently, the Algerians were able to launch sudden and devastating raids on many parts of southern and western Spain, and regularly struck at Portugal and Sicily, too. Not content with disrupting Spanish trade and communications in the Mediterranean, they were beginning to venture into the Atlantic, with damaging effect. The temperature of apprehension was increased several degrees by the belief in Madrid that both France and Algiers were plotting with the Morisco communities within the peninsula, who were numerous and well organised in the strategically sensitive areas of Valencia and Aragon. When the close political relationship which had often existed between France, the Barbary states and the Ottoman Empire was taken into account, the monarchy's situation appeared infinitely precarious.

Only calculations of this nature – a threat of this magnitude – could in my view have justified the concessions made to the United Provinces by the Truce of Antwerp. These included, for example, the abandonment of the king's own Catholic subjects marooned without protection in the northern regions of the republic, a compromise of principle which deeply disturbed Philip III himself. It is generally believed that some connection existed between the truce and the decree which ordered the expulsion of the Moriscos from Spain, which was signed on the same day of 1609. It is probable that the real nature of this connection has been missed, since it is difficult to accept that the expulsion was a crude grab at a kind of 'psychological' compensation for Spain's frustration in the wars against the northern heretics. Madrid certainly needed an armistice on other fronts so as to mobilise sufficient resources, and to carry out the massive operation (which took five years) relatively undisturbed. But even more may have been involved; it may be (tentatively) suggested that the events of 1604-9, incorporating the peace with England and the agreements with the Dutch, were part of a profounder reappraisal of defence tactics, by which the monarchy turned back to its 'historic' destiny in the Mediterranean. As it happened, good financial arguments could be advanced for such a course. The Italian provinces, as well as those of eastern Spain, would be much more likely – indeed, to some extent, obliged – to contribute to its support, thus providing some relief for beleaguered Castile and the royal treasury. The heritage of crusade against Islam was still very much alive in Castile; and perhaps the pope would lend a more sympathetic ear to new proposals for taxing the Spanish Church, in a cause rather nearer his heart than others engaged by Madrid in recent years. It would also offer to the whole military establishment a more promising field of endeavour than the unpopular, cold, soggy and fruitless fields of Flanders. Such campaigns would take place in what was, so to speak, their own milieu, and held out the prospect of legitimate booty as well as glory and eternal salvation.

Be this as it may, it remains clear to the present writer that to regard financial factors as the sole dynamic of events in the Spanish system is essentially simplistic and reductive. Of course, the crown had to choose between alternatives, and the question of available financial resources was present in the mosaic of arguments from which the decision emerged. Naturally, too, those who served its policy in hundreds of different capacities had (on the whole, and eventually) to be paid. Contemporaries were well aware that money was 'the sinews of war', but the suggestion that it decided matters so profoundly bound up with belief, duty and honour would have been regarded as blasphemous, if intelligible. In respect of money, as in all other respects, God would provide for the triumph of His cause. If, on the other hand, *nuestro Señor* withheld His basic support – as He apparently had, for His own inscrutable reasons, in the campaigns of 1588-1609 – then no amount of money would bring victory. Indeed, to Philip the Pious, as to many of his advisers, the coincidence of unparalleled wealth with unprecedented setback in the 1590s may have served as a warning that the monarchy was pursuing a misguided course.

Policy and Prejudice

Christopher Marlowe's Faustus was, it appears, a Dutchman and a patriot. Nevertheless, such was the power of Spain in contemporary

Europe that it could only be countered by magic and necromancy. Should Mephistopheles's spirits materialise, ruminates Faustus:

> I'll have them fly to India for gold . . .
> I'll levy soldiers with coin they bring
> And chase the Prince of Parma from our land.

Marlowe himself, an English spy (and even, perhaps, a double-agent) was well abreast of political developments. The context of this passage from his *Tragical History of Doctor Faustus* (*c.* 1590) suggests on the surface that Philip II and Parma were evil influences; underneath, his attitude was more equivocal, reflecting a certain admiration. Yet he correctly identified the source, and thus the Achilles' heel, of Spain's strength, since Faustus's infernal slaves would be used to drag 'from America the golden fleece/ That yearly stuffs old Philip's treasury' – an aspiration eventually achieved by the Dutchman Piet Hein in 1628.

Spain's European hegemony gave rise everywhere to sentiments much less ambivalent than Marlowe's. They were founded on a fear which was real and urgent, whatever hindsight may tell us about its justification. They were developed and strengthened through printed literature and via the Protestant pulpit. Local rumour and exaggeration lent them colour and vitality. The longevity of Spanish supremacy was important to the slow formulation of national awareness, a catalyst which produced from the primaeval soup of regional loyalties the raw material of European nationalism. Anti-Spanish attitudes are often referred to, collectively and for convenience, as the 'Black Legend', a term which tends to reflect the outraged sensibilities of the modern Spanish intelligentsia. It is so much a part of the intellectual and ideological heritage of European civilisation that its effects can still be observed at work today, both amongst historians and a wider public.

The Black Legend can be studied in the extant literature of early modern Europe, and not only in that which served an overtly propaganda purpose. The hatred and suspicion it encapsulates was a perfectly understandable reaction to the behaviour and pretensions of Spaniards. Many of the soldiers, bureaucrats and emissaries of the monarchy were imbued with a self-righteousness which bloated them with effortless superiority and arrogance. Despite their obeisance (which was something more than lip-service) to the ideals of the Christian Commonwealth, they never doubted their own qualifications to lead and inspire it. Moreover, they were (perhaps paradoxically) beginning to cultivate the usage of *españa* and *español*, to distinguish the race which had conquered empires, humbled the Turk, and spiked the guns of heresy, from the lesser auxiliaries of their European empire – the *naciones* as they were referred to in a term of deprecation which would seem odd to later generations. Consider the words which Marlowe's contemporary, Lope de Vega – greatest Spanish dramatist of his age, who had besides sailed against England with the Invincible – put into the mouth of Hernán Cortes (in his *Arcadia* of 1598):

> Spain has been given triumphs and palms
> The most glorious success to her arms,
> Her king has gained infinite goals,
> And to God brought numberless souls.[2]

Assertions of this kind, or rather the assumptions they voiced, were answered by the foremost minds amongst Spain's rivals. In 1595, on the occasion of England's official declaration of war, Francis Bacon pronounced upon 'the ambition and oppression of Spain':

> To begin with, the Church of Rome, that pretended apostolic see is become but a donative cell of the King of Spain. The Vicar of Christ is become the king of Spain's chaplain . . . The states of Italy, they be like little quillets of freehold being intermixed in the midst of a great honour of lordship. France is turned upside down . . . Portugal usurped . . . the Low Countries warred upon . . . the like at this day attempted upon Aragon . . . The poor Indians are brought from free men to be slaves . . . [3]

Bacon's highly colourful tourist's brochure illustrated the view that Spanish tyranny was universal and ubiquitous, and moreover (like all such regimes) it abused its own subjects as much as it threatened outsiders. The reality was of course less clearcut, as we may discover by examining in turn the English writer's areas of obloquy.

Though Madrid ceaselessly strove to explain itself to the pope, and to enlist his support, the Vatican cannot be regarded as a kind of Spanish department of state. So far from being a supine satellite, the incumbent at the time of Bacon's rhodomontade, Clement VIII, was on the contrary a politician in what might almost be called the tradition of anti-Spanish pontiffs. Clement was a professed Francophile, especially after the conversion of Henry of Bourbon to Catholicism, an achievement for which he personally claimed the credit. His promotion of the French cause, like that of a similarly minded successor a generation later, potentially undermined the 'Spanish peace' in Italy, and was a reminder to Madrid that Rome was never prepared to accept its Italian hegemony with complete equanimity. It cannot be denied, on the other hand, that a special relationship existed between the Spanish court and the curia, from which the former often derived material as well as spiritual sustenance. In the very year of Henry IV's famous 'mass', for example, the following news item was reported from Rome: 'The disputes which have so long prevailed among Christian powers about precedence at sea have now been settled. Only the

Pope and the king of Spain can sail their galleys with colours flying. If they meet they must salute each other. All other nations must yield precedence to these two.'[4]

Italy gave birth to the Black Legend, since it was here that the painful impact of the *tercios* was first experienced, in the opening years of the sixteenth century. For many Italians, the Spanish claim that their presence in the peninsula was part of God's obvious design was a sacreligious insult. Propaganda disseminated from the courts of Venice and Savoy, in particular, maintained that Castile's rule of her Italian dependencies was illegal, and imposed by the power of the pike alone. Moreover, it was denounced (in terms reproduced by a later generation of Italian historians) as inimical to the physical well-being as well as the psychological self-esteem of the people. Others, however, with an equal admixture of altruism and self-interest, acknowledged the benefits of Spanish patronage; an unparalleled period of peace and security, a minimum of interference with domestic institutions and internal administration, and (not least) a striking absence of fiscal exploitation. Though none of these was destined to remain inviolate long into the new century, they by no means exhaust the list of advantages brought by loyalty, or at least complaisance. For many Italians – businessmen, soldiers, artists, lawyers, engineers, churchmen – the Spanish system offered matchless opportunity for reward and fulfilment. This contradistinction can be seen in the attitudes of two writers whose influence on matters of morality and policy had dominated the later Renaissance, the Florentine contemporaries, Guicciardini and Machiavelli. To the former, Ferdinand of Aragon, architect of Spain's dominion in Italy, was an impious charlatan who advanced his own interests under the cloak of religion; for the latter, these same tendencies suggested Ferdinand's greatness, making him a hero of *raison d'état* second only to Cesare Borgia, and the creator of a polity which it would be both honourable and expedient to serve. Neither of these commentators was himself a subject of the monarchy, but their own princes, the Medici dukes of Tuscany, generally followed Machiavelli's advice. In this, they acted in like manner to dozens of lesser north Italian seigneurs, lords of Bacon's 'little quillets of freehold', whose wisdom was reinforced by regular pensions – or, if you prefer, bribes – from Madrid. The disbursement of annual *condotte* to princelings such as the Lord of Urbino (5,000 *escudos*), the Duke of Modena (12,000), and the Prince of Mirandola (7,500), cost the Spanish Treasury over 100,000 ducats, but it helped to guarantee the political stability of an area crucial to the strategic basis of hegemony in Europe as a whole. Even as things stood, the Duchy of Milan, bordered on three sides by unfriendly and constantly intriguing powers, was the linch-pin of a structure that was difficult to maintain.

The kingdom of Naples in the south of the peninsula (commonly called the Regno) was, unlike either Milan or the strikingly loyalist island of Sicily, actually a centre of anti-Spanish disaffection. Chronically difficult to govern, riddled with disorder and organised crime, hopelessly in debt, the Regno contained an active 'underground resistance'. As recently as 1585, the citizens of Naples had risen in a spectacular, if short-lived, insurrection, brutally suppressed by the Spanish authorities. In subsequent generations, the spirit of popular opposition was kept alive, apparently deriving comfort and example from the progress of rebellion in the Netherlands (G10). Small and dormant as this 'movement' was, it was supported by some members of the Neapolitan intelligentsia, who advanced dissident ideas under the very eyes of the Inquisition by the use of a series of elaborate codes. On the other hand, whether such examples are sufficient to justify Braudel's sweeping assertion that in the Italian provinces 'hatred of the Spaniard began to smoulder everywhere' towards the end of the sixteenth century must surely be held doubtful (B10/II). Even in Naples it was to take a prolonged period of intense material exploitation (during the Thirty Years' War) before the unprivileged masses again rose in revolt.

The polarities of feeling to be found in Italy were present more openly and violently in a France 'turned upside down' by religious conflict. Despite the new-found orthodoxy of the Bourbon monarchy, many social groups and regional areas of Catholic fanaticism continued to look to the court of Madrid rather than that of Paris for guidance and even leadership. Ravaillac, the assassin of Henry IV, like his predecessor who struck down the last Valois king in 1589, was a representative of the so-called 'good Catholics' who were opposed to both the centralising absolutism of the crown and to the pro-Protestant policies which (in their eyes) rendered it tyrannical. Paradoxical as it may seem, amongst such men, unconvinced by Henry's conversion, and including some of the most eminent clerics and nobles in the kingdom, Spain was regarded as the champion of liberty as well as of true religion. Even as Ravaillac waited his moment in 1610, the churches of Paris were echoing to the pulpit denunciations of Henry's plans for war against Spain. No amount of 'reason of state' could justify (according to this view) aggression against France's natural and proper ally in the struggle with heresy. A myriad personal and local vested interests also militated against the extension of royal authority which the Bourbon programme involved. Even the position of the Huguenots, by a supreme irony, was in practice anomalous, since the more that royal absolutism flourished by the prosecution of an anti-Spanish policy, the less solid appeared the foundations of their autonomy, enshrined in the Edict of Nantes. The events of 1610 delayed the operation of this logic for many years; but in the late 1620s it worked itself out fully, when the Protestant Dutch aided the French government in the Huguenot war and the siege of La Rochelle, whilst Madrid tried ineffectually to supply the rebels. Though Bourbon government and its embryonic new bureaucracy was, therefore, committed to a phased resistance to Spanish hegemony, for most of the first half of the century Spain was more the subject of a White than a Black Legend inside the borders of the French kingdom. And by the time anti-Spanish attitudes took firm root in the French consciousness, in the reign of Louis XIV, they did so in somewhat altered form.

Leaving aside Portugal (a special case in which treatment is best deferred), we turn next to the United Provinces, still in the 1590s an object of Bacon's sympathy, as of that of most Englishmen. Here the situation is, naturally, less complex. With the possible exception of the Calvinist Palatinate in the Rhineland, the provinces of Holland and Zeeland were the main centre of dissemination of the Black Legend. The pamphlet presses of the embattled republic thundered ceaselessly against 'the ambition and oppression of Spain', above all, perhaps, with copies of William of Orange's own *Apologia* (1583), the most celebrated of all attacks on the father of lies, Philip II. This document provided the twin pillars on which all subsequent versions of the legend were based, the personal attack upon a vicious king and his corrupt court (from which even today Philip's reputation outside Spain has hardly recovered), and the assertion that Spain's ultimate objective was world dominion. In the 1580s, under Parma's terrific onslaught, the rebel provinces had their backs to the wall – or rather, the sea – and the latter claim was an essential element of their rallying cry for international assistance. By the end of the century, partly indeed owing to the widening of the war, this pressure had been considerably relaxed, and the Dutch cause on the contrary was thriving in terms of international esteem, political security, and (not least) economic well-being. It is notable that around this time the torch of resistance passed out of Dutch hands, into those of their strange and passionate political disciples, the courtiers of the Elector Palatine. Though intensely Calvinist, the Palatinate had never been threatened by the Spanish system. Yet now Heidelberg became an ideological power-house of anti-Habsburg activity, attracting to itself the most gifted and the most lunatic zealots in western Europe.[5] As the United Provinces, under the guidance of their pensionary Oldenbarnevelt, moved steadily towards an accommodation with the Spaniards, the agents of the Elector Frederick were at work everywhere canvassing a renewed alliance against the common enemy. Though much of the resources of this small but prosperous principality was devoted to the campaign, thankfully for Madrid its political effect was circumscribed. In particular, the Palatine message was ill-received by his colleagues in the Imperial Diet, especially amongst the Lutheran princes who were profoundly distrustful of his religion and motives. In times of crisis, some of their number allowed the Dutch to recruit troops in their lands, but few wished to go further in irritation of Habsburg authority, either in Germany or Spain. Nevertheless, the commitment and frustration of the Heidelberg court must not be underestimated, for it eventually issued in Frederick's fateful decision to intervene in Bohemia in 1618.

Almost everywhere save in these two areas, therefore, Protestant hatred of Spain existed cheek-by-jowl with grudging respect and even admiration. In the English court this dichotomy was particularly marked, and those modern documents of the Black Legend, the cinema epics (such as the Hollywood *Sea Hawk* of 1940 and the already cited *Fire over England*, to name only two of the swashbuckling genre) do not err in making some characters pay tribute to the better qualities of the Spaniards, whether as friend or enemy. In declaring English aid for the Dutch in 1585, Elizabeth herself caused a gratuitous compliment to Parma to be included in the proclamation! On the other hand, since the experience of the so-called 'Marian reaction' in the 1550s, suspicion of Spain had taken a firm grip upon the cultural and political awareness of Englishmen in the south and east of Elizabeth's kingdom (H4). A spate of propaganda culminated in the publication of a work destined to become the decalogue of the Black Legend in the English-speaking world, Bartolomé de Las Casas's account of the misdeeds of Spanish administration in America, rendered into English as *The Spanish Colony* (1583). The Las Casas chronicle, all the more authoritative because witnessed at first hand by a Spanish cleric, became a hardy perennial of Anglo-Spanish hostility, being reissued at the outset of every new war, in 1625, 1655 and 1699. (It was even republished in New York in 1898, at the beginning of the last war against the colonial empire of Spain.)

As our text from Bacon suggests, during the 1590s another area of Spanish malfeasance came to rival mistreatment of the American Indian as a subject for English outrage and horror – the province of Aragon. As in the case of the New World, a Spaniard was on hand to provide unimpeachable testimony. This was the lionised ringmaster of anti-Spanish propaganda, Antonio Pérez. What better evidence could there be of Spain's criminal ambition than that provided by this talented politician and accomplished publicist, one-time private secretary to King Philip himself? It was in escaping from the clutches of his ex-master that Pérez took refuge in his native Aragon, thus sparking off the so-called rebellion of 1591. In fact the desperate gamble of a group of noble bandits, and treated with an astuteness bordering on liberality by Philip II, this event was brilliantly pictured by Pérez as the cruel and deliberate suppression of a liberty-loving people. In 1593, he arrived in England, to become patronised by the Earl of Essex, and close colleague with the two Bacon brothers (also dependants of Essex) in the task of propaganda. His defection, as notorious in its day as any spy scandal of our own time, was extremely inconvenient for Madrid. By the time of Philip II's death, Pérez was popularly believed to have been instrumental in all Spain's misfortunes – the anti-Spanish alliance 'network', the success of the Bourbons in France, and (especially) the disastrous and degrading sack of Cadiz in 1596, executed by Essex himself. Pérez's *Relaciones*, a scathing account of Madrid's 'Cabinet secrets' was widely translated and became a European best-seller. Its author passed into Spanish folklore as a puissant traitor, occupying the place in Spanish history that Benedict Arnold does in that of the USA or (say) Kim Philby in our own.

Though he enjoyed for a time a dazzling second career, Pérez's actual influence was limited, and he died in poverty and obscurity. For during the peacemaking era following the Treaty of Vervins in 1598, the war of words and ideas also, naturally, abated. This did not signify any relaxation of entrenched positions, but it did involve the more politic control of the firebrand confessional exiles on both sides. The court of Heidelberg, and that of Savoy, with its powerful ambitions in Italy, were, perhaps, exceptions to this rule. In the west, however, the lists of *condotte* paid by Madrid were steadily extended to include almost every major courtier at Paris, London and even The Hague. James I and his chief ministers, the queen regent of France and her favourites, Prince Maurice of Orange, all became highly paid pensioners of Spain. They were not thereby rendered impotent or reduced to puppets like the minor Italian princes; but they were less likely, all things considered, to be swayed by, or be tempted to exploit, the passionate protests and wild schemes of the fanatics.

CHAPTER 1

From Little Wars to Total War 1610–28

To the most high and mighty king, whose greatness is without
equal; who shines over the whole globe as powerfully as the great
Alexander; who has the sun for his sombrero, and in whose
shadow lives the whole of Christendom; master over all his lands,
whose subjects are as numerous as the stars of heaven. (The Shah
of Persia to Philip III, 1610)[1]

Why have we made war for sixty-six years in such a naturally
intractable land as Flanders, from which we have derived no
benefit? Christ did not recommend that his law should be imposed
by artillery, pikes, and muskets. (A Spanish official, 1624) (E23)

Introduction

The first eight years of this period coincide with the closing phase of the
administration of the Spanish monarchy by the Duke of Lerma; the
last six with the opening phase of its government by the Count-Duke of
Olivares. Dividing these two vastly different men, whose view and
exercise of the office of *valido* provides such a dramatic contrast,
elapsed some four years (spring 1618 to autumn 1622), which can be
regarded as a kind of interregnum. It is important to note that during
this politically confused period, when Lerma's grip on power had been
prised open, and with Philip III afflicted by serious illness, was taken
the most momentous single decision ever arrived at by a government of
Habsburg Spain. For at some indeterminable stage – probably in the
winter of 1618–19 (E12) – it was settled upon that if the United
Provinces did not agree to renegotiate the truce of 1609 along lines
more favourable to Spain, it would be allowed to expire in 1621, when
war would be resumed against what was still (and emphatically)
regarded as a rebel community. A few weeks after these events duly
occurred, Philip IV, a young man acutely conscious of his responsibilities in the Low Countries, succeeded to the throne.

This still-obscure 'conjuncture' has naturally been seen as a point of
no return, at which the monarchy again took up its cross, the *damnosa
hereditas* of the Netherlands, and resumed the stations to inevitable

crucifixion. Other less immediate factors have been adduced in support of this view. The 'crisis' years of 1618–22 witnessed a sudden and intense economic depression in western and central Europe. Probably connected with this was the equally unexpected (and as it proved, permanent) drop in the level of bullion imports at Seville. Spain suddenly found herself forced to subsist upon approximately one-half of previous expectations from what one commentator in 1617 called 'Castile's annual American harvest'.[2] These years are also accepted as marking the culmination of crisis in the native Castilian economy: a twenty- or thirty-year period during which indigenous investment and manufacture ceased on any scale, economic institutions became moribund, staple trades had relapsed into atrophy, all accompanied by widespread agrarian failure. Seen together with the immense demographic setback of 1599–1614 (the great plague of Castile and the Morisco expulsion), it indicates that the Spanish economy, possibly along with that of the western Mediterranean as a whole, had entered a condition which at best could be called comatose. The corollary was that 'age of disillusion' expatiated upon by Pierre Vilar and John Elliott, the era of Don Quixote and the *arbitristas*, when the prevailing *mentalité* was one of doubt and depression bordering on despair (B1; B8). Suddenly, however, and without any alteration in the basic socio-economic picture, this orgy of introspection gave way to a mood of renewed dedication and optimism. Under a young king and a new minister, Spain 'found herself' again in the struggle against rebellion and heresy, and an age of passivity and torpor was succeeded by one of dynamism and reform.

One does not have to suppress reservations about the analysis of 'collective psychology' in order to acknowledge that this interpretation has much to commend it. At the level of government, the difference in personnel, in attitude, even in atmosphere between (say) 1617 and 1623 cannot be denied. Yet in a sense, the change is primarily one of emphasis and not of nature. The policy of the Olivares regime – as Professor Elliott himself has shown – was deliberately to exaggerate the contrast between the new reign and the old (E9). In effect it transmuted the criticism of the *arbitristas* into condemnation of, and thence into propaganda against, the latter. In fact, however, many of the policies normally associated with Olivares can be traced back to the period before his influence, even to that of Lerma. As this observation implies, there is an important line of continuity linking the two *validos*. In spite of its lack of striking military achievement and reforming zeal, the last decade of Philip III was not all literary pessimism and official peculation. The *Pax Hispanica*, as it has been (somewhat hyperbolically) called, was arguably the period in which the positive achievements of Habsburg Spain were most widely experienced and deeply admired amongst its European neighbours. The conception of their responsibilities held by Philip III and Lerma may not have been identical with that of their successors, but it was no less valid, and (as it happened) was much less disastrous. Moreover, the break between them on the ultimate question involved in the identity of the monarchy, that of defence, was not as sharp as might be supposed. Just as some key men of the Lerma period survived the proscription of the new government to foster opposition, so the decisions of 1618–21 were in no sense regarded as definitive or permanently binding. War was a business prosecuted on a short-term contract; the question of winding it up, on one front or on all, was hardly ever absent from the agendas of the councils and juntas of state. Though ideal long-term objectives existed, they could always be compromised when such action was consistent with honour or necessity. With hindsight we can see that Habsburg ministers – those of Philip III as much as those of his son – in practice had to choose between the glorious failure of war and the mundane failure of peace. It was not a wide spectrum of choice, and involved no fundamental or intrinsic differences beyond those of temperament. For these reasons, and others which will become evident, much of what follows in this chapter attempts to place stress on the elements of homogeneity in the period it covers.

Narrative of Events

As Roland Mousnier has amply demonstrated, the assassination of Henry IV of France was an event of such profound significance that it alone provides justification of 'the history of events' from the scorn of its critics (H11). For our immediate purposes, it is enough to observe that Ravaillac's thrust gave a new lease of life to the Spanish monarchy, guaranteeing the survival of its hegemony for perhaps a generation. It provided a breathing-space in which Spain – if she wished – could maintain peace in Europe, whilst ameliorating the terrible aftermath of Philip II's wars within the Spanish system, its administrations, societies and economies.

There could hardly be more convincing proof of the supreme priority of Spanish government than the uses to which it put this unique opportunity for respite and reform. As long as 'war' is understood as a synonym for 'defence' or 'security', government in Madrid was government of war, for war, and by war. In the decade following 1610, peace prevailed only in a very relative sense, and the *Pax Hispanica* is meaningful only when placed against the comparative standard of the 1590s and the 1620s – periods of *comprehensive* war. Castile still regarded itself – an idea that was certainly not simple paranoia – as being potentially threatened by jealous neighbours and disloyal forces inside and outside the monarchy. Consequently, at no time in this 'peaceful decade' were all its provincial centres and military outposts simultaneously at rest. The *Pax Hispanica* therefore was entirely analogous to the *Pax Romana* of the Antonines. The graceful arts of court and society which commentators have seen as reaching an apex in this period, did so behind a frontier which constantly seethed with political intrigue and military action.

To begin with, the sequential closing of the northern fronts in the first decade of his reign offered Philip III the chance to tackle a problem widely regarded as the most insidious and dangerous facing Castile. For forty years a 'final solution' to the Morisco question had been continually postponed by Madrid because of other more urgent concerns (G2). Thus, even as Henry IV was beating his drum in Paris, the whole military and naval establishment of metropolitan Spain was mobilised in the immense operation required by the Decree of Expulsion signed the year before. The collection, transportation and shipment of more than a quarter of a million Moriscos from all parts of central, southern and eastern Spain was, in effect, a series of full-scale military campaigns lasting continuously from 1609 until 1614. We must not be misled by the absence of pitched battle and the (relative) lack of blood; and neither is it purely Quixotic fancy to speak of complete victory, for Habsburg Spain was utterly convinced of its necessity and devoted huge resources to its achievement. Though it was doubtless exaggerated, both at the time and subsequently, the Moriscos represented a real threat to integrity and security. Our own natural horror at the ruthless inhumanity of the deed must not blind us to the fact that no contemporary society, granted the power to do otherwise, could willingly tolerate the presence of such a substantial minority of culturally unassimilable, yet powerful, aliens. In the context of the major theme of this study, and for all the long-term economic results of the expulsion, Spain was a more viable unit in 1614 than it had previously been.

The additional price of such security was eternal vigilance. And there is no denying that – given the lax nature of the Lerma regime – vigilance frequently spilled over into activity of a more positive, even provocative, kind. The flashpoint of danger in 1614–18 was Italy, and in particular the Duchy of Milan. It was here, not in the Low Countries, far less in Germany, that contemporaries expected the coming of a crisis which might drag the interested parties into general war. Milan was sandwiched between two hostile minor powers, Venice and Savoy, but behind them loomed the United Provinces and France – not to mention the Protestant states of Rhineland Germany – to whom they were tied by commercial and diplomatic links. The pulsating ambitions

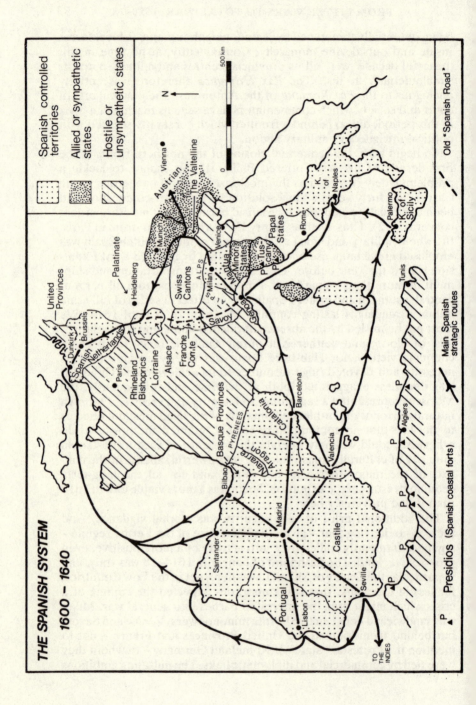

THE SPANISH SYSTEM
1600 – 1640

Spanish controlled territories

Allied or sympathetic states

Hostile or unsympathetic states

500 km

N

United Provinces

Spanish Netherlands

Dunkirk

Brussels

Paris

Rhineland Bishoprics

Lorraine

Alsace

Franche Comté

Palatinate

Heidelberg

Munich

Austrian

The Valteline

Swiss Cantons

ALPS

ALPS

Savoy

Genoa

Venice

Mantua

Minor States

Papal States

Rome

P. Tus-
P. cany

Vienna

K. of Naples

Palermo

K. of Sicily

Basque Provinces

PYRENEES

Navarre

Aragon

Catalonia

Barcelona

Valencia

Bilbao

Santander

Castile

Madrid

Portugal

Lisbon

Seville

TO THE INDIES

Tunis

Algiers

P

P

P

P

P

P

P

P

Old "Spanish Road"

Main Spanish strategic routes

P   Presidios (Spanish coastal forts)

of Carlo Emanuele I of Savoy, whose conspiratorial stamina represented a maverick element in European politics for nearly half a century, kept Spanish officials in Italy permanently on their toes. 'No slavery', he wrote to his son, kept hostage in Madrid as surety for his good behaviour, 'is more onerous than that of subjection to Spain' (G12). On more than one occasion he fell victim to his own loud and insistent propaganda, portraying him as the selfless hero of Italian liberty, and having failed to elicit support from the obvious candidates, took the field alone against the Spanish oppressors. Although this uppity princeling was soundly thrashed for his pains, and brought to heel for the time being by the Peace of Asti (1617), the enmity of Savoy rendered Milan vulnerable and sensitive. It was extremely unwise, therefore, for the so-called 'Great Duke' of Osuna to persist in attempting to alienate Venice, from his viceroyalty in Naples. Time was to prove that Venice, so unsympathetic to the Spanish presence in north Italy, was never prepared to act accordingly ('she is an enemy merely by estimation', as Antony Sherley put it).[3] Osuna's actions went far to achieve the contrary. Not perhaps, through the notorious 'conspiracy of Venice', since evidence of a Spanish-inspired plot to subvert the Serene Republic (though it formed an important article in the common European indictment of the monarchy) has never been discovered. But Osuna certainly encouraged the Vatican in its sacerdotal struggle against Venice, and, more seriously, waged indirect war on the republic's trade by his patronage of the Uskoks, a highly successful band of Adriatic pirates. Here, and on Venice's alpine frontier, where several Spanish–Italian *tercios* were engaged against her on behalf of the Archduke Ferdinand of Austria, a sinister element of co-operation existed between the two branches of the Habsburg House.

The standstill in the north was followed by a more forward policy in the Mediterranean generally. Of a piece with the expulsion of the Moriscos and the strong intervention in Catalan politics associated with the viceroyalty of Alburquerque (1615–18), were the expeditions aimed at flushing out various enclaves of Ottoman influence in north Africa and the central Mediterranean islands. A mighty handful of amphibious operations was launched, with considerable success, against the Barbary coast and Malta (1611), Tunis (1612) and Morocco (1614). The timing was propitious, since the Turkish empire was preoccupied with war against the Persians on its eastern frontiers, as well as being seriously disturbed by internal problems. Although the 'Barbary pirate' states of north Africa continued to be a thorn in Spain's side for more than a century to come (and Madrid was aware of their contacts with the Dutch) by 1618 the nexus of trade and communication in the western Mediterranean basin was more secure than ever before, a factor of inestimable importance in view of forthcoming events.

The constant energising of the Spanish system which such events illustrate seems not to accord with the conventional picture of the limp, complaisant government of Philip III and Lerma. Pierre Chaunu refers cryptically to this period as a 'Mediterranean interlude' in Spanish policy (C9), and indeed it may prove on closer investigation that a guiding principle of Madrid's role in these years was one of reorientation towards the south – a conception of the monarchy which most historians believe to have been definitively abandoned by Philip II in the 1570s. But in any case, even the more well-trodden paths of research show few signs of the purposeless inactivity which was once an emphasised characteristic of the reign. It is now accepted as the classic era of Spanish diplomacy, and certainly Madrid was never again able to deploy this most brilliant and intangible of its resources to such good effect. It was multitalented statesmanship of a very high order which ensured that out of the peace settlements of 1598–1609 was produced a situation where (in Trevor-Roper's striking if exaggerated phrase) 'the universal victor was the power which had been universally defeated' (C1). Though the millions of words of their extant correspondence (and, naturally, those of subsequent biographers) persistently overestimate the personal element in the achievements of such men as Gondomar (in London), Oñate (in Prague and Vienna), and Bédmar (in Venice and Paris), the negotiations in which they were involved substantially altered the European political balance in Spain's favour. The astonishing amount of vitriolic literature inspired by Gondomar's embassy is sufficient testimony to the feeling of one section of English opinion that their influence – and that of England herself – had been sterilised by Spanish flattery, bribes and promises. At the imperial court, Zúñiga and Oñate carefully re-forged the political links of the 'great House of Austria', reactivating an association which had almost withered away since the 1560s (E5). Oñate's agreement with the Archduke Ferdinand in Vienna (1617) indicated how far the two Habsburg minds were beginning to meet, and provided the strategic and financial basis for much subsequent collaboration. In this manner were repaired two damaged lines of political and military logistics. If the flanks were more secure, so was the centre, for at Paris, Cárdenas and Bédmar built on the Franco-Spanish double marriage treaty of 1612, creating a pro-Spanish party by the use of all available arguments, both material and spiritual. Such groups, more or less active in London, Paris, Prague and Vienna, existed by the 1620s to lobby and pester their governments in favour of neutrality, complaisance, or even co-operation with regard to Spanish policy.

By 1618, therefore, the old anti-Habsburg front of the late sixteenth century, never perhaps solidly substantial, had been broken up. In the last analysis, diplomacy is a kind of political salesmanship; but who would deny its usefulness, even when the quality of the product – in this case Spain's wealth, power and determination – was generally acknowledged? Certainly the skill with which Garret Mattingly's beloved galaxy of ambassadors exploited the conflicting fears and aspirations of the courts to which they were accredited has few equals in the history of this particular political science. Can we go further, and suggest that these men planned – or plotted – the events of 1618–21? This seems unlikely; but all were acutely conscious of the pressures upon the fabric of the monarchy; of the motives which inspired connections between these pressures; and, above all, of the facts that Louis XIII would not remain a minor for ever, and that the Truce of Antwerp was due to run out in 1621.

What is certain is that Spain in 1618 had, as it were, a geopolitical footing upon which could be based a response to the emergency in central Europe. Assurances of support against the Bohemian rebellion therefore reached Vienna almost by return of post from Madrid in the summer of that year, and Spanish troops took part in the earliest manoeuvres of the Thirty Years' War. The subsequent decade was one of virtually uninterrupted success for Spanish arms. The visitor to Madrid's world-famous Prado museum enters by a chamber in which are displayed ten of the twelve huge canvasses commissioned by Olivares from the finest painters of the monarchy to adorn the new palace of the Buen Retiro which he built in the 1630s. Each of them celebrates a major victory of the first half of the Thirty Years' War on one of the monarchy's world-wide battlegrounds. Indeed the scope and scale of its concerns is difficult to convey in the present restricted compass. Spanish fleets and armies traversed half the globe: in 1620 the *tercios* were instrumental in the decisive defeat of Czechs at the White Mountain; the crucial Valtelline passes of the Alps were occupied by Feria; Spínola performed the same for Alsace and the Lower Palatinate. The end of the Dutch truce was closely followed by a defeat of the enemy fleet in Spanish waters, and the victor here, Fadrique de Toledo, was on hand to repulse a Dutch assault on Brazil in 1625. At the same time, considerable aid was despatched to the beleaguered Portuguese outposts in the Persian Gulf and at all points east. In the main German theatre of war, successive Dutch-supported Protestant champions advanced (Bethlen Gabor, from the east; Count Mansfeld, from the west; Christian IV of Denmark, from the north) and rebounded from Catholic armies stiffened with Spanish pikemen. In 1625 came the *pièce de résistance*, Spínola's reduction of the Dutch fortress of Breda, family seat of the Orange-Nassau Stadtholders themselves. Velázquez's painting of this event, master- and centrepiece of Olivares's commission, celebrates the most prestigious of all the triumphs of the *época de triunfo*, which, coming a century after the battle of Pavia, was extolled as the greatest blow for the faith since that of Lepanto.

The fall of Breda created an arc of Spanish strongpoints around the United Provinces. The Archduchess Isabel and Spínola were thus in a position to enforce an extremely stringent economic blockade, not only of the continental river trade of the Dutch, but also of their ports and fisheries, thanks to the rapid development in Flemish shipyards of a superb new armada of modern frigates. For most of this decade, indeed, Spain held the initiative in the North Sea (a position hardly even contemplated by Philip II), and the effect on Dutch commerce was truly devastating. The armada of Dunkirk, and the overall naval effort of which it formed a part, were in turn the main weapon in Olivares's maritime-centred programme for the defeat of the Dutch by fully orchestrated economic warfare (F8). The year before Breda, the count-duke had set in motion this hugely ambitious design, known in Spanish as the *Almirantazgo* (or Admiralty) project. It was a revolutionary concept in Spanish strategy, by which the established continental power went over to the defensive on land (protected by the famous 'Union of Arms', a scheme of collective security in which all the monarchy's dependencies would join) and engaged by sea in a massive guerrilla operation aimed at the economic strangulation of the main enemy. The key campaign, however, involved a strike towards the Baltic, without which no overall success was possible. Unfortunately, it was precisely this area which was largely outside Spain's control. For these plans to reach fruition, Olivares depended on the unpredictable figure of Wallenstein. Nevertheless, for a time at least, the twin pillars of Dutch wealth and power – the Baltic trade and the North Sea fisheries – were in mortal danger. Perhaps at no other point during the whole course of the 'eighty years' war' for independence, was the Dutch republic so close to extinction. Conversely, the triennium 1624–6 was, if not the Everest, surely the Eiger of the Spanish system's military and administrative achievement.

As in the 1580s, however, the alarm bells sounded in London and Paris. In 1624, as Olivares's planning matured, Richelieu assumed the chief ministry of his king, whilst across the Channel, Prince Charles and Buckingham were badgering theirs to declare war in vindication of England's honour. A series of Franco-Dutch agreements provided for Bourbon aid to the beleaguered republic (especially the Treaty of Compiègne, 1625) and a French partnership with Savoy was struck at Rivoli the same year. By 1625, indeed, both France and England were at war with Spain. The targets of the first Franco-Spanish war for a generation – essentially a diversionary effort in favour of the Dutch –

were Genoa and the Alpine passes. For a time, the Genoese republic, too, was besieged, until a joint operation by Feria's Milanese army and the Mediterranean fleet under Santa Cruz could be mounted. Once the Spanish system rumbled into action the result was hardly in doubt; decisive defeat for the French and Savoyards was registered in the virtual *diktat* of Monzón (1626). Similar treatment was meted out to the ill-organised English contribution. A combined Anglo-Dutch amphibious expedition against Cadiz – in terms of size, at least, one of the grandest of the century – was routed and repulsed by the local militiamen of Andalusia. This was a dramatic reversal of events thirty years earlier. During the next few years, England's continental and coastwise trade was severely mauled by Spanish maritime forces. By 1629, Charles I (who had meanwhile also blundered into war with France, thus upsetting the anti-Habsburg applecart) had learnt his mistake and was ready to sue for peace. It was little wonder that in 1626 Olivares prepared an ecstatic self-congratulatory speech for his young master to deliver to the Cortes of Castile; 'all the might of France, England, Holland, and Denmark, could not save Breda from our victorious arms' (D2/11).

By now, however, Castile itself was showing signs of serious fatigue, ominously akin to that of the 1590s. Olivares's attempts to relieve the pressure on its precious resources of men and money – to which both the Union of Arms and the *Almirantazgo* project clearly relate – had not been successful. The scheme to place royal finances on a securer basis, through a central bank and reformed taxation, had run into a morass of political difficulties. These setbacks forced a resort to floods of *vellón* coinage and increases in crude sales taxes, both inimical to the welfare of the Castilian peasant and businessman. In addition, during the mid-1620s, harvests were uniformly below par. The unprecedented cost of the Breda campaign led directly to the first 'bankruptcy' of the reign in 1627, that is to say even before the stunning blow of Matanzas, the Dutch capture of the silver fleet, in 1628 (G5). In these years, Spanish forces in all landward theatres were so passive that the situation amounted to one of armistice. It is true that this position accorded with the overall strategic thinking of the count-duke, but it is also notable that a prolonged bout of stocktaking was engaged within the government. These deliberations were punctuated by the news of the death of the Duke of Mantua, pro-Spanish lord of two important chunks of territory in north Italy. His heir was a French nobleman – worse, a protégé of Richelieu and Father Joseph. The calm was shattered by the precipitate military action of Córdoba, governor of Milan, taken to preserve Spanish interests on the spot. His trumpets blared out the danger to prestige, the threat to a position gained by ten years of unrelenting effort. The monarchy resumed its ride to the abyss.

Resources

When the infant king Louis XIII of France became the son-in-law of
Philip III in 1612, he entered the protection of a man who was, to
quote the marriage contract

> King of Castile, of Leon, of Aragon, of the two Sicilies, of
> Jerusalem, of Portugal, of Navarre, of Granada, of Toledo, of
> Valencia, of Galicia, of Majorca, of Seville, of Cordera, of Cór-
> doba, of Gorcega, of Murcia, of Jaén, of the Algarves, of Algeciras,
> of Gibraltar, of the Canary Islands, of the East and West Indies,
> and of the Atlantic Islands. Count of Barcelona, Lord of Biscay and
> of Molina, Duke of Arbenas and of Neopatria, Count of Rosellón,
> Marquis of Oristan and of Gocceano, Archduke of Austria, Duke of
> Burgundy and of Brabant and of Milan, Count of Flanders and of
> Tyrol.[4]

Even this list was not exhaustive! Such an enormous aggregation of
power naturally excited the elemental fear of some observers, and the
admiration of others. Two of the latter, writing in this period, considered that the extent and variety of the monarchy qualified it for
universal dominion. More significant (for our purposes) than any of
the Castilian *arbitristas*, are the works, more political than economic,
of Antony Sherley and Tommaso Campanella. Sherley's father had
sailed against Spain with the Elizabethan seadogs; Campanella personally led a rebellion against the Spaniards in his native Naples. Both,
however, believed that the Philippine monarchy was a potentially
coherent and self-sufficient unit, if not actually a homogeneous one.
They therefore discussed resources, Sherley from the strictly material
point of view, Campanella from a vantage more spiritual or
philosophical. The former's great memorandum, *Political Power in the
Whole World*, was addressed to Olivares in 1622, and has with justification been seen as one of the earliest expressions of *Weltpolitik*. The
ultimate fulfilment of the monarchy, Sherley argued, could only be
achieved by economic autarky. He examined its widespread natural
resources in detail, suggesting that the proper exploitation and
exchange thereof could liberate it from dependence on the resources
of its rivals in the constant struggle to feed and clothe the peoples of the
monarchy, to stimulate their economies, and to supply their defence
requirements.[5]

Whilst Sherley was, perhaps, the most thoroughgoing of those who
viewed power through the lens of mercantilism, Campanella's dimension was different, but no less comprehensive in scope. In several
utopian works, including *Concerning the Spanish Monarchy* (c. 1610),

he apostrophised the Spanish empire as capable of uniting diverse talents and interests in a common purpose, the creation of a peaceful and spiritually centred world community: 'The Portuguese and Genoese have the mastery of trade and navigation; the Netherlanders everything to do with manufacture and machines; the Italians, problems of administration; the Spaniards, those of war, exploration, diplomacy, and religious affairs (H9).' Though his ideas were tinged with millenarian madness, Campanella went even further than Sherley in one material respect. For him, the future lay with science and technology, and the more the patronage of Spain encouraged development in these areas, the more its universal destiny could be realised. In particular he advocated the foundation of schools of seamanship, 'for the master of the sea will always be master of the land'. On this point his ideas coincided exactly with those of his English contemporary, for Sherley also envisaged maritime development as the highroad to political influence.

The optimism of such thinkers may be interpreted as a counterweight to the gloomy diagnosis of the native political economists of Castile. But, in practice, however much Olivares and others might dream of it, the luxury of such a programme was never permitted by the context of recurrent emergency in which Spain was governed. The 1620s witnessed the final abandonment of any attempt to run the Spanish system in all its facets through the official agency of government – the directly bureaucratic approach known as *administración* – and the general resort to its weaker and less reliable alternative, the *ad hoc* contract with private enterprise, or *asiento*. This is one of the many paradoxes of Olivares's policy, and Dr Thompson is surely right to regard 'the inability of Madrid to tap to the full the resources of the Monarchy' as a major cause of the decline of Spain in Europe (G1). By this criterion, indeed, Olivares was attempting the impossible, and it may therefore be correct to judge him by how close to the impossible he came.

In demographic terms, at least, available resources experienced no major setback between the plague of Castile (1599–1601) and that of Milan (1628–30). However, although most Moriscos were not eligible for military service, the expulsion was bound to place a further indirect strain on the capacity of the peninsula in this respect. As it proved, the monarchy was not to confront insurmountable problems of recruitment until the 1640s, but the populations of Spain, Italy and Flanders had ceased to expand, and replacing the continuously depleting ranks of the *tercios* was never less than a painful and doubtful exercise. Between 1607 (date of the first armistice with the Dutch) and 1621, the problem was a mild one; when it increased in pressure, inexorably and without respite in the 1620s, two factors may have eased the perennial quest of the *maestro de campo* and his drum-sergeant. First, the constant drift of the population to the towns perhaps reduced the necessity to scour the outlying districts of Castile and Naples in the kind of counterproductive invasion later to become ubiquitous. And second (since we are being speculative), the economic depression itself, by increasing unemployment, may have had the effect of releasing men to the colours.

We are now much more aware of how war could be self-perpetuating in the context of early modern society. The 'travelling' destruction of armies caused regular local dislocation, which in turn forced men to enlist through the lack of other means of subsistence. It is equally possible that the profound slump of the generation before 1621, reaching an acute point (especially in northern Italy) in 1619–22, had a similar effect. In other words, the phenomenon of 'trailing a pike in Flanders' (to be observed all over western Europe) may have had similar causes to the noticeable increase in vagrancy and banditry in the Mediterranean of this period. If this was the case, it may be suggested that economic decline actually assisted the Spanish war effort, at least in the short to medium term. The hypothesis seems particularly to make sense in the Italian dependencies, where agrarian depression set in around 1590, spreading gradually to the towns and manufacturing centres up to the crisis of 1620. In 1591, the Italian element of the army of Flanders comprised a mere 2·6 per cent; by 1601 this figure was nearer 5 per cent, and by 1610 had reached 10 per cent, continuing to grow during the whole of the Thirty Years' War (F1).

Be this as it may, Spain's military establishment was exceptionally healthy during the opening campaigns of the war. Madrid was in control of four operational field armies, in Flanders, the Rhineland, central Europe and Italy, each around the optimum size of the period (20,000), in addition to twice as many garrison troops. Moreover, a virtually new navy had been created since about 1617, some fifty galleons being built, fitted and manned for service in the *Armada del Mar Oceano*, not to mention other auxiliary squadrons such as that of Dunkirk. All in all, there seems little reason to doubt Philip IV's boast in 1626, that the monarchy had no less than 300,000 men under arms.

The inevitable consequence of this massive military expansion was an increasing shortage of supply, and in the 1620s a gap quickly opened up between the numbers conscripted and the ability to feed, clothe, equip and pay them. Even if Olivares's domestic programme had not been faced with insuperable political difficulties, it would probably never have had time to mature and take the strain now being placed upon the Spanish system. Various improvised orders were issued in the spirit of the nostrums of the 'reform memorandum' which emanated from the Council of Castile in 1619, and the *arbitrista* ideas which lay behind it. Apart from the fiscal measures already mentioned, there were the sumptuary laws associated with the *Junta de la Reformación*, attempts to tighten up import restrictions and tariff barriers, and to encourage home industries (such as leather, steel and shipbuilding). The total embargo on trade with the Dutch was a very successful offensive weapon, but proved completely unrealistic in terms of the essential needs of Spanish commerce and the Andalusian economy. Consequently this, like all the other long-term objectives of Olivares's 'economic planning', was continually shelved, waived, ignored or undermined in practice, not only by harassed local officials, but by central government itself. The task of resuscitating an economy which had already been moribund for a generation was quite beyond an administration that operated permanently under emergency conditions, which needed to plug gaps and to carry out running repairs with any materials which came to hand.

These materials were all too often foreign-, or even enemy-controlled. The decline of textile and metallurgical manufacture in both Spain and northern Italy, meant an increased dependence on German and other sources of supply in northern Europe. As war became general and transport a lottery, the cost of fire- and side-arms escalated and the search for supplies preoccupied the officials of Olivares's juntas. As early as 1623 the need for mass-production of gunpowder led to the formation of a junta charged with the stimulation of Spain's dormant centres of manufacture. Of still greater importance was the exhaustion of timber stocks in the peninsula, due to the deforestation occasioned by the various naval programmes of Philip II. This had wideranging military implications, since wood was necessary for pikes, guns, carts, barrels, and for all kinds of siege- and defence-works which comprised the indispensable hardware of an army. The shortfall in this area was even more critical in the maritime theatre. Indeed, the rapid development of a new navy took place against the background of an almost complete *falta de medios*. Spain's Mediterranean provinces simply did not possess in any quantity the raw materials to construct or maintain it. As early as 1623, for example, it was not possible to provide or replace masts from indigenous sources: 'Since we cannot obtain these from Holland', Philip IV minuted, 'we must write to our ambassador in England, and ask him to arrange a contract with merchants there, or from the Hanse towns, for the delivery to Lisbon of a quantity of masts – as long as they are not carried in Dutch ships.'[6] The same applied, however, to rope, pitch and tar; in practice 'the Dutch connection' could not be avoided, and Madrid constantly had to fall back on the middlemen of Amsterdam. The dominant trinity of grain, copper and timber, all essential to the smooth working of the Spanish system, was a Dutch preserve (stemming from their monopoly of Baltic trade). Dutch business was actually anxious to co-operate, for they had almost equal need of salt (for their fishing industry and other ancillary trades) from the rich deposits of Portugal and Murcia. Through this contact, and a variety of frauds and deceptions, many of them perforce connived at by the Spanish authorities, the Dutch presence in north Europe–Seville trade (and consequently in that of Seville in the Atlantic) was maintained. 'Despite the prohibitions on any kind of dealing with the Dutch', complained one official in Brussels, 'they are in fact allowed to compete for our business on even better terms than his Majesty's own subjects.'[7]

The great resolution to forego Dutch goods and services in the actual process of reducing the republic to terms therefore broke down, but it came too close to success in the middle years of the decade for it to be written off as a chimera. The more we know about the industry, imagination and consistency of Olivares's 'grand design', the more impressive it seems. Nevertheless, by the late 1620s his attempt to catapult Spanish power into the Baltic, to asphyxiate the Dutch, and fulfil Sherley's dreams, had to be called off. Though some elements were persevered with, the economic blockade – the count-duke's 'continental system' – was allowed to lapse, and Brussels was permitted once more to subcontract with the Dutch, and to raise much-needed revenue by the sale of licences and trade-passports. Meanwhile, Olivares's brother-in-law, the Marqius of Leganés, was reduced (in his capacity as captain-general of artillery) to arranging an agreement with Simón de Silveira, most prominent of the new Portuguese business allies of the crown, for an equal division of guns and specie which could be salvaged from wrecks in Spanish waterways. 'He is able to do this by the use of newly designed instruments and machines.'[8] It was not, perhaps, exactly what Campanella had envisaged, but it had its place in the scheme of things.

Questions connected with the material supply of the armed forces of the monarchy are still, to my mind, in need of further detailed research, and may reveal much more about its inner workings. Those of financial resources, on the other hand, are better provided for by modern investigation. Admittedly some elements of budgeting procedure are still a mystery, but at least we now have a basic outline of how things were managed and fairly reliable estimates of the sums involved. Olivares's government was persistently able to solve the problems of war financing, though only through intense effort and at tremendous cost. Estimation of need, negotiation of *asientos de dinero*, transfer of credit and specie, went on continuously, in an atmosphere never less than critical, often frenetic. It took ten years of comprehensive warfare, and the appalling expenditure of 1625, before the over-heated engine seized up for the first time in 1627. This is all the more remarkable in view of the fact that the two wars of 1618 and 1621 – to name only the major commitments – were embarked upon in full cognisance of the swingeing drop in bullion imports during the previous quinquennium. Of course, the chorus of demands and complaints over subsidy and supply was unceasing; there was not a moment of rest from the open beaks of the imperial eaglets. In much of this, of course, there was an element of tactical exaggeration, by which it is easy to be misled; and it seems that, unlike the metropolitan defences studied by Dr Thompson, those comprising the actual theatres of war were – to judge by the absence of mutiny at least – sufficiently catered for.

By far the greater proportion of the revenue on which subsidies were secured was derived, directly or otherwise, from the Castilian taxpayer. This fact raises the interesting question: how necessary was a healthy economy to the prosecution of war? One way of answering is provided by Professor Alcalá-Zamora:

> There is no doubt that the economic structures of our country left much to be desired in 1620; but it is certain also that it possessed enormous reserves of energy, which were expended during the following 40 years in the most continuous and disproportionate effort ever made by a people. An exhausted nation would have succumbed to the strain well before it did. (F6)

This certainly takes us part of the way, though it still seems to beg the essential question, which the present writer has attempted to tackle elsewhere (C8). For it is arguable that the Spanish system simply did not, at any point in its existence, rely on what we would regard as a normal economic infrastructure, but rather on a peculiar, indeed unique, combination of unlimited deficit-financing and extra-economic revenue. During the years covered by this chapter, speaking approximately, the annual royal budget expanded from 12 million to more than 15 million ducats. Roughly one-half of this had to be written off to service the crown's debt – a practice regularly adhered to up until 1627; and even during the comparatively quiescent years of Philip III, recurrent military spending wavered between 4 and 5 million ducats – that is to say a further third at least. During the last three years of the reign, money contracts rose in value by over 50 per cent to some 7½ million. The following decade was the most profligate, in terms of borrowing, in the whole of the Habsburg period; taking 1621 as the base year (= 100), it reached 240 in the year of Breda (1625). This represents an increase in expenditure of 250 per cent (1615–25) as against one in revenue of 25 per cent! After the double blow of 'suspension of payments' and Matanzas in 1627–8, the crown was never again able to raise credit on such a scale.

Nearly all the methods adopted in order to negotiate loans were in some way inimical to the Castilian economy. The coinage of *vellón*, for example, wreaked havoc with the rate of exchange, confused the monetary system, and put capitalism on the rack. Moreover, much of the copper used in the process had to be purchased from Sweden through the good offices of the Dutch! But it brought in 2.6 million ducats per annum to the treasury in 1621–6. It was then replaced by commensurate increases in the *millones*, an extraordinary sales tax utterly hostile to business and investment. In addition, the dynasty gradually reduced itself to penury and political impotence during the Thirty Years' War. In his early years, Philip IV reduced his own annual household expenditure by 75 per cent to some 300,000 ducats. He regularly resorted to alienation of his own *patrimonios* (royal estates), and likewise mortgaged many other sources of regular income. Hundreds of regalian rights and petty feudal privileges were abandoned in the search for ready cash, in a process which gradually undermined the very stability of government. Like economic matters themselves, considerations of political husbandry were not allowed to obstruct the juggernaut of war.

One apparent innovation in the fiduciary field must be briefly considered. The strength of Spain's position in Italy may be judged by the military contribution made, not only by the direct dependencies, but also by the satellite princelings, to the army which threw the French out of Genoa in 1625. Before this period, however, the temptation to exploit the Italian provinces financially had been resisted through fear of prejudicing political control. This principle was deserted for the first time in 1620, when an *asiento* of a million ducats was raised on the royal rents of Milan, specifically for use in Flanders. This was quickly followed by the imposition of new war taxation, at first both sporadic and modest in scale, on Naples and Sicily. As Philip IV put it to the President of his Council of Italy: 'The present state of the affairs of my kingdoms compels me to seek all possible means of raising revenue with which to defend them. One of those regarded as most suitable for this purpose is the extraction of a million ducats from the kingdoms of Naples and Sicily.'[9] The sum involved in both these transactions suggests that Madrid was aware of the actual extent of the slump in bullion returns, which ran out at a million ducats a year; and that Italian sources were envisaged as a substitute for what was assumed to be a temporary embarrassment. In fact – a syndrome with which the modern taxpayer is all too familiar – it was to prove permanent, indeed (without exaggeration) a breakthrough into a new era of war financing for the monarchy. The Old World was to be called in to redress the balance of the New.

As for the famed wealth of the Indies, engrossments of silver never represented more than a fraction of the funds managed by the royal *Hacienda*. On the other hand, its value as security for loans gave it a considerable premium value over all other sources of revenue. In the years leading up to Breda, price inflation, exacerbated by the wars, again reached the peak levels of 1603, and this, plus monetary inflation, increased the value of specie. Partly for this reason, the German and Genoese bankers of the crown were always prepared to do business. Even after the serious breakdown of 1627, the rickety system was capable of repair, so long as the annual arrival of the plate fleet at Seville remained, as it had for over a century, as certain as the day itself. In the negotiations of 1627, when some great Genoese houses went to the wall, Olivares persuaded a branch of the Fuggers to keep its hand in, and arranged a big new *asiento* with a group of Portuguese-Jewish financiers. Things seemed set reasonably fair for the campaigns of 1628 – the year of Mantua and Matanzas.

Policy

For this period, the influence of two powerful favourites in the making of policy was firmly established. The Duke of Lerma's authority was enshrined in a 'constitutional' instrument in 1612; Olivares had completed the manoeuvres necessary to his position by 1623. It is, however, no contradiction to state that to a very large extent, responsibility for decisions remained a collective one, even if this in practice meant the defeat of one group or 'interest' by another. All major questions of peace and war, treaties and alliances, were invariably referred to the Council of State, either in the first place or at a later stage. The opinions of other councils or of individuals were also often canvassed. In this manner a wide variety of ministerial and professional advisers were permitted to address a question, down to 1630 or so even if predictably unfavourable to the 'governing' interest. For the king and his *valido* to act in flagrant opposition to majority opinion, formally expressed in a *consulta* (or report) was a difficult and risky operation (E13). The reliance of the crown on the great clerical and secular lords who staffed the council was a painful reality in a whole range of affairs. In the course of these twenty years, nevertheless, a definite regression in the authority of *Estado* can be discerned. Until about 1622 it was both consultant and executive in function, consistently with the political style of Lerma and Philip III; under Olivares, it was almost imperceptibly stripped of executive power, and eventually lost much of its consultative role also. By the 1630s it had become a mere appendix to government.

Of course, the crown could always work to ensure a compliant response, by the exertion of the kind of pressure familiar to any student of modern Cabinet government, and this was often enough for the *valido*'s purposes. In particular, the government was able to exploit the tension between the Councils of State and Finance, arising from the latter's constant attempts to intervene in, or to usurp, the functions of the former (analogous to the relationship between the Cabinet and the Treasury today). Intractable difficulties with either committee – or, more awkward still, with both – could be surmounted by recourse to *ad hoc* juntas, small groups of handpicked supporters. The proliferation of such bodies is rightly associated with the Olivares regime, but their use was by no means peculiar thereto. Both of Philip IV's immediate predecessors had utilised them when necessary, and it might be felt that government by junta was essentially a response to war rather than a characteristic of a style of politics *per se*. The more war, the more juntas, of course, and under Olivares they became the rule and not the exception, established as well as improvised – a feature to which the prolonged lives of the *Junta de Estado* and the *Junta de Medios* amply testify. Though often a mark of exasperation, and always politically tactless, such methods were part of the royal prerogative, and certainly made administration more flexible; no inherent rights, either of collective authority or individual membership, attached to the 'official' councils, as Olivares reminded them in a circular as early as 1623.

Another point may be made in modification of the still-prevalent view of rule by *valido* as the total delegation of *all* executive power. The role in government of the kings themselves is coming to seem considerably greater than earlier writers had supposed. The whig-liberal attitude, which, with its moralistic overtones, dominated nineteenth-century work, and could speak via the pen of E. J. Hamilton as late as 1938 of 'the progressive degeneration in the characters of the monarchs' (B7) now appears in need of radical revision. Whilst such routine judgements are still a feature of the textbooks, recent detailed studies of Philip III and his son are virtually unanimous in revaluing their administrative abilities. In the case of the latter, indeed, the reappraisal is complete. According to Alcalá-Zamora,

> Philip IV took part in, kept himself informed of, and himself decided upon, all the affairs of government. Those who have worked on the original papers are continually surprised by this, and become aware of having been deceived by references to his 'indolence'. At least during the first twenty years of his reign, the king's workrate bears comparison with, and often exceeded, that of his grandfather. (F6).

Since the king can no longer be regarded merely as a passive element in the partnership, the 'institution' of the *valimiento* itself seems not to conform to previous views. As a working method of government, it can still be seen as delegation of authority, but not as abdication of responsibility. Olivares's own ingrained belief in his master's sacred duty to rule is attested by the king's minutes, comments and signature on numberless documents of the reign, ranging from the weighty to the trivial. To sum up, it can be stated that, for this period at least, policy was a matter for a flexible apparatus, which, however hierarchical in structure and oligarchical in nature, was committee-oriented and based on consensus.

Such a system appears to epitomise the unity of purpose felt by almost all levels of society during the opening years of the new reign. Official memoranda, political pamphlets, sermons, dramatic and poetic effusions, all were instinct with the sense of mission, and bewailed the outraged honour which the withdrawal from the north had brought to the monarchy. The determination of the new regime 'to seek the bubble reputation even in the cannon's mouth', was doubtless popular, for the early 1620s were filled with 'an almost revolutionary enthusiasm' (F6) for war against heresy, a campaign which was associated with the rooting-out of Lerma's supporters from government and bureaucracy. A partial corrective to the impression given by this strange and partly 'inspired' phenomenon is given by Professor Domínguez Ortiz:

[Lerma's policy] was certainly not one of cowardice, or of renunciation, or of bowing to the force of destiny. It was more a dangerous conviction that the empire could cease to be a dynamic enterprise, perpetually recreated by daily sacrifice, and that it would be enough to maintain the position already acquired, taking small defensive measures, with an occasional demonstration of power in order to preserve prestige. (G5)

Lerma's vision, therefore, was clearly more limited than that of many other ministers; and his fall in 1618 was bound up with his defeat in the Council of State over the German question, and the victory of Zúñiga, Olivares's uncle, and the most well-placed and ruthless spokesman of the 'hawkish party'. In effect, however, the duke's position had been previously undermined by this group – which included Feria and Oñate, as well as Osuna, later ironically proscribed as a client of Lerma. It had its plans firmly fixed on the option of a renewal of full-scale war in 1621. As early as 1617, Oñate's treaty with Ferdinand of Styria laid down the basis of future Habsburg collaboration. In the same year, the decision was taken to revive the sadly neglected navy, and the first contracts for a new *Armada del Mar Oceano* were duly signed. From Naples, Osuna raved about the gathering designs of Spain's enemies. 'This pacifist attitude serves only to oppress my soul', he berated Philip III, 'and to give comfort to those who are jealous of the monarchy ... all that is needed is for Your Majesty to have resolution, and Spain will not fail you.'[10] Osuna's views were a known quantity; more telling was the support of the Archduke Albert and Ambrogio Spínola, from Brussels, for intervention in Germany in 1618. These men had been the chief proponents of the Truce of Antwerp, and in essence they saw the need to take precautionary measures in the Rhineland as a 'police-type' operation which would safeguard that settlement, and encourage the Dutch to renew it on terms more favourable to Brussels. Nevertheless, they subscribed to the so-called 'domino theory' of containment of Spain's enemies, popular amongst the 'hawks', and later perfectly elaborated by Olivares: 'Major and fundamental dangers threaten Milan, Flanders and Germany. Any such blow would be fatal for this monarchy, since should we sustain a great loss at one of these points, the rest would follow, and after Germany would fall Italy, after Italy, Flanders, then the Indies, Naples, and Sicily' (E9).

The crucial problem for Spain's relations with all its neighbours was that defence of this principle necessarily involved the constant protection of the corridors of communication *between* its dependencies – especially those in the Alps, the Rhineland and the English Channel. It was here that containment – to keep up the Cold War analogy – shaded into the more aggressive approach of 'roll-back'. This, however loath they were to accept it when it came to the Low Countries themselves, was the logical conclusion of the line supported by Albert and Spínola. The two most recent Spanish authorities agree that, whatever the ultimately defensive preoccupations of Madrid, its politico-military tactics in 1618–21 were unavoidably provocative (F6; E13). On the other hand, the very success of these tactics steadily improved Spain's negotiating position with the United Provinces. In the event, far from achieving terms more flattering to her *reputación*, these negotiations proved disappointing, even in some respects humiliating. The failure of diplomacy again brought into play all the material arguments for war which its success, and the consequent boost to prestige, would have discounted. The dramatic advances made by the Dutch in Asia, their increasing presence in Spanish commercial life, their suppression of the staple trades between north Spain and the Netherlands, even the ill-timed launching of a West India Company in Amsterdam; all these could well have been overlooked had The Hague been prepared to accommodate the honour of Spain in ways which were no longer seriously prejudicial to Dutch political integrity and economic prospects. In the meantime, Madrid prepared for the worst, and with hindsight we can interpret Philip III's visit to Portugal in 1619, a duty he had delayed for over twenty years, as being symbolic of 'a turn to the north', like his father's original pilgrimage forty years earlier. In Lisbon, the king was taken dangerously ill, and Zúñiga interrupted his efforts to enlist local support for a tough line against the Dutch, to write to the Archduke Albert concerning the heir: 'The prince is of good temperament and very healthy . . . God keep him so, for he's a quick-witted lad and has an extraordinary aptitude for things.'[11]

The relative status of 'reasons' for the renewal of war with the United Provinces can be judged from the fact that diplomatic contact of some kind was never entirely discontinued, except for a short period at the height of Spanish success in 1624–6. Though the truce expired in the spring of 1621, and both sides were tensed for the struggle, active military campaigning did not begin for over a year. In 1623, whilst rejecting a Dutch overture for talks, Philip IV noted that 'we must act carefully, for experience suggests that to keep the door open can only be beneficial'.[12] For his part, Olivares never wavered in his insistence on the 'three-point plan', the Spanish terms found unacceptable in 1619–21. These were, recognition of Habsburg sovereignty (if only in the weakest possible manner); freedom of worship for Dutch Catholics; and restoration of trade access to Antwerp through the Scheldt. It is clear, however, that reasoned opposition to this policy never disappeared from the central councils, even during the culminating years of the count-duke's grand strategy. Harassed as he was by the many competing demands on his time, Olivares could not relax his campaign of persuasion, cajolery and threats, nor stint his attendance at committees and audiences. His patience with this situation, often wearing thin in the 1620s, was afterwards to be eroded completely. In the meantime, two issues illustrated the co-existence of two distinct elements in the policy-making of Madrid, neatly epitomised in the attitudes of Lerma and Olivares. For almost throughout the whole of the Habsburg period, can be discerned a conflict between those who favoured diplomacy and retrenchment and those who advocated applied power and the primacy of *reputación*.

The first of these concerned the alliance with the German emperor, stemming from Oñate's and Zúñiga's work, and regularly renewed down to the end of the Thirty Years' War. This was the only major new factor in the alignment of power when compared to the 1580s; whereas (as critics pointed out) at that time France and England had felt it necessary to enter the lists even without the threat of a Habsburg family campact. Olivares was completely committed to the link with Austria, and brushed aside all objections. In 1623 he sacrificed the friendship of England, so painstakingly nurtured during the previous decade, by rejecting the suit of Charles I for the hand of the infanta, whom he designated as strengthening the bond with Vienna. He ignored the gradual revival of the old Franco-Dutch connection once Richelieu had taken control in Paris in 1624. 'It is not possible', he arrogantly informed Philip in this year, 'to gain the co-operation of lesser princes without purchasing it at an inflated price, for since you are so superior in power and wealth, you shall find none prepared to make accommodation on equal terms.'[13] The count-duke failed, however, to apply this argument to the emperor, a point duly made by his critics, such as Montesclaros (President of *Hacienda*), Don Augustín Messía and Pedro de Toledo. The Austrian alliance was expensive; between 1618 and 1628 about 350,000 ducats a year in silver were carried across the Alps for Tilly's and Wallenstein's armies. There was a danger, as Montesclaros put it, 'of Your Majesty bearing all the costs of the war, but only the imperialists deriving the benefit . . . such a thing', he continued, doubtless acutely conscious of the expense of the Breda campaign, 'will make the pacification of Flanders almost impossible'.[14] Unlike some other followers of an independent line, Montesclaros was a firm supporter of the war in Flanders, despite the nature of his office, which ought (at least according to the thesis of those experts who class finance as the only key to policy) to have made him otherwise. It was all the more important, therefore, for Olivares to obtain an Austrian declaration of war against the Dutch rebels, just as Spain had assisted Ferdinand against those of Bohemia. Such a commitment was continually evaded by the imperialists and the leaders of the Catholic League. As Philip himself admitted in 1623, 'it is a terrible thing that the German armies, who are so obliged to us for help in all that concerns the integrity of the empire, should refuse to join us against the Dutch, maintaining neutrality in the face of such infamy'.[15]

This deviation by the king brought what amounted to a reprimand from the count-duke: 'It ought to be understood', he announced, 'that your Majesty's armies have never yet failed, and will not fail on any future occasion, to go to the assistance of the emperor and of the Catholic League'.[16] It is easy to understand Olivares's obstinacy on this point, for Austria and Bavaria were a vital link in the only remaining chain of landward communications with the Rhineland and the Low Countries, via the Valtelline passes of the Alps, so stubbornly defended since their occupation in 1620. Agreement with Ferdinand II also guaranteed (through the holding of the Lower Palatinate and Alsace) Spain's position in the Rhineland itself. Above all, Germany was Olivares's only hope of a successful conclusion to his war programme, since it alone offered the means by which Spanish power could advance to the Baltic.

This was the Protestant lake in which (Olivares and his closest aides believed) lay the lodestone of Dutch power and wealth. There was much to justify this conclusion. Amsterdam capital and shipping dominated the Baltic economy, almost to the point of monopoly. The Dutch had cornered strategic (especially maritime) materials, such as timber, hemp, tar and copper, through their strong presence in Sweden. They dictated conditions of supply of grain to needy southern Europe, through their direct intervention at Danzig. By the mid-1620s, Olivares's anti-Dutch programme had made encouraging advances on most fronts. Several tentacles of the enemy's economic octopus had been sliced off or lacerated. They had been crushingly repulsed in Brazil; new regulations had harassed the whole of their Mediterranean enterprise; a continental blockade was asphyxiating Dutch river-borne trade with their central European markets; their fishing industry was being severely mauled by the devastating raids upon the trawling grounds in the North Sea. The perpetrators of this last tactic, a superb new frigate squadron based at Dunkirk, had also been used to strike at Dutch routes to the north. In this essential theatres, however, everything depended upon access to the Baltic, denied to Spain by the Dutch–Danish control of the Skaggerak. The count-duke's design thus rested upon the subversion of this obstacle, by means of Wallenstein's offensive and the capture of a naval base in north Germany. The emperor was content that a Habsburg navy in the Baltic would be built up from Spanish resources and Flemish knowhow.

In this sense, at least, Olivares could argue that Vienna *was* engaged against the United Provinces. But this was a point which was obscure and elusive for those many councillors who were not on his wavelength. The German aspect of his policy remained a sore point with his critics throughout, and even beyond, the count-duke's period of office. For too many, it seemed gratuitously and dangerously to revive the kind of commitment to Germany which helped stimulate the revolt of the *Comuneros* (1520), and which had remained unpopular in Castile ever since. Many influential nobles and clerics felt that the affairs of Germany were, on the whole, not the concern of the monarchy: it was a feeling curiously akin to that often expressed by the patriarchs of Catalonia and Portugal, concerning other commitments of a type regarded as more acceptable by the Castilians themselves.

It is probable that some of Olivares's opponents would have been won over by a more overtly 'religious' element in Spain's stance towards the war. But although Olivares exploited the combative confessional atmosphere of the early 1620s, his own position was somewhat lukewarm, at least in the opinion of his more extreme clerical critics. The count-duke was anxious to arrange a specific coalition treaty which would bind together Spain, Austria, Bavaria, against all

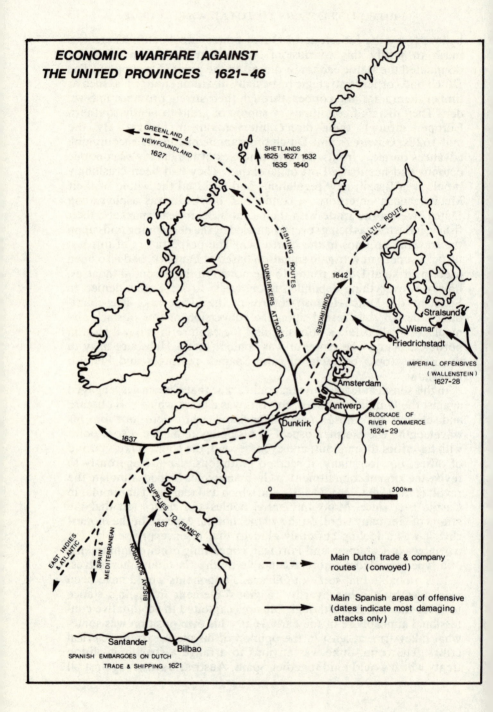

ECONOMIC WARFARE AGAINST
THE UNITED PROVINCES 1621–46

GREENLAND &
NEWFOUNDLAND
1627

SHETLANDS
1625 1627 1632
1635 1640

FISHING ROUTES

DUNKIRKERS ATTACKS

BALTIC ROUTE

DUNKIRKERS

1642

Stralsund
Wismar
Friedrichstadt

IMPERIAL OFFENSIVES
(WALLENSTEIN)
1627–28

Amsterdam
Antwerp
Dunkirk

BLOCKADE OF
RIVER COMMERCE
1624–29

1637

0   500km

EAST INDIES
& ATLANTIC

SPAIN &
MEDITERRANEAN

SUPPLIES TO FRANCE

BISCAY SQUADRON

1637

Santander   Bilbao

SPANISH EMBARGOES ON DUTCH
TRADE & SHIPPING 1621

Main Dutch trade & company
routes (convoyed)

Main Spanish areas of offensive
(dates indicate most damaging
attacks only)

comers. At first glance this seems to justify the 'clash of two worlds', the grand religio-cultural struggle discerned by writers such as J. V. Polisensky (C3). In practice, however, Olivares stoutly resisted such a reductive and inflexible approach, rejecting Montesclaros's call for an exclusively 'Catholic' confederation which would perhaps enlist the patronage of Rome, but would certainly alienate the Protestant princes of Germany whose complaisance was so essential to his plans. The second divisive issue of policy to be discussed here is closely connected with this. Although Olivares was aware of the ultra-Catholic opposition to Richelieu within France, the position of the Huguenot faction was of far greater interest to him because of its solid material base and strategic potential. Throughout the 1620s, therefore, he pushed for an agreement with the Huguenot leaders which might keep the fires of resistance to Paris burning in Bordeaux and Languedoc. The suggestion was anathema to the 'traditionalists', and was thrown out of the Council of State by a large majority in 1624. But the *valido* was not deterred, and, whilst little more than moral support was offered to the French 'good Catholics', financial assistance was provided for Rohan and the other Protestant chieftains. In 1629, when he felt more politically secure, Olivares offered the latter the huge subsidy of 600,000 ducats a year. But by then it was too late; the fall of La Rochelle (1629) and the Day of Dupes (1630) spelled the effective end of resistance to Richelieu from both religious elements in French national politics, and the Mantuan war was to demonstrate the consequences for the Spanish war effort. But it illustrates, too, that rigid ideological patterns ought not to be imposed on the complex rationale of policy-making. For Olivares, as for Richelieu, reason of state undercut other considerations, and this reason was nothing other than the logic of war.

Attitudes

In his popular stage presentation *A Game of Chess*, an extended metaphor of Spanish influence in the English court, Thomas Middleton described the sinister machinations of the pawns of the Black (or Catholic) king:

> ... they're not idle
> He finds them all true labourers in the work
> Of Universal Monarchy, which he
> And his disciples principally aim at.
> Those are maintained in many Courts and Palaces
> And are induced by noble Personages
> Into great Princes' services, and prove
> Some Counsellors of State, some Secretaries,
> All serving in notes of intelligence.[17]

Madrid, indeed, was the best-informed court in Europe. Never before, and not again until the heyday of Louis XIV's influence, had a government so much 'intelligence' at its disposal. The quality of the material fed into the unceasing treadmill of its administrative apparatus was not uniformly high, but very little was regarded as beneath attention, and the base of collection was extremely wide. The supply of news, analysis and prophecy was in part professional. The official diplomatic system (and, in the dependencies, that of regional administration) provided information gleaned at the level of 'national' courts, but also processed the reports of hundreds of agents who operated lower down, in ale houses, lodging places, churches, theatres and bourses. The monarchy also enjoyed the assistance of many others in addition to these payroll functionaries: religious sympathisers, acting out of essentially personal motivation; 'defectors' from rival states; hundreds of travelling personnel who had a contractual relationship with the Spanish system such as traders, financiers and priests (E2). Many of these naturally expected reward or preferment, but as often they collaborated according to a moral imperative which gave a different tenor to their information, a tenor of blind and often distorting fanaticism.

There was, therefore, an element of tangible reality behind the fears and accusations to be found in the anti-Spanish propaganda which forms almost a distinct subgenre of Elizabethan and Stuart literature. Covert emissaries of Habsburg power lurked, if not everywhere, certainly in many places; and if not explicitly engaged in subverting the integrity of the host country, they were undoubtedly assisting the policy of Spain. All over Europe, in the years after the death of Henry IV of France, pro- and anti-Spanish groups can be identified, and sides were taken (on the evidence of 'popular culture' like the plays of Shakespeare and Jonson) amongst sections of society not usually regarded as politically interested. The various themes and shibboleths were common to many European capitals. In this late flowering of the Counter-Reformation, virulent religious hatreds associated with Rome, the Jesuit order and the Holy Inquisition. In the interval between two prolonged wars against Habsburg hegemony, profound political apprehension. Because of Castile's determination to preserve its monopoly rights over limitless resources of overseas wealth and trade, commercial envy and ambition. Each of these had its counter-argument among the supporters and beneficiaries of Spanish power, providing the kind of debate which has ever since revived whenever the balance of political influence in Europe appears seriously disturbed.

The background to this polarisation of attitudes was an astonishing permeation of Spanish culture, a powerful (if occasionally two-edged) weapon in itself. In this area, at least, the mercantilist ideas of the *arbitristas* had been accidentally adopted through the 'isolationism' of Philip II. European ideas were no longer imported into Spain; but those of the peninsula were exported in quantity – here, as elsewhere, the future was being mortgaged. Whilst Shakespeare had to wait for two centuries to achieve an impact on the Continent, Cervantes's *Don Quixote* was translated into English during the author's own lifetime. All the major picaresque novels of the 'golden age' appeared in English and the other major European languages, shortly after original publication. Such writings, like the less 'literary' works of Bartolomé de Las Casas and Antonio Pérez, often presented a highly critical picture of Castile and its preconceptions which (as we have seen) could provide fuel to Spain's enemies. On the other hand, dozens of works of jurisprudence and piety, volumes of mystic poetry, the dramas of Lope de Vega and the canvases of Spanish painters were also widely imitated and admired, forming an influence which radiated through the entrepôts of the southern Netherlands and northern Italy. Spanish volumes – or at least those from the Spanish-dominated culture of the west Mediterranean – sat on the shelves of many influential families' libraries in Prague, London and Paris. The seductive (if intangible) effect can be observed in the behaviour of men as diverse as Martinitz, Corneille, Charles I and Richard Crashaw. This 'cultural' ambience of the *Pax Hispanica* had its material side also; in many aspects of fashion and taste, Spanish luxury was *à la mode*. As Ben Jonson put it in *The Alchemist* (1610):

> Your Spanish jennet is the best horse. Your Spanish
> Stoup is the best garb. Your Spanish beard
> Is the best cut. Your Spanish ruffs are the best
> Wear. Your Spanish Pavan the best dance . . .
> . . . And as for your Spanish pike
> And Spanish blade, let your poor Captain speak.[18]

The interplay of forces involved in attitudes to the monarchy was naturally a more complex phenomenon than is suggested here. But without question, the reaction of different communities, often starkly polarised, was the greatest talking point of the day, an issue in which the tension once again steadily mounted in the years leading up to 1618. This was the case particularly in the United Provinces. Of course, there was no 'party' or interest in the republic which could accurately be termed 'pro-Spanish' in the sense which existed elsewhere. There was, however, a part of the political nation, especially in the state of Holland, which inclined to moderation. It was around the eminent figure of Grand Pensionary Oldenbarnevelt that – partly against his will – this group clustered. Oldenbarnevelt was the statesman to whom, together with William the Silent, belonged the credit of leading the republic out of the wilderness of subjection to Spain: but, on the other hand, he was strongly associated with the decision to accept the truce of 1609. His supporters were satisfied with the Truce of Antwerp as a permanent settlement of Dutch differences with the Habsburg dynasty, and were prepared to write off the southern Netherlands as beyond the recall of the nation. They included that section of Dutch business life with established interests in trade with the Mediterranean, and other essentially European concerns.

As so often in this period, division of opinion was expressed through the medium of religion. Indeed, it is a salutary thought that the political situation in the republic, which became tantamount to civil war, was focused around an academic dispute between two professors of theology. The movement of 'conservative reform' of the Reformed Church to which the Oldenbarnevelt faction inclined, stemmed from the tolerant and Erastian ideas of Arminius, and wished to resist the pressure of the Calvinist synods for a renewal of holy war and colonial expansion. Their opponents, rigidly orthodox in religion according to the stand taken by Professor Gomarus, turned for political support to the alternative source of authority, the stadtholder-prince, Maurice of Nassau. They wanted no truck in religion with what they regarded as crypto-Romish ideas, demanded a challenge to the Spanish monopoly in the Atlantic (after all, an invention of the pope), and a full-scale assault on the Jesuitical Habsburg regime of Brussels which oppressed the southern provinces of the fatherland. To them, Oldenbarnevelt was, in the words of one anti-Arminian pamphlet, 'the Spanish Counsellor'. The struggle that ensued was one of the most profound to afflict the republic in its entire history, since it was concerned with the very nature of the Dutch state and society. Here, as in England, where for a generation the term 'Arminian' was to signify a fellow-traveller of papistical tyranny, the challenge provided by the Spanish monarchy asked questions about the very identity of the community.

Contacts between England and the United Provinces – as between the latter and the German and Baltic states – existed across a wide range of cultural and economic points. It is true that the crusading fraternity of earlier days had been largely dissipated; the jealousy and frustration amongst many English merchants caused by the mushroom growth of Dutch trade since 1590 or so, was not easily assuaged by appeals to religion. This was an attitude encouraged by the barely disguised contempt of James I for the republican burghers of Holland. Nevertheless, Spanish spies like Manuel Sueyro in The Hague and Jacob van Male in London, reported assiduously upon the arrivals, businesses and departures of one country's soldiers and divines amongst the other. For, in the last analysis, the crude strategic realities of the sixteenth century had been little altered. As it was put by Thomas Scot, the most dedicated of anti-Spanish writers, 'it behoves us to look to ourselves when our next neighbours' houses are on fire'.[19] In addition to this, the interests of English and Dutch met in the specific and emotive issue of the Palatinate. Frederick, the Winter King of Bohemia, took his wife (plus limitless emotional sympathy) from England, and his political counsel (plus limited financial subsidies) from the United Provinces. The Elector Palatine and his Stuart princess were the focus of Protestant hope in England even before the tragic events of 1618, whilst after it the influential 'Palatine lobby' was a thorn in the sides of Gondomar and James I. The storm of antipathy aroused by the Spanish ambassador is unique in English history, and the priest-tormented Thomas Scot is only the best-known of dozens of writers whose views reflect a popular hatred of Spain in this period. For Scot, Gondomar was 'the Spanish Machiavel', and the devil, in a cardinal's hat, supervised the conclaves of Madrid.[20] In the early 1620s, after excoriating the failure of James to support his son-in-law, he escaped into exile in Holland, one of a generation of English religious radicals (to which Cromwell's intimate Hugh Peters belonged) who dedicated their lives to maintaining that identity of interest between the 'sister republics' which offered the only sure hope of security for both.

The attraction of the southern Netherlands for the other end of the English ideological spectrum again underlines the importance of the Low Countries in crystallising attitudes towards the Spanish monarchy. It was through the seductive agency of the brilliant court of the Brussels' archdukes, and its powerful religious establishment, that so many of England's Catholics were, in Cromwell's beautiful word, 'Spaniolized'. For every writer's pen and soldier's sword offered to the Dutch, one was also consecrated to the interest of Albert and Isabella: 'You ask me about the desire shown by some English gentlemen to serve me in the Netherlands', wrote Philip III to Albert in 1619. 'It seems a good idea to examine what they have to offer, for, should they prove good soldiers, such assistance could be valuable when the truce with the Dutch expires'.[21] It was in the Low Countries, therefore, that what might (with some exaggeration) be called a dress-rehearsal took place in the 1620s and 1630s, of the armed conflict which was to break out in England itself in the following decade. In the sieges and marches of the Dutch borderlands, not only Englishmen, but French and Germans faced each other in opposite camps. The grizzled veteran of the Flanders wars became a stereotype in the literature and painting of all western Europe, not just in that of Castile.

In France, the role played by the ultra-Catholic party, supported by the Spanish envoys Cárdenas and Mirabel, was consistently helpful to

Madrid. Often *dévots* of the Counter-Reformation Church, and deeply influenced by Castilian mysticism, they were distrustful of the Bourbon dynasty and its heretic origins. Whereas in England it was the anti-Spanish interest which opposed the growth of centralised royal power, the reverse was the case in France. Such men included sympathetic elements among the great provincial magnates, many prelates, and princes of the blood. They envisaged a policy of co-operation with Spain in the stand against heresy. During the regency of Marie de Medici the influence of this group was all-pervasive; after Richelieu's accession to power they resisted his policies tenaciously. The authentic flavour of the *odium theologicum* which rent French politics can even today be tasted in the works of historians:

> There were many, even in France, who equated Catholicism and Spain in their zeal for religion, giving unquestioning allegiance to the Spanish king who seemed its living embodiment. Spain disguised her true aims under a cloak of religious propaganda . . . casting a specious hue over the intrigues of Spanish policy. Every act of disloyalty, perfidy, corruption and cruelty committed by the Spaniards was condoned by the French who were convinced it was done 'for the sake of peace and Holy Mother Church'. (H11)

Even such a man as François du Tremblay (later, as Father Joseph, to be Richelieu's principal assistant and a veritable hammer of the Habsburgs) was in his early years a subscriber to the attitudes here described. Not so, however, the cardinal himself; in a brief stay in office in 1616 he ordered a French envoy to the German princes to 'tell them that France does not support Spain in any way, and offer (with discretion) to assist any who will oppose Spanish machinations in Germany' (E6). Virtually his first act upon re-entering the royal council in 1624 was to grant the Dutch request for subsidies which had been ignored by his predecessors. These were two areas in which the kingdom of France could help to bring about a gradual exhaustion of Spanish strength. The major strategic objective, however, was one in which no amount of 'war by proxy' could be decisive: as Richelieu claimed to Louis XIII on assuming office

> It cannot be doubted that the Spaniards aspire to Universal dominion. Until recently, the main obstacles to this end have been the physical separation of their territories, and the [individual] lack of population within them. But now, with the acquisition of the Alpine passes they are able to remedy both these deficiences.[22]

To Richelieu, then, the security of France, and thus the successful establishment of royal government and authority to which all his ends were bent, depended on the severing of the communications of the Spanish monarchy. The cardinal's obsession with the Valtelline, involving France inevitably in the theatres of south Germany and north Italy, dominated his strategic thinking. He was certain – rightly on all the evidence – that so long as Spain could hold its system together by these thin but far from fragile threads, she could remain at war in Europe *ad infinitum*. For the Bourbon kingdom, the gigantic problem posed by Spanish power was to be the engine of development – economic and social, as well as political – for the ensuing generation.

Germany provided Richelieu with solid ground for progress. In the 1620s, in contrast, it seemed that Italy was a quagmire of his hopes. Of all the influential princes of northern Italy, only the arch-intriguer Carlo Emanuele of Savoy returned more than polite evasions as France attempted to build up a platform of support. The fact was that the Spanish position in Italy had guaranteed the stability and security of the peninsula for more than half a century, and this, along with the huge vested interests it involved, suited most Italians perfectly. In the writings of an earlier school of liberal historians one frequently encounters passionate expressions of distaste for the arrangement by which Italian 'liberty' (and, of course, democracy) was thus delayed. 'Italy', according to one such author, 'was ruled by Spanish methods, by Inquisition and espionage, by the extinction of liberty both of thought and action.' This was doubtless the reason why 'in contemporary writings we find few allusions to the disadvantages of the Spanish domination, and many to the advantages of a continuation of peace' (G12). Such opinions tend to echo the contemporary propaganda of Carlo Emanuele, who, in his own words, fought 'for the honour of the Italian princes and their common liberty', whilst they themselves were content with 'servile acceptance of promises and bribes, offices and titles, in return for oppressing their own nation'.[23] Indeed, more recent studies of the Italian dependencies have illustrated the social solidity of the whole apparatus of Spanish government, from Milan to Sicily. By 1628, admittedly, the crown's policy of financial exaction had not really begun to bite; but even when it did (with the result of popular rebellion) there is little evidence of a change of loyalty on the part of the ruling class, nor even in the root attitudes of the *populari* itself. Richelieu's breakthrough in Mantua was to come, not because of the weakness, but in spite of the strength of the Spanish–Italian Raj.

The year 1618 was the point of explosion for all the seething elements which made up the compound we have been discussing. In Prague, and in Amsterdam, the issue was decided in favour of the hard-line anti-Habsburg groupings. The Bohemians, Martinitz and Slavata, in whom Oñate reposed so much hope, became a rare example in history of ministers who were literally thrown out of office. In the United Provinces, the execution of Oldenbarnevelt and the proscription of the Arminians at the Synod of Dort (1618–19) meant the victory of the hardliners over negotiation with Spain. After the Franco-Spanish Marriage Treaty of 1612, Philip III (signing himself *vuestra buen padre*) kept up a regular correspondence with his son-in-law, Louis XIII. This exchange was interrupted on the Spanish side for two months on the receipt of news of the rebellion in Prague. 'You have good reason to be annoyed with me for not writing', Philip remarked on its resumption, 'but we have been very concerned with what is happening in Germany. Please God this matter can be settled without too much disturbance.'[24]

Conclusions

In so far as such an aspiration can ever be counted successful, Spain's attempt to preserve its European hegemony came closest to success with the surrender of Breda in 1625. The massive and slow operation by which Spínola invested the great fortress created a kind of war-maelstrom into which were sucked the military resources of both sides. The confrontation engaged the attention of all Europe, and (in comparative terms) was fought on the scale of Verdun and achieved the symbolic significance of Stalingrad. Observers like Jacques Callot, mordant 'official' artist of the Thirty Years' War, recorded its glories and its horrors. The effort involved almost broke the spine of the monarchy, but it seemed justified by success. In fact, it was a pyrrhic victory if ever there was one. When the Marquis Spínola's exhausted, undernourished, ragged soldiery entered Breda, they marvelled at the strength of its defences, and the veritable cornucopia of its stocks of food and materials. From the point of view of contemporary Madrid, however, the long-delayed verdict of heaven on the Dutch rebels, as on those of Bohemia, seemed about to be issued. It seems an appropriate point to pause, and to examine the nature of Spanish policy in this *época de triunfo* when its forces seemed to be carrying all before them.

All modern Spanish authorities agree that Spain's was intrinsically a defensive motivation. 'The political ideal of Habsburg Spain', says Jover, 'was the *status quo*, tranquillity, stability, peace' (H10). Fraga Iribarne, present conscience of Spain, and biographer of that conscientious diplomat Saavedra Fajardo, fleshes out his description with rather more dubious claims; policy was based on 'a series of convergent theses: religion, peace, moderation, public faith, dynastic legitimacy, respect for treaties' (E6). Other experts maintain that the Spain of this period merely reacted to consistent (if inevitable) pressure on its system. More recently, Ródenas Vilar and Alcalá-Zamora have revised this position to some extent, pointing to the belligerent nature of much Spanish thinking (E13; F6). The latter even claims that the renewal of war with the Dutch may have been influenced by a kind of conspiracy of various interest groups within the monarchy who stood to gain, materially and/or emotionally from the return of large-scale hostilities.

Identification of the actual point at which defensive thinking shades into the aggressive, preservation into aggrandisement is, of course, a subjective process. But few can doubt that such a point was reached and passed by Spain in the 1620s. Whether one follows Marañón in posing Charles V as the inspiration of Olivares's ambition (E10), or accepts Elliott's alternative suggestion of Philip II (E9), the effect is the same – a grand geopolitical strategy, directed, it might be felt, with an energy and a vision surpassing either of these models. The execution of such a design affected the interests and prestige of many innocent bystanders amongst the states of Europe. Of course, the Spaniards could always plead a legal extenuation of their actions; in many cases they applied one of the age-old nostrums, self-incurred punishment of rebellion, or defence of an established right against encroachment. Such pleas are not always wholly convincing, as in the case of the occupation of the Valtelline in despite of its rightful, and innocent, over-lords. The great advocate of this tactic, the Duke of Feria, was impatient with legal niceties, 'to abandon these passes is to facilitate the designs of our enemies, to hold them will render their designs fruitless . . . are we to suffer this little piece of earth to stick in the windpipe of the monarchy?' The Council of State, target of this expostulation, replied firmly that 'the laws of God cannot be balanced by reasons of state'; but the operation to take the passes went ahead all the same.[25] Even more provocative, if perhaps less 'morally' dubious, was the invasion of the Rhineland states in the same year (1620). Madrid's reluctance on this issue was overcome by Bédmar's pragmatism; apart from their strategic necessity, the provinces were 'populous, fertile, and very rich in revenue' (F6). It may be reckoned, moreover, that some aspects of Olivares's Baltic design, and his policy of aid to the Huguenots, are difficult to reconcile at least with Fraga's ideal statement of the Spanish case. But even Philip III had attempted to underwrite the *status quo* in the Mediterranean by forming an alliance with the infidel empire of Persia.

'Gradually', says Alcalá-Zamora of the 1620s, 'Spain was drawn into a policy of violence, prestige, and energy' (F6). By 1625, the year of Breda, the spirit of *Weltpolitik* seemed to have triumphed in the Council of State. At this moment – ephemeral though it proved – the fundamental gravamen of the charge levelled against Spain by her enemies, the lust for universal empire, is not easy to refute. The outstanding prophet of such a consummation was Antony Sherley, whose influence on Olivares was, surely, a substantial one. Though his work is always eclectic (and often downright plagiaristic) its personal synthesis of ideas is developed into an overt programme of global power. Although at base Sherley was, paradoxically, a Mediterranean-centred thinker who could not adjust to the emergent significance of the north, his knowledge of the international scene was profound. In surveying all of Spain's rivals in turn – France, Holland, Venice, England, Denmark, and even Sweden – he displays a keen (and 'modern') eye for distinguishing the strengths and weaknesses of their political systems, strategic potential, and economic and demographic reserves. He clearly identified France with her huge population and agrarian wealth as the main threat, in spite of internal divisions and the poor quality of her fighting men. Sherley's adoption of the theme of maritime power, elaborated by several other important memorialists, has already been noted. Only by a forward policy of alliances and 'preventative war' could Spain, in his view, put the integrity of its empire, and the permanence of its hegemony, beyond challenge from so many determined opponents. 'All the monarchies in history which have proved durable had the same objective, and that was supreme dominion.'[26] The consequence of such reflections was a policy of 'overkill', leading eventually to 'over-reach'. And in addition to the physical exhaustion which Spain faced during the War of Mantua (1629), Philip IV felt keenly the fact that the feeble nature of Spain's justification in the issue had swung the pendulum of much European opinion behind the policy of France.

CHAPTER 2

The Empire of Olivares
1628–43

In Navarre and Aragon
Nobody gives a *real*;
Catalonia and Portugal
Are of the same opinion;
Only Castile and León,
With Andalusia's noble soldiers,
Carry the cross upon their shoulders. (Francisco de Quevedo)[1]

Concerning the state of this kingdom, I could never have imagined to have seen it as it now is, for their people begin to fail, and those that remain . . . are quite out of heart. They have not one man of quality fit to command an army. The king's revenue, being paid in brass money, will be lessened a third part being reduced into silver. They begin already to lay hands on the silver vessel of particular men, which, together with that in the churches, is all the stock of silver in the kingdom. Justice is quite extinguished here and the people become almost desperate. . . And the greatest mischief of all is that the king knows little of all this and the count-duke is so wilful as he will break rather than bend, so as your Honour may be confident this monarchy is in great danger to be ruined. (Hopton to Vane, 1641)[2]

Introduction

The two crises of 1629–33 and 1639–43 mark out clearly the parameters of Olivares's empire. The first of these was a personal misjudgement, by which he incurred the criticism of the king and his fellow ministers, not to mention the pope. His reaction was to impose his control of affairs up to and beyond the point of outright dictatorship. And, like the more familiar dictators of our own century, his inner world became steadily more unreal, composed of absolutes and surrounded by a wall of suspicion. The second hammer-blow of 1640 reduced even this great man, the most profound and visionary statesman that the Spanish monarchy ever produced, to impotence, though never to apathy.

The count-duke's lifelong enemy, the writer Matías de Novoa, recorded his death in 1645 with the comment, 'the fatal favourite of these crowns at length came to an end, as he had brought everything in them to an end. His passing was the cause of universal satisfaction.' Both opinions enshrined herein were to become orthodox in succeeding generations. Even the latter, however, was not entirely just; some supporters, like his Italian aide Virgilio Malvezzi, survived to protect Olivares's reputation with rather more skill than the author of the patently tendentious *Nicandro*, the famous exoneration which he caused to be issued from his exile. Moreover (as we shall see) a clique of his political associates resisted the attempts of the *antiolivaristas* to remove them from government after 1643. The controversy over Don Gaspar de Guzmán has continued ever since, and for two centuries the prejudices of Novoa held firm sway:

> He was a man of rigid, vain, and presumptuous character, irascible, insulting, and vengeful in his manner and bearing. He deprived the king of his crown, weakened the kingdom and destroyed its reputation. His incompetent rule lost us part of the Low Countries, Catalonia, Portugal, the Azores, and Brazil. He inundated the monarchy, and the whole of Europe, with war.[3]

When the first modern historian of Spain's *declinación* began to write, he gave a further echo to these judgements. As Antonio Cánovas del Castillo matured, however, and particularly as he himself assumed the cares of office and the burdens of statesmanship, he modified his opinion. In his great (if somewhat ramshackle) study of Philip IV's reign, Cánovas registered the count-duke's serious personal flaws, but also noted his political sagacity and integrity, exposing the bias of Novoa as a protégé of the dispossessed Duke of Lerma (E14/2). Moreover, as interest revived in the literature of the period, it was realised that other scathing critics of Don Gaspar – for example, Quevedo, the most mordant satirist of Spanish letters – nursed an animus arising from similar faction allegiances. All the same, Cánovas's rehabilitation was too provisional to survive a new onslaught caused by the profound trauma of 1898. Spain's humiliating defeat in her last major colonial war (against the United States) brought a reaction against the whole heritage of empire. Down to the 1930s, the Spanish intelligentsia regarded the imperial past as the *fons et origo* of their country's mental lethargy and economic backwardness. The celebrated 'generation of 1898', who now came to dominate Spanish historiography, were men of liberal-democratic leanings, to whom the Catholic imperialism of absolute monarchy was anathema.

In a standard textbook which first appeared in 1926, Deleito y Piñuela actually compared Olivares's policies to those of the unfortunate ministers of 1898, as inspired by a 'flagrant imperialism', so unenlightened as to be deserving of disaster.[4] To the list of high crimes and misdemeanors of the count-duke catalogued by Deleito, the first (and as yet, only) biography by the physician-historian Gregorio Marañón added further indictments in 1936. Though Marañón had very little to say about Olivares's political career or ideas, his prodigious researches produced many unsavoury details concerning his character and private life (E10). It is true that the *valido* was cleared of some of his enemies' wilder accusations (for instance, that of sorcery!). But, for Marañón, Olivares remained a half-possessed megalomaniac, with a sick craving for power, and a Quixotic obsession with reviving the faded imperial glories of Charles V.

As the work of E. J. Hamilton made its impact in Spain, and the writings of the *arbitristas* on Spain's economic decline were unearthed and published, Don Gaspar began to appear as the anachronistic figure who led Spain into an impossible and fatal crusade at precisely the time when reform and retrenchment were needed. Even the postwar emergence of a 'new school' of Spanish history did little to rescue Olivares. Under the inspired leadership of Jaime Viçens Vives, this group was influenced by French interest and methods in social and economic problems, and, being centred in Barcelona, retained a healthy Catalan suspicion of the man who first attempted the so-called 'Castilianization' of the peninsula, in a ruthless struggle to impose a centralised absolutism. Indeed, in this context it may be said that the count-duke's modern successor, the dictator Francisco Franco (d.1975) did encourage an atmosphere which proved more favourable to his reputation. The Franco regime, doubtless for purposes which were often undesirable in themselves, stimulated a revived respect for Spain's religious and imperial traditions. The deposit of this, however indirect, is detectable in the work of many Castilian historians of the early modern era, and in particular that of Antonio Domínguez Ortiz on several aspects of the government of Olivares. Domínguez's contribution culminated in 1960 with his monograph on the policy and treasury of Philip IV, which consistently illustrated the cogency and range of Don Gaspar's strategic thinking, supported as it was by enormous administrative grasp and energy (G5). Valiente's study of the *valimiento* as an 'institution' also made us aware of Olivares's sheerly political talents as chief minister (G4).

For the non-Spanish student, however, rehabilitation of Olivares became reality with the publication of J. H. Elliott's masterly book *The Revolt of the Catalans* (1963), which was far from being restricted to the subject of its title. It was this that brought our attention to the variety, intensity, and above all the intractability of the problems which Olivares attempted to grapple with, revealing (to the surprise of many) his intellectual kinship with the *arbitristas* and his qualifications to be regarded as a genuinely reforming minister. To date, Elliott's study remains the only one of the count-duke 'in the round' as it were, but it has enabled historians to revise their appraisal, almost to the extent of moving him out of the shadow of Richelieu. (It is interesting that even the doyen of Habsburg Spain, Fernand Braudel, now refers to Olivares as 'the not always unsuccessful rival of Richelieu, and very nearly a great man') (B10/2). Of course, any final judgement must fall short of canonisation, since, to borrow a phrase from Don Gaspar's great English contemporary, he must be seen 'warts and all'. But it seems unlikely that any future research will fundamentally alter the assertion, first made by Cánovas and now returned to in full circle by a young modern scholar, that 'it is inadmissable and even childish to picture a Spain which was destroyed by one ambitious minister' (F6).

Narrative of Events

In 1628 Spain's war effort seemed poised on the brink of real and concrete achievements. Only two years later her fortunes had ebbed to such a degree that, in both the struggle with the Dutch and over the affairs of Italy, the initiative was never recovered. Though some recent views have demurred on this point, it is difficult not to regard such change as a significant watershed in the story of Spanish hegemony. In the spring of 1629, the almost incredible news of Matanzas arrived in Madrid. For the first time the security of the Atlantic *flota*-system had been breached by the Dutch raiders. Almost simultaneously, the enemy began a great offensive in Flanders, the result of long and careful planning during the lull which followed Breda. Again Spanish defences were pierced, causing panic in Brussels. In the north, Wallenstein retired, licking his wounds and shortly to be relieved of his command, from his attempt on the Baltic ports. As if this were not sufficient, the position in Milan suddenly and dangerously deteriorated.

The governor of Milan, Gonsalvo de Córdoba, was, unfortunately, not made in the same mould as had produced his famous namesake, founder of the *tercios* and of Castile's Italian empire. Nevertheless, his pre-emptive military move, to support the Spanish candidate for the succession to the disputed territories of Mantua and Monferrat, was consistent with the attitudes of Madrid's mandarins in Italy since the turn of the century. This area was Spain's barrack square (*plaza de armas*), nerve-centre of communications and of the whole war-machine. No challenge to its security could be tolerated for a moment.

Yet, from the French point of view, Mantua offered a singular opportunity to make strategic capital. With established influence here,
Richelieu would have a chain of enclaves, connecting his ally Savoy, on
the western frontier of Milan, with a promising client, Venice, to the
east. Not only Milan itself, but the key Alpine passageway of the
Valtelline could be put under serious threat. 'You can never hold the
certain arbitration of Italy', the Duke of Feria had brusquely informed
Philip IV in 1623, 'unless you are the sole protector of the peninsula'.[5]
This was the logic of Córdoba's assault upon the main fortress of
Mantua, at Casale; of Olivares's immediate and blanket approval of
the action; and of Richelieu's equally rapid pledge of armed support
for those prepared to resist it. A two-pronged French offensive on
Mantua and the Alpine roads was quickly set in motion. By the
summer of 1629, Córdoba had been repulsed from Oasale and Milan
itself was in danger.

Circumstances favoured the French. Richelieu had just completed
his statesmanlike settlement of the Huguenot problem, ending a
decade of sporadic civil war, and enlisting many experienced officers
and men of the defeated armies under the Bourbon lilies. For the first
time since the death of Henry IV, France was politically stable, and a
trained royal army was available. The diplomatic situation was equally
propitious. Two outstanding 'neutral' forces, Venice and the Vatican
(at loggerheads on so much else) were united in support of the French
legal case over the Mantuan succession. Moreover, France's overall
strategic security seemed guaranteed by Frederick Henry's offensive
in Flanders and Richelieu's increasing political influence in Rhineland
Germany. Even so, the cardinal's gamble may have failed. The war
against Spain brought palace intrigue in Paris to a head, and on the Day
of Dupes, Richelieu only narrowly escaped from the clutches of his
pro-Spanish adversaries in the royal family (1630). In addition, the
Emperor Ferdinand, as overlord of Milan, chose this moment at last to
reciprocate the support vouchsafed his affairs by Philip IV since 1618.
In 1629, an imperialist army under Pappenheim and Gallas (lieutenants respectively of Tilly and Wallenstein) made its lumbering way
across the Alps. For the first time since 1527 a German army was in
Italy, and the pope trembled upon his throne: had not Wallenstein
remarked 'Rome has not been sacked for a hundred years. It must be
richer than ever'? (E13).

Indeed, as on that infamous earlier occasion, the Germans proved a
liability to Madrid, despite the fact that, in principle, Ferdinand's
intervention was the only solace that could be derived from the whole
imbroglio. Spain was completely unprepared for the Mantuan war.
Her trained veterans were all in Flanders. In any case, Olivares had for
some time been developing, at considerable cost, an essentially

maritime emphasis to the war effort, which, though making sense in the Flanders/Baltic nexus was of little use in this new emergency. The government's finances were in difficulty, and in the period following Matanzas it was impossible to raise the rapid and extraordinary *asientos* needed to launch an effective response to the military challenge. The local situation was little short of desperate. A sequence of poor harvests had escalated into a subsistence crisis in the Milanese countryside. Starvation was widespread, and the towns were in tumult as food stocks became exhausted. In the summer of 1629, plague, the awful outbreak known in Italian history as the *peste di Milano* (and chronicled so movingly in the pages of Manzoni's great romantic novel *The Betrothed*) took a firm grip on northern Italy, ravaging equally the predatory troops and their village victims. After three generations of tranquillity, hell, in the shape of the Thirty Years' War, had returned to Italy.

Paralysed by plague, desertion, and lack of supply (all compounded by administrative incompetence on an unusual scale) the Habsburg generals could make no impression on the French positions. After the poor campaign of 1629, Spínola was despatched in person to co-ordinate matters, and great hopes were placed upon this master of siege warfare. The return of the native to northern Italy was no triumph: Spínola, victor of Ostend and Breda, found Casale too tough a nut to crack, surrendering his life in the attempt (1630). The French continued to hold the initiative, whilst the Dutch were in process of reversing Spínola's achievement in Flanders. Bluster and threaten though he may, the count-duke had to admit defeat. Worse, he was forced into accepting the arbitration of the Vatican, which under Urban VIII, was known for its inclination to Paris. Thus called upon to resolve openly and fairly between the two eldest daughters of the Church, Urban obligingly sent his emissary to supervise peace terms, and it was thus that Guglielmo Mazzarini made his debut upon the stage of European politics. Not surprisingly the Treaty of Cherasco (1631) represented Richelieu's first international success, a real breakthrough not least in terms of estimation and prestige. The chagrin of the Spaniards was all the more bitter since – as French propaganda hurried to proclaim – God had favoured right against might. Spain's abasement was moral as well as material, and seemed to reflect backwards (not altogether unjustly) on to all her enterprises since the start of the wars. The Holy Father himself had reputedly referred to Philip IV as Polyphemus (that is, the Cyclops), reserving for Ulysses (Rome) the honour of being devoured last of all his victims. What would today be called Spain's 'credibility' in Italy was seriously undermined, moreover, since she had been found to be most helpless precisely in the area where she should have been most strong. But we must not exaggerate the difficulty this caused; Madrid retained overall control, a vital consideration in view of increasing material dependence on the Italian provinces.

Once the dust of Mantua had settled, certainly, its consequences caused less immediate concern than the equally dramatic volte-face in the Low Countries. The Dutch offensive culminated in the capture of their main target, 's Hertogenbosch (Bois-le-Duc) in 1629. This opened a period of severe internal crisis in Spanish Flanders. With Spínola absent, and the Archduchess Isabel too old and feeble to stem the tide, Brussels drifted into limbo. Losses at the front were compounded by a collapse of morale amongst both military and civilian personnel. The army of Flanders was mutinous for the first time in a generation, a tendency exacerbated by the choking-off of supplies and reinforcements following Mantua and Matanzas. Covert disloyalty threatened amongst indigenous commanders and administrators. The 'obedient provinces', disillusioned and exhausted, began to lend at least one ear to the suasions of their rebellious relations in the north. Olivares had been alerted to some of this even before the setbacks of 1629, recalling Spínola for discussion at Madrid, and placing the question of a renewed truce with the Dutch on the agenda of the Council of State. During 1629 itself, however, full authorisation was given to Isabel to initiate negotiations with Frederick Henry. These orders became more insistent and concessionary as Matanzas was succeeded by the fall of Pernambuco in Brazil, giving the enemy their first foothold on the mainland of America (1630). In the talks which began at Roosendaele, the United Provinces held the whip hand; a new arrangement with France, and their foreknowledge of the impending Swedish military intervention, helped to make the Dutch attitude uncompromising and inflexible.

The situation of 1625 had thus been completely reversed by 1630. The defeats of 's Hertogenbosch and Pernambuco had effaced the triumphs of Breda and Bahía, and it was Flanders, not the United Provinces, which was now in a state of siege. In 1631–2 a treasonable conspiracy, neither widespread nor popular but none the less ominous in the circumstances, was discovered. Isabel and Aytona, her main Spanish adviser, could not halt the spread of discontent in the army, nor prevent the spontaneous assembly of the southern Estates to consider the question of the war, and by implication, of the whole political future of the southern Netherlands. The Dutch offensive continued, with Maastricht falling in 1632, and only petered out with the capture of Rheinberg a year later, just a few weeks before Isabel's death. For a time it seemed that the final moment of reckoning had arrived: there was even a minor rebellion, in the Basque country (the first in metropolitan Spain since 1591), to make the monarchy's foun-

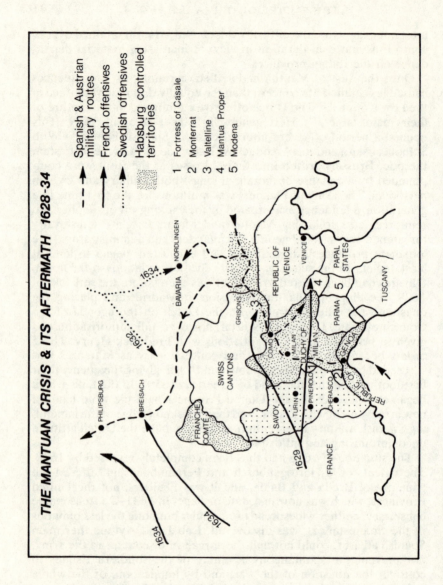

THE MANTUAN CRISIS & ITS AFTERMATH 1628-34

Spanish & Austrian
military routes

French offensives

Swedish offensives

Habsburg controlled
territories

1 Fortress of Casale
2 Monferrat
3 Valtelline
4 Mantua Proper
5 Modena

dations quiver. And it was at this infinitely delicate moment that the Swedish landing in Germany added a new dimension to European politics.

As his grander visions faded, Olivares was acute enough to realise that the preservation of essential routes of communication was the prior guarantee of survival. For whilst the Swedish army was demolishing the structure of Habsburg authority in Germany, moving with unexampled swiftness from the Baltic to the Swiss border, Richelieu exploited the confusion by making his first positive moves in the Rhineland. These developments conspired to block Spain's road to the Netherlands by 1633. The story of her reaction – limited and ephemeral though it was to prove – is by any standards an epic one. Don Gaspar's own contribution to Spain's recovery was crucial, characterised as it was by an almost frenzied expenditure of energy. By 1632, Olivares, Oñate and Feria had agreed that Germany was to be the fulcrum of the monarchy's effort, since here was the key to affairs both in Flanders and Italy. The process of raising fresh armies in Castile and Naples was begun. Meanwhile, the attention paid to the navy since 1621 proved after all a wise investment, for the efficient squadrons in Santander and Dunkirk not only kept open the sea-lane to Flanders, but actually took the war to the enemy with startling success. Partly for this reason, Brussels continued to resist Dutch military and political pressure. Likewise, the concentration on protecting the Valtelline – an objective successfully maintained even during the Mantua fiasco – proved prescient. Via this avenue, Feria was able to launch the first counter-attack in 1633, aimed at liaising with the imperialists, clearing the Swedes from the Rhineland, and securing a passage for the main Spanish army.

The second wave (also prepared in, and launched from, Milan) was commanded by Don Fernando, Cardinal-Infante of Spain, the king's younger brother (b. 1609). His designation as governor and captain-general in Flanders was a piece of inspiration on Olivares's part to match his meticulous planning. By late 1634, Don Fernando was installed in Brussels, riding beneath Rubens's triumphal arches to the relieved acclaim of the population. *En route*, he had capitalised on the brilliant successes of Feria's vanguard by smashing the Swedish army at Nordlingen (September 1634). The Swedes and their allies broke up into small uncoordinated bands, pressure on the Rhineland lifeline was relieved. Initiative was restored to the Habsburgs with an emphasis which put an end to procrastination in Paris. In the spring of 1635, with a touch of mediaeval romance which aptly illustrates the lingering preconceptions of dynastic authority, Louis XIII's herald arrived before the gates of Brussels to issue his master's challenge. After the bouts and passes of *toreros* and *picaros*, the matador had entered the ring.

Once there, however, he was to be rudely buffetted, tossed, and all but gored (like any *novillero*) for his temerity and lack of experience. In this same year the German princes made their peace with Ferdinand (at Prague) leaving the latter's hands relatively free. Consequently, the Habsburg confederates were able in the following campaign to mount a joint invasion of France from Flanders and the Rhineland, a pincer movement which nearly reached Paris, and reduced Richelieu to despair. 1636 – the 'year of Corbie' – ranks in French history alongside 1792 and 1914; but not, fortunately for the cardinal, 1870 and 1940. For with immense logistical problems, the stout resistance of Corbie itself, and the inevitable onset of disease in the ranks, the offensive faltered. Richelieu and his master were able to rally, to the extent that by 1637 France had been cleared of the invaders, and in the following campaign was preparing to move into the attack. This almost regular fluctuation of fortunes, like the swing of a pendulum or the movement of the tides, was to be a recurrent feature of the whole twenty-five-year duration of the Franco-Spanish war.

In the Italian theatre of this struggle, the war of succession in Savoy after the death of Vittorio Amadeo (1637) engaged the attention of both major protagonists. Again, however, Mantua, and in particular the fortress of Casale, proved vital; by the time of Richelieu's death it had resisted several further sieges, and it was becoming clear that the French were assured of a foothold in Italy from which they could harass and embarrass Spanish dominion. Meanwhile, Castile's relations with the principality of Catalonia were reaching the point of violent breakdown. In a somewhat desperate attempt to inspire loyalty amongst the Catalans, the count-duke had created an army to be stationed on the Franco-Catalan border, designed initially as the anvil for Don Fernando's hammer in the campaign of 1636. The plan misfired badly. Though a number of local troops were recruited, the army never achieved a half of its optimum size and was quickly depleted by desertion and vicious squabbles among the *naciones*, not to mention the appalling conditions of war in the Pyrenees. Far from being capable of mounting an invasion of France, it was too weak even to defend the frontier, or (more vitally) to keep open its own lines of supply, amidst an increasingly hostile population. Nevertheless, for some reason – perhaps attracted by the potential of a region which had already actually been in revolt – Richelieu failed to exploit the rising tension in Catalonia, preferring instead to make his main thrust in the Basque country. This proved an error on his part, for the invasion of Spain and siege of Fuenterrabía (1638), sparked off exactly the kind of mass patriotic reaction in the rest of Spain that Olivares had vainly looked for in Catalonia. The relief of Fuenterrabía in August was a heady triumph for the latter, and for his scheme of the 'Union of Arms'.

Inadvertently, however, this particular setback could not have worked more perfectly to Richelieu's advantage had it been a deliberate piece of bluff. Lionised in Madrid as a result of what seemed to be a definitive answer to mounting criticism, much of Olivares's earlier ambition came flooding back. The loss of the indispensable fortress of Breisach (in Alsace) caused Olivares to write off the possibility of reopening the land lines to Brussels. Though the tendency has been present since the mid-1620s, the late 1630s witnessed a radical shift of Spain's strategic thinking to the maritime quarter. In 1638–9 two huge amphibious naval expeditions were planned and launched. In what proved the last great actions of Spain's geopolitical empire, armadas were sent to defeat the Franco-Dutch fleets in the North Sea, and across the Atlantic to throw the enemy, bag and baggage, out of Brazil. Both these expeditions met with disaster, involving a terrific and irreplaceable loss of scarce human and material resources.

The monarchy was therefore already in a debilitated condition when, in the spring of 1640, the bushfires burning along the Pyrenean foothills suddenly burst into a general conflagration. The escalation of violent exchanges between 'foreign' soldiery and the local peasantry, combined with economic dislocation and political grievance in the towns (especially Barcelona itself) caused that peculiar coalescence of events, the revolt of the Catalans. By the late summer, the principality had effectively seceded from the monarchy, and Olivares had decided on repression, not compromise, committing Castile to full military intervention. This decision provided a supreme opportunity for those who had been plotting rebellion in Lisbon. Olivares's tactless demand for Portuguese assistance against the Catalans resulted only in a further secession, and one with which he simply could not cope. The Castilian defeat at Montjuich, outside the walls of Barcelona, (early 1641), doomed the peninsula to a generation of internecine war, a 'Spanish civil war' which consumed the entrails of the monarchy. The empire of Olivares, at least, was finished, the fall of its master and inspiration only a matter of time. In the winter of 1642–3, the king bowed to the pressure of a group of aristocrats, the *antiolivaristas*, who undoubtedly represented a consensus of their caste. The count-duke was politely relieved of his duties.

Resources

So many are the difficulties and obstacles in my way, that I feel like throwing myself upon my bed and hoping for death. (Olivares to Don Fernando, 1632)[6]

To examine the crisis of the Mantuan war is doubtless to become aware of the practical limitations upon the operation of the Spanish system. Yet, whatever Olivares's own responsibility for the débâcle, it certainly emphasised his case over the Union of Arms, that streamlined programme of contribution and distribution of forces, by and between the various dependencies of the monarchy, upon which he pinned his dearest hopes for reform and victory. If such a scheme had been in existence by 1629, a 'reserve army' may have been available for use in Milan. The plan was for each province permanently to maintain an auxiliary force as part of a pool and as follows:

Region	Fully equipped men (in thousands)
Castile	44
Catalonia	16
Portugal	16
Naples	16
Flanders	12
Aragon	10
Milan	8
Valencia	6
Sicily	6
The Islands	6
Total	140

The Union of Arms was both paradoxical and anomalous. As many contemporaries remarked, the monarchy had large latent resources; yet (which was less appreciated) was genuinely unable to meet such targets. As a means of reconciling the contradiction between potential strength and actual weakness, the instrument was crippled more by the failure of supporting reform legislation in other areas than by any inherent flaws. As a 'planning' statesman, Olivares (it must be remembered) was a little before his time. Local resistance was, of course, fierce and unrelenting. The figures stipulated may have been unrealistic, as much for Castile itself as in the much more celebrated case of Catalonia. That given for Sicily almost certainly erred in the opposite direction, since the island was much more populous and prosperous than officials in Madrid believed. On balance, the question of the numbers envisaged as performing 'national service' was less critical than that of the local financial effort demanded by their support over an unspecified period (G9). For this reason, in his search for regular recruits, Olivares was obliged to turn to the nobility as well as to the regional authorities. But it is perhaps easier to understand the general attitudes of a man who believed that the monarchy was capable of such an effort.

The reasons for the failure of the Union of Arms are well known, the progress made towards its achievement considerably less publicised. From the late 1620s, unceasing negotiation went on with all the provincial Estates, persuasion being backed up with threats and bribes. In Flanders, for example, Olivares's special envoy, the Marquis of Leganés, promised economic concessions in return for agreement, but warned that, in the last analysis, 'nobody would be allowed to inhibit the establishment' of the Union.[7] The scheme was duly accepted in 1627. Thereafter, one by one, the Italian provinces, Aragon, Valencia, the Basque country, and eventually even Portugal, followed suit. It is true, of course, that most agreements finally reached involved substantial reductions in the crown's targets; that Catalonia's recalcitrance thoroughly vitiated the whole basis of the programme; and that the process was much too prolonged. But during the Fuenterrabía campaign, few of Philip IV's dominions failed to make *some* contribution to the common cause, an illustration, salutary in view of the disaster only two years later, of what might have been.

Though even rough estimates are at present impossible, the sequence of military setbacks in Flanders and Italy (1629–33) had involved serious casualties in the military establishment. A great effort was made to replace these by building up the new army in the Milanese, and of the 25,000 men who crossed the Alps with Feria and Don Fernando in 1633–4, Castile and Naples between them provided more than four-fifths. Consequently, for the first time the Council of War began to encounter insuperable difficulties in recruitment. From 1634 on, when only the sea route was available, small but regular shipments of reinforcements were made to Flanders, and down to 1643 perhaps 20,000 Spanish and Neapolitan levies were transported in this manner. A similar number was raised, from the same sources, during the campaigns on the Catalan frontier (1638–40), and additional armies had to be improvised for the interventions in Portugal (1637) and Catalonia (1640). All in all, it may not be too wide of the mark to guess that over 100,000 military personnel were conscripted from greater Castile in the fifteen years 1628–43. This figure was matched by the kingdom of Naples, which sent 50,000 men to Spain or Milan in the first half of the 1630s alone. Alcalá-Zamora is perhaps guilty of an anachronism in writing of 'general mobilisation' (F6); but the impact of this blood tax on the socio-economic structures of the monarchy was certainly greater than a proportional loss would have in later centuries. In 1637, a subcommittee of the Council of War regarded as simply impossible a royal requisition for a fresh levy of 6,000 men in Castile, an indication of the prevailing levels of depopulation and disruption.

In the midst of the frantic chaos of 1640 in Madrid, Arthur Hopton the English ambassador, reported on these and other problems.

I hear of nothing but preparations [for the invasion of Catalonia] and this without all consideration of the want of people in the country; [they are] taking tradesmen out of their shops and husbandmen from the plough, the most of them such as leave young women and children unprovided, which would cause general disconsolation but that they hope the business will be short, wherein they may be deceived. Nor will it secure these men from being sent to Italy in case they could be spared here, for I hear the Marquis of Leganes's army [in Milan] is much diminished, and that the kingdom of Naples is so exhausted as it grows unable to furnish any more men.[8]

A partial solution to this problem was to encroach upon the legal immunities of the great nobility and their vassals. During the 1630s, Olivares threw more responsibility upon the local aristocracy as a means of relieving pressure on the royal *alfareces* (not to mention the Treasury). In 1634, for instance, the immensely wealthy Duke of Medina Sidonia was obliged to raise and maintain 3,000 men for service within the peninsula, and the less eminent were imposed upon *pro rata*. The count-duke also began to investigate the hiring of mercenaries on a regular basis from extra-monarchial sources. Several schemes were considered for the provision of Irish levies in quantity, a theme that was to swell in prominence during the next decade. The great advantage of Irishmen was, of course, their religion. Up to this point, the principle of recruitment only from Catholic states had been strictly adhered to, and indeed was reiterated forcefully in the important articles of military reform issued as late as 1633. It became more honoured in the breach than the observance, and by 1641 Philip IV was reduced to juggling with both his armies and his conscience. As he wrote to his brother:

The extra soldiers you offer me for use in Spain would probably be heretics. Since men of a contrary religion are more acceptable in my armies which operate outside the peninsula, it would be better not to send them here, but to attach them to the army of Flanders, sending me instead an equal number of Catholic [i.e. Walloon] troops.[9]

Much of the foregoing illustrates the hardening of Olivares's dictatorship. Don Gaspar was becoming daily less tolerant of the lukewarm and the incompetent at all levels of the king's service, and his complaints about disloyalty and self-interest were ubiquitous and harsh. There is evidence for his belief that the aristocracy of Castile was losing its enthusiasm for the eternal conflict, though whether this was a cause or a result of Olivares's autocracy is difficult to decide. At any rate, as early as 1636, the count-duke referred to the 'falta de cabezas de calidad'.[10] By this he meant the absence of staff officers of Castilian (and especially noble Castilian) origin, not – as often implied – the lack of crude quantities of men. Feria's army of 1633 had not contained a single regiment commanded by a native Castilian, and the following year Don Fernando expressed concern at the absence of Spanish captains in the army of Nordlingen. It is true that Belgian and Italian officers usually proved effective substitutes, at the top of, as well as lower down, the chain of command. The Fuenterrabía campaign, too, witnessed a veritable surge to the colours of younger sons of the nobility. This was not enough for Don Gaspar; in March 1640, he brought the issue before the Council of State: 'during the recent misfortunes of the monarchy, our nobles have been extremely discouraged, and they need to pull themselves together. It is not necessary actually to volunteer, nor to contribute great expense, nor even to be absent long from one's family, in order to do one's duty and at least to show willing' (E14/2). A few months later, faced with the crisis in Catalonia, Olivares offered the ultimate insult to the *nobleza* by virtually compelling them to fulfil their ancient feudal obligation of enlistment. It was a move which helped to settle the fate of its author.

About this time Hopton made the apparently strange observation that 'they [the Spaniards] have both their hands full of work, yet I find not that their money fails them'.[11] It seems to me that this observation is important and accurate. For M. Chaunu, the general setback to the Habsburg cause in 1629–33 is easily understood; 'it was the loss of eighty tons of silver [at Matanzas] that caused the defeat of Spain, and guaranteed that Germany would not be converted by the booted missionaries of Wallenstein' (C9). Conversely, Alcalá-Zamora points out that two of Spain's most successful military phases (those of 1624–6 and 1634–6) coincided with 'good' sequences of silver imports at Seville (F6). It is difficult to think of Wallenstein's captains as missionaries, booted or otherwise, but (more seriously) the teacher's task would be a straightforward one indeed if historical phenomena were susceptible of such simplistic analysis.

We may agree that finance played a vital role: 1629 was one year in which Olivares, despite intense efforts, was not able to negotiate *asientos* on the necessary scale and for this, Matanzas was to blame. But a partial, if drastic, remedy lay to hand. Over 2 million ducats in pure silver was expropriated from private interests at Seville and despatched directly to Milan. 'The Marquis Spínola', reported one delighted observer in 1630, 'goes within a few days to Milan, and with him one-and-a-half million ducats in money and silver bars'.[12] Even including a nearly equal contribution from Naples, this was not enough fully to meet the campaigning needs of the 40,000 men of the army of

Italy for two years. Furthermore, important supplies to Brussels and Vienna were inevitably interrupted. But none of this absolves us from the task of examining political, strategic and socio-economic conditions bearing heavily upon events, especially in the local context. In any case, the silver shortfall was continued, if in ameliorated form, well into the next decade. On several occasions, Caribbean hurricanes destroyed individual galleons of the silver fleet. In 1633, Feria's little 'army of Alsace', which crossed the Alps, swept the Swedes from the Rhineland, and fought a savage winter campaign in Bavaria, *received no payment* except incidental expenses which were met from its general's own pocket. In all this time, their discipline and comportment – not to mention fighting quality – were reported as exemplary.

By the mid-1630s, however, the revenue situation was stabilised, mainly through a swingeing programme of new and extra taxation, coupled with private imposts and forced loans, rather than improvement in silver receipts. The Castilian Cortes granted a new subsidy of 10 million ducats (for four years) in 1633; the Vatican was persuaded to allow fresh ecclesiastical taxation (worth 600,000 ducats per annum). Don Fernando's own benefices made a huge contribution to the Nordlingen campaign. Olivares introduced a tax on salt (in 1630) and one on paper (*papel sellado*, 1636), to mention only the most effective and unpopular of his fiscal expedients. In the same period, coinage of copper was again resorted to, after an abstinence of nearly a decade. Above all, it was Naples which provided a lifebelt in the swirling tides of war. In the late 1620s, the ordinary *servicio* of the province was 1·2 million ducats; ten years later the annual regular contribution was worth three times this amount. In 1632, during preparation for the counter-offensive in Germany, the Viceroy of Naples was ordered 'to put in hand all possible means of raising money for the royal armies, and in case present levels are insufficient, you may begin to sell and alienate rents, feudal dues, townships and villages, and any other effects of the royal patrimony'.[13] As late as 1633, a 'voluntary' donation from the local nobility and bankers could raise over 50,000 ducats. By 1638, however, when the new viceroy was ordered to procure an extraordinary *asistencia* of 2·5 million ducats, their patience was becoming frayed. Nothing, however, could hold down the escalation of extortion. One Neapolitan banker rapidly rose to the position of handling greater contracts than any of his colleagues in Madrid (G10). Funds from the Regno helped the crown to raise 30 million ducats in *asientos de dinero* in the six years 1632–7 alone.

Once relieved of the pressures of the Mantuan war, Philip IV began to reconsider the concessions he had envisaged making to the Dutch in order to obtain a truce. His accountants now reckoned that a warchest of nearly 7 million ducats would be available in each year for the next six. 'The rebels' peace terms are at present unacceptable', he wrote to the Archduchess Isabel, 'but during these six years we can promise ourselves very great progress. Therefore, the enemy will appreciate the great amount of treasure with which we can oppose their designs, and will be forced to change their tune.'[14] As the allotted period elapsed, Madrid was continuing to spend approximately one-half of this overall total in the Netherlands; no progress had been made, and there were few signs of a change of heart in The Hague. The war with France, and the rebellions within the peninsula, elbowed the Dutch to the sidelines, a position which they found perfectly comfortable. The dogs of war had finally arrived to howl on Castile's doorstep, and Madrid was now in need of material sustenance from Flanders. In June 1641, for example, Philip sent his brother a list including no less than 15,000 variegated firearms, 'besides many other supplies which I order you to send to the ports of Cantabria at the first available opportunity'.[15] Don Fernando was already on his deathbed when he sent the forlorn response, 'our own shortages are getting worse daily, and if the wars continue these provinces are destined for complete ruination'.[16]

Policy

Many years after the war over Mantua, as the Count-Duke of Olivares lay dying, disgraced and periodically insane, Philip IV defended his own conduct towards the kingdom of France. Writing to his new confidante, Sister María de Ágreda he explained that the *present* war had been launched by Louis XIII as an act of unprovoked aggression, and that Spain's policy had been one of conciliation, both before and after the events of 1635. Since, however, every letter to this correspondent was effectively an act of confession, he was obliged to admit that 'the previous wars which took place in Italy over Casale and Monferrat are more difficult to excuse. For although I have always followed the counsel of my ministers in affairs of such moment, if ever I have erred, and given God little satisfaction, it was in this'.[17] As it happened, Olivares, too, had recently defended his record on this same question, in the *Nicandro*, 'an antidote to the calumnies' perpetrated by his enemies. The Mantuan war, he maintained, had been precipitated unilaterally by Gonsalvo de Córdoba, and it had been impossible to prevent its development into a major confrontation. As these two statements indicate, this issue was the first to cause a breach in the relationship between king and *valido*. Philip, indeed, wished for a compromise, even causing a draft agreement to be drawn up. The count-duke, however, reacted in favour of a crushing demonstration of power, even to the point of unlimited war between the Habsburg confederates and the French. It is equally significant that neither man had any doubt as to the significance of the defeat, especially in terms of the monarchy's *reputación*.

Olivares's decision in 1628 was all the more startling in view of its immediate political context. For his clearest arbitrary act came at a time when, far from opening another front, an overall peace settlement was under discussion in the Council of State. It seems possible that Don Gaspar deliberately seized the opportunity offered by Córdoba's initiative, in order to head off a growing mood of war-weariness and retrenchment amongst his fellow-ministers, an embryonic consensus carrying an implied threat to his policy, and even to his position. In 1628, the arrival of Spínola, a man of known moderation and vast prestige, inspired a bout of reappraisal in Madrid. In April the *Junta de Estado* unanimously accepted Spínola's recommendation of diplomatic overtures to the Dutch; so also, a few months later, did the plenary Council of State, with only two dissenting voices. The count-duke felt obliged to bend before the prevailing wind; but (probably confident of their rejection) insisted on two basic preconditions for negotiation – reopening of the Scheldt and religious freedom. 'In such a case', he argued, 'we will retain our reputation without giving away anything to the rebels.'[18] His select Junta accepted this significant rider, and so, too, (despite strong opposition led by Spínola) did the full council. Though peace was still to be moderated by honour, it is notable that these deliberations took place well before news of Matanzas. Despite them, no diplomatic contact was in fact made until the Italian emergency – not Matanzas – increased the urgency of a settlement. An immediate armistice with the Dutch now became desirable, not so much because of the situation in the old war, as that created by the new – the likelihood of a major rupture with France. By the spring of 1629, Spínola was begging for permission to return to Flanders, and to negotiate 'a long truce . . . to enable us to make preparations in case of a break with France'.[19]

This new calculation rose rapidly to the point at which it dominated Olivares's thinking. Even in 1629, he was apparently willing to avoid particular humiliation in Italy even at the cost of generalising the conflict (this, it is true, before the Swedish irruption). When Philip instructed his aunt, the archduchess, to make contact with the Dutch as a matter of urgency, he expressed desire 'to relieve my subjects of this burdensome and costly war' but also added that 'as soon as an armistice is agreed, as many men as possible must be assembled on the frontier with France'.[20] After several changes of mind, and following the end of the Italian diversion, Brussels was again required (January 1632)

. . . to proceed [with negotiation] in all secrecy . . . since with the present threats it would be useful to reduce commitments in Flanders and apply our resources to other, more convenient, purposes. We may believe from the proceedings of the French that they will soon openly break with us . . . Doubtless Your Highness has already ordered the strengthening of frontier posts.[21]

In view of this (and much similar) evidence, there seems little doubt that the chorus of self-righteous outrage with which Spanish propaganda reacted to the eventual French declaration of war in 1635, was at best disingenuous, and at worst hypocritical. Olivares, as paranoiac abroad as at home, had decided not merely to risk, but actually to force a showdown with France. Just as the Spanish case in 1635 represented a pathetic attempt to put France in the wrong, in order to recoup European moral estimation, so was Olivares's actual policy highly contingent upon his abasement of Cherasco. French moves in Italy and Germany since 1624, Richelieu's constant support of the Dutch, and finally his provision of Gustavus Adolphus's warchest (Treaty of Barwälde, 1631) had in any case convinced the *valido* that an all-out trial of strength was inevitable. As he wrote to the pope, in response to an offer of arbitration (in the circumstances a trifle tactless) in 1640:

The French are struggling all over Christendom on behalf of heresy, which would never have made such inroads upon our faith without their encouragement. This was the case even before they began the war against my master. What difference would it therefore make to our security and interests were we to have a formal peace?[22]

By 1633, Olivares was aware that Spain's counter-offensive in Germany was bound to confront Richelieu with the supreme moment of decision. His offer of aid to the emperor against Sweden was conditional upon joint contingency planning over 'the real enemy', France. Forcing the cardinal's hand would not only transform an insidious threat into one which was open and declared, but could also take place in circumstances favourable to the Habsburg side. The purely German settlement of 1635 allowed Ferdinand to join a full offensive and defensive league, creating precisely such conditions, and incidentally (by altering the focus of the partnership from the United Provinces to France), providing the correction to what had always been a serious flaw in Olivares's strategic premises. At last there would be genuine and fully orchestrated Habsburg collaboration. Ironically, as the talks at Roosendaele broke down, the Spanish–Dutch conflict was fading into the background, ceasing to be a 'hot' war (except in the maritime theatre) and, by default, conditions approximating to those of armistice held sway until the Treaty of Munster. In some ways, therefore, the great military effort of 1633–4 in Germany must be seen as ambiguous; for here (as it were) the monarchy was shifting on to its other foot, so as to confront the decisive challenge to its European hegemony.

The invasion of France, the great gamble of 1636, nevertheless failed. Subsequently it becomes difficult to keep track of policy-making in Madrid. Now the slave rather than the master of events, Don Gaspar's perceptions and objectives, once so clear and firm, degenerated into vacillation and uncertainty. In the space of weeks, even of days, his mood was capable of change from exultation to despair. At times – the Fuenterrabía crisis or the planning of the ill-fated armadas of 1639 – he could still display astonishing organisational energy and grasp. But policy ceased to have any long-term meaning. 'If I am not out of my mind', he protested (revealingly) to a French agent in 1637, 'I believe firmly that the Lord Cardinal and myself could reach agreement in one day, since there is no outstanding matter of difficulty between the two crowns.' Not long afterwards, in an amazingly puerile outburst, he told the junta that 'Richelieu is a dissembler, and wishes only to fool us . . . the answer is to prosecute the war with greater fury than ever' (E14/1). The body which listened to such assertions, and rubber-stamped the count-duke's decisions, was by now sadly reduced in size and function, a mere cabal of *apparatchiks*. The conciliar aristocracy, its advice ignored, abused to their faces, impoverished by forced loans and fines at the *valido*'s fiat, were voting with their feet against his regime. The 'strike of the grandees' (in Marañón's famous phrase) saw them withdraw from the performance of their offices. Don Gaspar's own camarilla of (not untalented) protégés – the nepotistical lieutenants he promoted to so many key positions – had been sent to the outposts of empire in Italy or Flanders, the better to guarantee local loyalty and efficiency. This made him vulnerable at court, and a close-knit group of malcontents led by the Count of Castrillo began to plot his overthrow. As Olivares repeatedly placed the responsibility for failure on the shoulders of the nobility, they responded by spreading the accusation that 'the fault in everything lies with the count-duke' (E10). By the summer of 1640, during the Catalan crisis, Olivares was reduced to dependence on the disillusioned king, on the one hand, and his secretarial factotum (some said grey eminence), Jerónimo de Villanueva, on the other. Failing in confidence at last he called upon the advice of the retired veteran, Oñate. 'It seems to me', commented the war-hawk of an earlier generation, 'that we have no choice but to look for a general peace, or at least a settlement in one or two of the wars in which the House of Austria is at present engaged.'[23]

Olivares, however, rejected this, along with Oñate's suggestion that no further resources be expended outside the peninsula whilst the

Catalan problem remained unresolved. On the contrary, he reaffirmed his determination to maintain his European strategy, and the war systems which supported it, to the utmost. The following winter, the defeat of Montjuich and revolt in Lisbon seem to have moderated this obstinacy; but it is significant that the bitter duty of supervising the search for peace was fobbed off on to Don Fernando in Brussels. Richelieu's terms were predictably harsh, and talks stagnated. Then, in 1642, an unexpected success at Honnecourt in Flanders again hardened Don Gaspar's resolve. It was this victory, more than any defeat, which influenced his fate. It seemed to underline the fact that only Olivares's dismissal offered a way out of the desperate plight of war on no fewer than six fronts. Though the finer points of the conspiracy are still obscure, by various means the king was eventually persuaded to part with the man who had guided him throughout his mature life.

The physical separation of the two in 1642, when Philip left Madrid for the Aragonese front, was no doubt important – a fatal parting of government and court. So, too, were the weighty and prolix moral and legal arguments put to the king against the very nature of the *valimiento*. True, these had been rehearsed long before, but only now seemed to receive the divine imprimatur, a judgement of such pragmatic emphasis that even Philip should have been impressed. There is, however, another factor which draws on both those already posited. As the king had come gradually to question the omniscience of his tutor, so developed his own desire to participate more actively in the monarchy's affairs, a tendency perhaps encouraged by the waning of his remarkable sex drive. It was Cánovas who (crying in the wilderness a century ago) first claimed that Philip became a *rey papelista* – a bureaucratic king in the tradition of Philip II (E14). Unlike his grandfather, however, Philip was taken with the idea of leadership on the battlefield as well as in the council chamber, and it was this, it may be suggested, which now came to the forefront. Perhaps this revealed the influence of the genes of Charles V rather than those of the personally unwarlike Philip II. As early as 1629, he had expressed a desire to take command in Flanders, the role in which Don Fernando was eventually substituted. In the subsequent correspondence of the brothers can sometimes be detected a note of envy on Philip's part that it was not he who rode, booted and spurred, at the van of the monarchy's defences. In 1642, his moment arrived in the protection of Castile itself against a threatened French invasion. Though never exposed to serious danger, he had Velázquez paint him with uniform and baton (the celebrated and symbolic 'silver portrait') perhaps as much as anything to impress his teenage son. It was possible to drop the pilot when the captain felt himself at the helm.

Attitudes

> You Spaniards always have God and the Holy Virgin on your lips
> and a rosary in your hands, but you never do anything except for
> worldly ends. (Richelieu to the Spanish ambassador)[24]

The war of 1635 was accompanied by the thunderous salvoes of the
partisan pamphleteers. France justified her action by posing as the
chivalrous liberator of Europe from Spanish tyranny, much as her
petty client of Savoy had always done in the Italian microcosm. Spain
was accused (justly) of fomenting disloyalty and disorder within
France, and (unjustly) of plotting the overthrow of her king and
national independence. Spain retaliated with accusations that France
was abetting the persecution of the true faith by Protestants and
Infidels, spreading heresy in the Rhineland and plague in the Milanese.
In 1630, during the Mantuan overture to the main item, a renegade
Spaniard domiciled in France tried to express the mutual and cosmic
antipathy of the two nations: 'God having set against a hell, heaven;
against a Lucifer, Michael; against vice, virtue; against the fire, water;
and finally against the Spanish, the French nation.'[25] Years later, in
conversation with his Spanish opposite number at the peace congress
in Westphalia, the French envoy d'Avaux reduced the matter to its
(more manageable) political essentials:

> He confessed to me that they had a profound apprehension of the
> power of the Austrian dynasty, seeing Spain and the empire acting
> in conjunction. I replied that of course the princes of the House of
> Habsburg had a close accord, being cousins and friends, but neither
> had ever nurtured designs against the interests of France. The
> proper fear that France should have was of the power of the
> Church's enemies, which threatened all three crowns, which should
> therefore unite and not destroy each other.[26]

There was here an unbridgeable gap of understanding. For the servants of the Bourbon monarchy, the Spanish system was something
which inexorably, even if incidentally, smothered its progress and its
pride. To those of the Habsburgs, it was difficult to accept that there
could be any necessary or fundamental incompatibility of interest with
France. Before 1630, Olivares was often criticised in some government quarters for being too patient (or myopic) in the face of French
provocation – a fact which helps to explain his bitter change of heart
after Mantua. Failing French collaboration in the work against heresy,
Spain would have been content simply to neutralise the policy of her
great neighbour by keeping her weak and divided. In effect, of course,

this itself was to conspire against French sovereignity, of which the declaration of 1635 was the inevitable reassertion. Perhaps the Habsburg invasion of France in 1636 was actually an abandonment of this principle in favour of a more radical solution, though it is hard to believe that Olivares aimed at anything more than a restoration of the *status quo ante* 1624. In any case, however tactically sound, the move was politically counter-productive. As it was put by Malvezzi, friend and servant of Olivares, 'it is an old and true saying that fear of an external enemy is the greatest remedy for internal dissensions'.[27]

Even as he wrote, however, Malvezzi's dictum seemed not to apply to the Spanish monarchy itself. Despite the external danger, there was an increasing level of internal protest. The revolt of Viscaya (1631), a sudden Portuguese insurrection (1637), pointed towards the crescendo of 1640 and the culmination of 1647. Amidst all the rumblings and earthquakes, it seems to the present writer that the Portuguese rebellion calls for comment at this point. Though it began as a simple and virtually bloodless coup, it ended by contributing more than any other single factor to the final dissolution of Spanish hegemony. It was the only one of all the mid-century upheavals of the seventeenth-century 'General Crisis' actually to achieve its objectives. It has received, if for good reasons, very little informed comment in English-language studies. But (above all) the Portuguese revolt against Castile expressed an attitude of exceptional vehemence towards the Spanish monarchy, more intense and wideranging than that subscribed to by any Frenchman.

As early as 1622, Antony Sherley had informed Olivares that 'Portugal is opposed to government by Castile, and *in everything* she remains an old enemy and uncertain vassal, changing her loyalties too easily'.[28] The Englishman spoke wiser than perhaps he knew. Treatment of the policies of Olivares's empire has come to be focused on the revolt of the Catalans, as a result of the magisterial work of J. H. Elliott, to which there is unlikely ever to be a Portuguese equivalent. Don Gaspar himself commented that 'the Portugal revolt is the affair of the Monarchy; that in Catalonia is my affair' (E7). Long before the outbreak of rebellion in Barcelona, he had regarded the Catalan attitude as treasonable, and to this he later added the charge of heresy. Both accusations were flung back in the face of Castile by the rebels. But this was small beer compared to the feelings of the Lusitanians, which in many ways were an even more trenchant comment on the count-duke's rule. The small group of aristocrats who, after long effort, finally persuaded the Duke of Braganza to proclaim himself as John IV of Portugal, were it is true motivated in part by grievances similar to those which concerned the Catalans, and (for that matter) their cousins amongst the Castilian nobility. Their revolt was also a reaction to the same events which precipitated insurrection and intrigue elsewhere. But these things must be set in a unique context.

At the psychological root of Portuguese attitudes was antisemitism, more virulent in Lisbon than anywhere else in Europe. Bitter suspicion and hatred of the Sephardic Jews was especially marked in Portuguese religious and civic life, and thence had percolated on to the popular plane. During the course of the Thirty Years' War it evolved into what can only be termed a conspiracy theory which in some respects anticipated the murderous myths of the modern era. Many of the Jews of southern Spain had taken refuge in Lisbon after the expulsion of 1492, leaving behind their crypto-Jewish relations – the so-called *conversos* – to survive as they might in the former Moorish kingdoms, now dominated by an intolerant Catholicism. In Portugal they were subject to the periodic persecution of the Inquisition, but nevertheless they flourished in the business life of Lisbon until the 1570s. At this point, the serious depression in trade arising out of the war in the Netherlands, followed as it was by the Castilian annexation of Portugal in 1580, forced many of the Lisbon Sephardim to emigrate once more, this time to Amsterdam, a perfectly logical step both in commercial and social terms. And it was not long after this last diaspora that the armed merchantmen of the Dutch began to attack the Portuguese trading empire in India and the Far East. By the 1600s this had broadened out into systematic conquest of the Portuguese factories and settlements. The Portuguese believed that their association with the monarchy, and in particular Madrid's renewal of the Dutch war in 1621, had brought this fate upon their empire. In addition, they accused Olivares of neglecting their defence needs in favour of Castile's irrelevant imperialism. On the whole, we can say with hindsight that neither claim was justified. What is certain is that Portugal's whole economy and national self-esteem had suffered considerably from the rise of the Dutch republic and its unprecedented commercial expansion.

In the opinion of Lisbon, the Jews were behind the whole disaster, forming an evil link between Madrid and Amsterdam in a plot to dismember the Portuguese empire for their mutual profit. The presence of Lisbon Jews in the mercantile community at Amsterdam was cited as a material reason for the extraordinary ease and efficiency of the Dutch *Drang nach Osten*. Portuguese-Jewish financiers had risen steadily in importance in Madrid, until in 1627 they emerged as the crown's main bankers. Olivares came to depend on such men for vital *asientos de dinero*, and naturally protected and rewarded them, despite the intense opposition of Castilian officialdom (G5). By the 1630s, several hundred Jewish business families were well established in Madrid and Seville, a fact connected in Portuguese grievance with the exactly contemporary Dutch move across the Atlantic, and the capture of Pernambuco. They pointed, moreover, to the fact that, despite official embargoes against Dutch interests, the element of clandestine and ostensibly private contact between the Spanish and Dutch continued to increase. The war between Philip and the Dutch heretic-rebels was thus an elaborate front, behind which lurked their common interest in betraying and subverting the Portuguese, true guardians of a pristine Catholicism in the wider world. And since the Jewish families, wherever domiciled, were all associated and in constant communication, obviously it was they who orchestrated the whole operation – Castilian overlords and alien heretics united in nothing less than a Jewish world conspiracy. Such haunted ideas were not wholly peculiar to the Portuguese. Francisco de Quevedo, a vitriolic opponent of the count-duke, was currently expressing very similar sentiments – for example in his satire-fantasy *La Hora de Todos* (1635) in which an international congress of Jews is pictured as pulling the strings of European war, at once leading Christianity to perdition and pocketing the profits of hatred.

In the late 1630s, the taxation programme associated with the Union of Arms screwed up the tension, since it was believed that the Jewish bankers who farmed the taxes were the ultimate beneficiaries. The Dutch conquest of Brazil was, meanwhile, proceeding apace, partly owing to the assistance of a 'fifth column' of Jews, to whom the Hollanders offered patronage and toleration (F2). The failure of the Pernambuco expedition in 1639–40 (to which Portugal, in fact, had made a rather inadequate contribution) appeared in Lisbon as the doom of the colonial empire. Olivares's peremptory demand for Portuguese levies to assist in the subjugation of the Catalans was the final straw. During the mob violence of the rebellion in Lisbon and other towns, fanatic popular feeling against all their enemies was whipped up by priests (especially Jesuits) and agents of the Inquisition. The anti-semitic myth now fused with another, equally powerful, legend which had general credence amongst the masses – the belief that Dom Sebastian, the unbalanced crusading hero, whose death in battle against the Moors in 1578 had led to the loss of Portuguese independence, would reappear one day to reclaim it, along with his throne. Faith in this unlikely messiah had sustained national feeling during the 'Sixty Years' Captivity', to the extent that Braganza, upon assuming the crown, was obliged to swear to surrender it when the expected event occurred! The peculiar intensity of national and colonial pride in Portugal can be gauged from the fact that hers was the first and also the last of European empires, having a continuous history of over half a millenium. It is worthy of comment, too, that the phenomenon described above was contemporary with the greatest of all antisemitic pogroms of the seventeenth century, the outbreak which accompanied the Cossack rebellion of Chmielnicki in the Ukraine. It is little wonder that the next generation produced a Messianic movement, that of Sabbatai Zevi, in Judaism itself.

The Portuguese revolt thus helped to seal the end of the empire of Olivares, by attributing to it more sinister geopolitical characteristics than any other of its European adversaries ever dreamed of. But the white-hot fanaticism of the Portuguese did not end there. They went on to challenge the progress of Dutch expansion, eventually succeeding where Castile had failed in bringing it to a term – a fact little noted in textbooks, perhaps simply because it *is* so surprising.[29] Moreover, simultaneously, they fought a tenacious war of independence against Castile, lasting for nearly thirty years. In the course of this struggle, Spaniards and Dutch were indeed effectively allied against them, though it is true that Portugal also received assistance from interested parties. As we shall see, it was this 'unknown war' which proved to be the insupportable incubus in the final death-throes of the Spanish system.

With material force and general opinion mounting against him in the 1630s, Olivares cast about desperately for support. An approach was even made to Hugo Grotius, eminent Dutch propagandist and legist of earlier years, now exiled because of his Arminian sympathies. But he and his associate (a son of Oldenbarnevelt) named too high a price for putting their knowledge and talents at the service of the Spanish monarchy. A rather more weighty area of sympathy for hire lay in the England of King Charles I. In fact the Caroline court (much to the disgust of many Englishmen) had been moving of its own volition back into the Spanish ambit since the treaty of 1630. Charles himself returned to his (and his father's) pro-Habsburg prejudices *a fortiori*, and most ministers and courtiers followed suit. There was more than a kernel of truth in the allegation, widespread in the ranks of opposition to the king's non-parliamentary government, that Whitehall was full of crypto-Catholics and Habsburg sympathisers. These developments were encouraged by the Bourbon queen, Henrietta Maria, a supporter of the anti-Richelieu faction amongst the French royal family. The king's artistic tastes were definitely inclined towards the Baroque cultural axis of the Spanish monarchy. In 1629–30, he had been captivated by the Archduchess Isabel's envoy, Peter Paul Rubens, the most celebrated painter of his day, who for many epitomises the ideology of the international ultra-Catholic movement which looked to Spain for guidance and salvation. Charles could not persuade Rubens to remain in England, and had to be satisfied with his pupil, Antony van Dyck. With the latter's collaboration, he began his career as the English Maecenas, building up an unparalleled collection of canvases mainly from Mediterranean sources. His agents and envoys, men like Francis Cottington, Francis Windebank, Walter Aston, Endymion Porter and Balthasar Gerbier, swarmed to the centres of Spanish power, in almost conscious imitation of Charles's own pioneer journey in 1623 to Madrid. Indeed, for a unique spell, Spain itself became a part of the incipient Grand Tour for younger sons of the court aristocracy. One such hopeful young royal servant was Richard Fanshawe, one of the founders of Hispanic scholarship in England: in 1635 he visited the infamous Escorial, headquarters of the system (which so many of his compatriots regarded as the inner circle of the inferno) and composed a descriptive poem, paying special attention to the paintings which he knew would excite his master's interest.

This interest had other directions, too. Though little research has been done on the theme, it is notable that many of the plans and stratagems of 'Thorough' seem to mirror the policies of the Olivares regime, in some cases (especially fiscal) down to the finer points. In any case, Charles's experiment in government stood in need of a powerful patron, and particularly one with whom profitable commercial links could be built up. Development of English trade in the Mediterranean was a major priority, both for Charles himself (as recipient of the controversial customs dues) and for many influential merchants in the City of London. The important expansion in English commerce owed a lot to the king's ability to exert some influence in Madrid and Brussels in this decade. Enterprising English capitalists began to compete successfully for *asientos* against Portuguese and Genoese in the management of the support systems of war. Indeed, Charles himself was chiefest among them: the Spanish attempt to keep open the Channel route to the Netherlands, though based primarily on their own considerable naval power, also came to rely on English co-operation. The English government supported the 'composition' trade between Dover and the Flanders ports, by which means war material was ferried across in English (i.e. neutral) ships, under the noses of the Dutch – even at times with the protection of the royal navy. What has been called an 'English road' came into existence in partial substitution for the blocked continental trails (F7). Supplies of silver were landed at Plymouth or Southampton and re-embarked at Dover – some of it actually coined in the London mint – for the pay of the army of Flanders. In this way, whilst Charles creamed off a useful percentage, the Spaniards were able to avoid the unwelcome attentions of enemy fleets in the Channel, not to mention its treacherous climate and navigational conditions. Even some regiments made their way to Flanders's fields by this route; and so it came to pass, in the bizarre manner of things, that fifty years after the Invincible Armada, the *tercios* of Spain tramped peaceably through the lanes of southern England.

King Charles's miserable failure (in 1639) to protect the last Spanish armada from a successful Dutch attack in English waters did not affect the fact of mutual dependence between the two crowns. After the Scottish rebellion of 1638, followed closely as it was by similar events within Spain, Philip IV's envoy to London offered a firm military alliance, 'against the conspiracy of revolution and heresy in our two kingdoms'.[30] Charles's asking price of over a million *escudos* in annual subsidies was too high for Madrid, and negotiations were still in progress when he was forced out of London and the civil war began. The loss of English collaboration in 1642 was another blow to Olivares's hopes of staving off the French challenge. In the meantime, the Stuart attitude to the Habsburgs had formed an intense, if often subliminal, undercurrent to the feelings which led to the great rebellion, and one which was to spring into a culminating prominence during the Cromwellian Protectorate.

Attachment to the culture and ideology of the Counter-Reformation baroque (though it was never an uncomplicated phenomenon, and did not necessarily predicate political support for the Spanish monarchy) thus stretched in a great geographical swathe from London, through Belgium and the Rhineland, to Bavaria and the Austrian lands, the Italian peninsula, and finally Spain herself. When we consider its many and powerful sympathisers within France, the profound apprehension of Richelieu is hardly surprising. Around this time he began to increase his efforts in the courts of southern Germany, and by the time of his death and Olivares's fall, had captured an important degree of influence. On the other hand, because of the latter's determined pursuit of his German policy the Habsburg confederation not only survived, but actually reached a point of apogee in the mid-1630s. The Spanish politico-financial apparatus assisted in the construction of a solid territorial base to its lobbies in Austria, Bohemia and Moravia. Not only did the armies of Wallenstein and the Catholic League find it impossible to operate without Spanish silver, but in the 1620s dozens of the Italian and Castilian officers of the great *condottiere* had been granted lands in the former rebel areas. Men like Marradas, Colloredo, Piccolomini and Gallas founded dynastic estates in the Austrian empire which have lasted in some cases to the present day. It seemed to some, like the Bohemian radical Jan Comenius, that their homelands had been conquered and occupied by the insatiable Spanish machine. (Comenius, who ran what has been called a 'post-office' for all opponents of Habsburg world dominion, was later to exercise considerable intellectual influence over the English revolutionaries.) After the murder of Wallenstein, the further division of his vast territorial acquisitions among the loyalist generals increased this impression.

Nevertheless, the constant internal preoccupations of Vienna – Swedes, Transylvanians and Turks amongst them – made it impossible for the imperialists to take a consistent part in Olivares's strategy. By the end of the decade they were longing to extricate themselves from commitments in western Europe – a situation that was to persist until almost the end of the century. Despite a strenuous attempt to counter the process from Madrid, Bavaria, too, was gradually detached from Olivares's empire, a severe strategic setback. The over-ambitious Duke Maximilian had learnt the lessons of neutrality after the thorough Swedish devastation of his possessions in 1632–3. Despite the ceaseless activity of his envoys in Germany, the count-duke was powerless to prevent the growth of contacts which finally brought about the assembly of European diplomats in the towns of Westphalia, beginning in 1642. This collapse of a costly policy, as unpopular in Castile as much as Paris and Prague, though not definitive until 1648, was another nail in Don Gaspar's coffin.

Conclusions

In 1628–9 only the remote outworks of the Spanish system's defences were penetrated. Grave matters though Matanzas, Mantua and 's Hertogenbosch were, in some ways the surprising thing was that they, or something like them, had not happened before. At any rate, the enemy was still at arm's length; by 1642 he had broken through, and was within the walls of the Spanish citadel itself. At the height of the earlier crisis, Philip IV had issued a decretal which amounted to a 'state of the Union message' akin to those periodically delivered to the Castilian Cortes. He assured his people that every effort was being made to stem the enemy's progress. Both in Italy and Flanders, greater armies were being assembled than for many years past. He professed not to be downhearted at the terrible coincidence of failure, 'since God has given me a strong heart, which is capable of bearing even worse afflictions without tiring'. Though time was fully to bear out this assertion, the king was nevertheless deeply affected by the affair of Matanzas in particular: 'I assure you that whenever I speak of it, my blood freezes in my veins, not because of the loss of the treasure, for this can be replaced, but because of the reputation which we Spaniards have lost as a result of that infamous retreat.'[31]

By the 1640s, prestige, that dynamic principle of so many of the crown's policies, had indeed been irrevocably lost. Consider the apocalyptic whirlwind of war and rebellion in which the monarchy was trapped in this decade. There were revolts or conspiracies in Catalonia, Portugal, Andalusia, Aragon, Naples and Sicily. In 1641 the first serious revolt in the American colonies for nearly a century broke out in Chile, perilously close to the silver mines of Peru. Theatres of war existed in Flanders, the Rhineland, northern Italy, Aragon and Portugal, not to mention the conflicts at sea in the Mediterranean, the North Sea and the Atlantic. The appalling strain, and in particular the calamitous collapse of the Seville–Atlantic trade in 1640, caused depression in the one remaining area of economic vitality, Andalusia. It was in this region that soon afterwards began the series of violent local protests which ruined Castile's strange record of stoic complaisance. Philip's dominions seemed about to disintegrate, the empire of Olivares had shrunk to the size of his (not inconsiderable) girth. The government which, little more than a decade earlier, had been planning to establish its power in the Baltic, and even more recently had been sending expeditions to Germany, the Shetland Islands, Greenland and Brazil, was now fighting for survival with its back to the wall. Castile itself was imprisoned between the Franco-Catalan armies menacing it from Aragon, and the fanatical Portuguese rebels on its other frontier. From infinite ambition it was reduced to infinite precariousness. The king whom Olivares had encouraged his propagandists to call *el rey planeta* had become *el rey aldeano* – king of the village.

Of course it would be idle to deny that the Spanish monarchy was never the same again, and ridiculous to ignore the long-term consequences of '1640' in terms of its prospects of survival. But it remains a fact that the structure did not suddenly subside into ruin. None of the events catalogued above immediately transformed the determination of Madrid to continue the struggle, at least to the point at which a settlement could be obtained which was consonant with duty and honour. As I have argued elsewhere, a sequence of defeats on the battlefield, and the (more vital) rupture of strategic communications, were not decisive (F9). The monarchy's fall from hegemony was like a slow-motion film of the demolition of a factory chimney; occasionally, even, the picture freezes; and when the dust settles, a substantial if truncated section is seen to remain standing, necessitating the repetition of the whole process.

CHAPTER 3

Years of Survival
1643–56

I am so grateful for your intercession with God on my behalf, since before everything must come the salvation of my soul; this is the first consideration, and after it the good and tranquillity of this monarchy. (Philip IV to María de Ágreda, 1645)[1]

God did not create kingdoms for the good of kings, but kings for the good of kingdoms. (The Count of Peñaranda, 1648)[2]

Introduction

Only in recent years have historians come to accept that the crisis of the 1640s, severe and damaging as it was, did not result in the abrupt collapse of the Spanish system. It is now equally clear that there was no dramatic 'Ascendancy of France', declining Spain's inseparable companion which sits at the other end of the see-saw in a familiar textbook image. Though (doubtless) such statements can be made the more confidently as a result of research progress on the infrastructures of French and Spanish power, the patient assembly of statistical detail has belatedly come to support a conclusion which ought to have been evident from long-established facts. Fernand Braudel, in his examination of 'the long sixteenth century', recognised this as long ago as 1949. Twenty years later, the Oxford scholar John Stoye sensibly deduced that the period covered by the present chapter witnessed 'the eclipse of France' and 'the survival of Spain' (C6). In 1971, Domínguez Ortiz strongly supported this view (D3). Meanwhile, research stimulated by the 'General Crisis' debate encouraged approaches which were essentially comparative and made still wider comparisons possible. By now, not only has much material been advanced to support the opinion summarised above, but the fact of Spain's decline has itself been challenged, and the very concept of 'decline' subjected to question (B2). In the process, many previous assumptions concerning the nature of the Spanish monarchy and the mainsprings of its policy have been undermined to a point where it seems best to discard them altogether.

In particular it now seems obvious that the monocausal economic explanation of Spanish failure, established by E. J. Hamilton, and resting upon the evidence of the effects of bullion inflation upon the economy, has had its day. The evidence itself has been exaggerated, both in relative and absolute terms. Moreover, the Spanish system and its policy-decisions were not in any immediate sense dependent on conventional economic criteria, and usually functioned without significant reference to their logic. Even the more sophisticated gloss on the economic thesis, that policy and power were governed by financial realities – the availability of liquid revenues – is something that must be used with caution and constant qualification. Particularly as advanced by M. Chaunu, such conclusions are too sweeping, because too mechanistic and exclusive, even where they offer a relevant and important component of analysis. No decade of the Spanish monarchy's history saw a more drastic diminution of such resources, especially of silver, than the 1650s. But this did not, in practice, drastically affect the monarchy's ability to wage war. For some fifteen years after the silver levels began to fall again in 1646, Spain maintained her war effort on a full footing. French power was continuously stalemated, even after the extra responsibilities of a war with England were added. Though it is true that peace negotiations with France were finally clinched at the lowest point of silver returns, it would be unwise to conclude that financial breakdown was the sole or even the major cause thereof. Indeed, it seems necessary to point out that in dealing with large-scale political phenomena, considerations of a political nature must assume primacy, so long as they are firmly placed in a relative and comparative context. Strategy, logistics, economics and finance all bear on them and help to condition the historian's balance and discrimination. The quack doctors of deterministic persuasions (ideological or otherwise) offer placebos for the headache caused by the need to understand the infinite complexity of historical processes. But the student must be wary of these analgesics, which come, like some television commercial, stamped with the spurious sanction of 'science'.

Narrative of Events

Following their breakthrough into Catalonia in 1641, the French gradually built up pressure on all the key strategic points of Spain's imperial defences. By the mid-1640s – approximately a decade after Corbie – Castile, in its turn, was hemmed in and apparently doomed. These years, when the Madrid government was new and inexperienced, certainly constitute the supreme military and political crisis of Habsburg Spain. The surmounting of it guaranteed for a further generation the survival of Spanish hegemony, if only by default of its enemies, and clearly in an attenuated and less vigorous form. What gave France the initiative in the opening phase was not only the sword pointed at Castile, but the piecemeal and skilful surgery performed on Spanish communications by Richelieu in the campaigns of the late 1630s. At their most vulnerable point – the Rhineland passages – this severance was definitive. The French presence in Alsace-Lorraine led to the fall of Breisach (1638) which spelled the end of 'the Spanish Road' to the Low Countries. Richelieu's new fleet had also contributed (by the destruction of a major Spanish force at Guetaria in the same year) to the yet more significant setback of Oquendo's armada at the Downs in 1639, which drastically reduced Spain's naval capacity. Such successes provided Cardinal Mazarin with a stable platform from which to mount his subsequent offensives on all fronts.

These offensives nevertheless met with stubborn resistance everywhere. Above all, the centre held firm. After the rout of Castile's punitive force at Montjuich, Catalonia was formally annexed to France, and a Bourbon viceroy was established in Barcelona. During the next two campaigns the principality was almost cleared of Castilian troops, and the Franco-Catalan armies advanced towards Aragon. Their capture of Lérida in 1643 gave them a very strong position, as it were undermining the outworks of Castile's defences. However, as they penetrated deeper into the peninsula, topographical and logistical problems slowed down the French advance. The Aragonese responded energetically to the prospect of invasion, and the king's presence in their capital much encouraged the spirit of resistance. Philip's involvement in the defence of the kingdom – and the transference of the court to Zaragoza – met with the desired patriotic response. The difficult terrain favoured the locals, and offset the French superiority in cavalry. Indeed, the war quickly became a familiar one of static fronts and sieges in which the Spaniards possessed greater experience, technique, and even equipment than their adversary. Mazarin found it increasingly difficult to supply his forces along dangerously stretched lines of supply which had to cross the Pyrenees (F12). Like their Castilian predecessors in 1636–40, they were obliged to turn to local resources, progressively alienating the Catalan population from the new regime. The French quickly found themselves operating – outside the towns at least – in a basically hostile environment. The defence of Castile-Aragon was aided also by the fact that it could be organised along internal lines of supply, the military factor which so often told in favour of the French kingdom in European wars. A further point in Spain's favour was her control of the Mediterranean, where her remaining armada strength was now concentrated. Not only were the French impeded from supplying Barcelona by sea (indeed finding their own coastline under constant threat), but the Spaniards were able to transfer resources from Italy to Valencia, and thus to endanger the French southern flank.

Though Lérida was regained in 1644, Castile was unable to take the offensive. The fortress sat for subsequent campaigns at the crossroads of a punishing and exhausting war, surviving long sieges by the French commander Harcourt in 1645 and 1646 – the latter lasting seven months. The turning point came in the following year. Mazarin, anxious to break the deadlock, and especially to gain a strong negotiating position at the conference tables in Westphalia, detached Condé from the Flanders front and put him in command in Catalonia. The Bourbon champion nearly brought off the recapture of Lérida, but was ultimately frustrated by a desperate relief expedition. Castile was now scraping the bottom of the barrel, but the effort was worthwhile, for the French setback had both military and political consequences. It marked the last serious French offensive, and influenced Mazarin to turn his attention elsewhere, particularly to Italy, where the situation was (in his eyes) ripe for French intervention. On the other hand, Condé, after a string of glorious successes in Flanders and the Rhineland, was bitterly disappointed by his failure in the peninsula and placed the blame squarely on the cardinal's mismanagement. As a result, he was attracted towards the movement of French aristocratic and civic leaders who were becoming disillusioned with the war and the regency government. The subsequent outbreak in France of the period of endemic disorders known as the *Fronde* (1648–52) considerably eased the pressure on Madrid. Simultaneously, Catalonia fell into the vicious grip of bubonic plague, an epidemic which originated in southeastern Spain and became rampant upon breaking through into the midst of a population debilitated by a decade of warfare. This rendered complete the dislocation of the principality, enabling the Castilians to push back the French line, now with much assistance from the natives themselves. Philip wisely adhered to the generous terms of nonreprisal which he had always offered the rebels, and by 1650 only the original centres of the revolt in Barcelona and the Pyrenean foothills kept alive the chimera of secession. Barcelona was gradually isolated, and after a prolonged and horrifying siege capitulated to the king's bastard son, Don Juan José, in October 1652. Contrary to the received impression, this event (though it ended the Catalan revolt) did not close the Catalan front. Sporadic and sometimes serious fighting continued in the mountainous no-man's-land of northern Catalonia, representing a continuous drain of energy and resources, until the settlement of 1659.

The dire emergency in the heartland of the monarchy naturally dominated the course of events in the Netherlands. For example,

Madrid was now making heavy supply demands on Flemish resources, both human and material, for the defence of Castile. Whilst Don Fernando remained in control at Brussels such requisitions could be resisted, or at least reduced in scale, by the authority vested in the royal blood; combined (in this case) with the personal reputation of its possessor. When the cardinal-infante died in the autumn of 1641, to be succeeded by the obscure Portuguese *caballero* Don Francisco de Melo, the military self-sufficiency of the Spanish Netherlands was further reduced. The redoubtable Dunkirk squadron, for example, was transferred to the Mediterranean, though not before it had ferried thousands of Walloon recruits to the ports of northern Spain. Moreover, the strict defence responsibilities of the army of Flanders were overtaken by the need to take the offensive, dictated by Madrid's precarious position and her demands for relief operations (F9). Not surprisingly, if it was not as weak as has often been assumed, Melo's army could not measure up to such requirements. After a deceptively promising victory at Honnecourt in 1642, it met with a sharp reverse on the 'immortal day' of Rocroi, at the outset of the next campaign. Though the consequences of this battle have been vastly exaggerated on the basis of legend, and the Spaniards quickly regrouped, Condé was able to make slow progress in subsequent years. He took Gravelines in 1645, and even succeeded (to the great rejoicing of the persecuted Dutch) in capturing that nest of privateers, Dunkirk – also, as it happened, Spain's most useful strategic harbour – in the following year. However, Condé's removal to Catalonia (described above), along with the exceptional demands on the French war-machine made by the events of 1647, provided Brussels with a timely breathing space. The respite actually became initiative by 1648, since the Treaty of Munster finally reduced the need for vigilance on the extensive northern frontier of Flanders, a factor which coincided with the outbreak of the Fronde. For many reasons, the Spaniards were slow to capitalise their advantage – a crucial, if understandable, failure. Nevertheless, with the defection to their ranks of both Condé and Turenne in 1650, and the recruitment of a young and capable Habsburg prince (the Austrian Archduke Leopold-William) to the governorship, a notable recovery began. By 1652, with the repossession of Dunkirk, most losses had been wiped out. Only two years later, the army of Flanders was once again able to pitch its tents on the soil of France.

The wheel of fortune which seemed to govern the tides of war in this decade turned through the same number of degrees in Italy. As in earlier and later periods, the history of northern Italy during the later stages of the Thirty Years' War appears on the surface a grim catalogue of violence and betrayal dominated by the greater ambitions of foreign powers, and ending in the awful dénouement of epidemic pestilence. All this is seen through a glass darkly (which adds to the Gothic image) since the Italian role in the Thirty Years' War has so far failed to attract more than passing attention from historians. What seems clear is that Guglielmo Mazzarini's promotion to supreme power in France had the effect of bringing Italy back into the European limelight. Just as for the United Provinces, during the previous generation, the major objective had been the capture of Peru and its silver mines, so Mazarin now schemed to conquer Naples, 'truly the best Indies that the king of Spain possesses', as he put it (G12). The architect of Cherasco knew better than most how precarious Castile's authority in Italy had become, yet how vitally important its resources were to the continuing viability of the Spanish system. The search for the *coup de grace* in military terms was, for Spain's various enemies identical with the search for the El Dorado – that Holy Grail or secret ring of profit and power, according to taste. So, like other adventurers who were in later ages to hold control of French destinies, the cardinal decided on a major intervention in the Mediterranean.

He first took a hand in the Savoyard civil war. This conflict had been smouldering for some years. The opposing sides had been espoused and aided in lukewarm and desultory fashion by the major adversaries. However, in 1645 the French attacked Genoa (still a loyal and useful ally of the monarchy), and followed this with an incursion into the Milanese. These moves preceded the launching of amphibious expeditions against the Spanish outposts on the coast of Tuscany, themselves envisaged as stepping stones to the Regno. The plan was to tie down the Spanish forces in the north, and to knock out their major naval and supply bases; which, coupled with control of Barcelona, would leave only Valencia (itself threatened by Condé) as an isolated centre of Spanish defence. What the French intended was nothing less than the destruction of the Spanish (communications) system in the western Mediterranean, to complement Richelieu's achievement in the northern theatre (E15). But Mazarin's enormous and immensely costly ambitions were thwarted. Despite an almost total moratorium on aid from Spain and Naples, the Marquis of Velada, governor of Milan, responded with vigour to the opening enemy gambits. Genoa was again bailed out by a Spanish army, and the French siege of Finale – the port in the republic through which passed the direct line of Madrid–Milan contact – weakly collapsed. Moreover, of the three *presidios* invested, whilst two (Porto Longone and Piombino) were indeed taken, the third and most significant, that of Orbitello, resisted stoutly, giving a Spanish squadron time to cut off and annihilate the besiegers. When, therefore, the moment arrived towards which all Mazarin's thinking (not to mention diplomatic intrigue) had been bent, the simultaneous insurrections of Palermo and Naples in 1647, his inter-

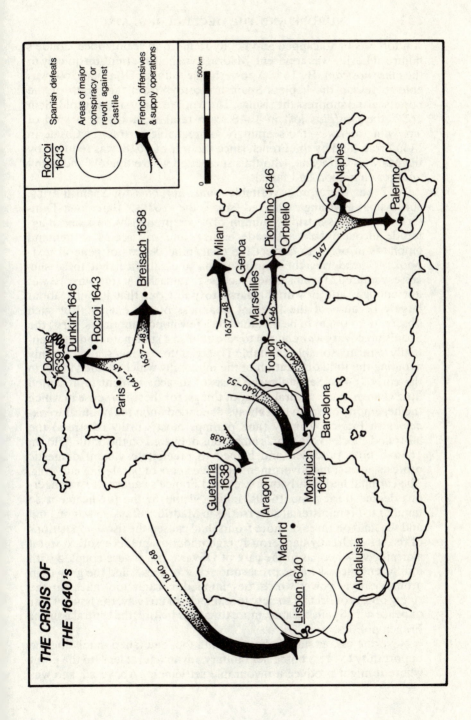

THE CRISIS OF
THE 1640's

Rocroi
1643   Spanish defeats

        Areas of major
        conspiracy or
        revolt against
        Castile

        French offensives
        & supply operations

0   500km

vention was handicapped and fatally reduced in scale. Once Condé's failure at Lerida was apparent, Madrid switched its attention quickly to the *mare nostrum*. By 1648 a powerful fleet under Don Juan José was able to rescue the hapless Spanish viceroys from the wrath of the populace and suppress the risings. The whole enemy strategy folded; in 1650, the *presidios* lost in 1646 were retaken, and – as a kind of 'crowning mercy' – the seemingly impregnable fortress of Casale in Monferrat, held by the French since the war of 1628, was reduced by the Marquis Caraçena, who thus succeeded where Spínola and many another champion had failed.

1652 was therefore a veritable *annus mirabilis* for Spanish arms, surpassing anything achieved since the 1620s. Barcelona–Dunkirk–Casale was a triple triumph of a comprehensiveness and magnitude inconceivable a decade earlier, and still seems to demand emphasis in order to correct the congenital defects of general textbooks. Considering the determination and sacrifice that these successes required, it seems almost tactless to remark that (of course) it was not enough, and downright harsh to point out that it came about largely because of the internal weakness of the enemy. But such observations ought to be modified by a few important riders. First, the Spanish recovery *was* enough to re-establish a stalemate leading eventually to the reasonably equitable Treaty of the Pyrenees, and certainly avoiding the total dissolution of the monarchy which seemed likely in the early 1640s. Secondly, the basis of its achievement represented little change in the natural order of things, for there is a sense in which the hegemony of Spain had always depended upon the political weaknesses of France. Thirdly (and perhaps most worthy of stress) the all-round check to Mazarin's ambitions delivered on the battlefields in 1646–8 both preceded and helped to precipitate violent domestic protests against his government and five years of paralysing civil war. The cardinal had clearly overstretched France's capacity to a dangerous degree during the 1640s, falling victim to the predicament so familiar to his ministerial adversaries in Madrid. Offensive war on land and sea, and on three or more fronts, had caused the fiscal impositions of the state, already dangerously high under his predecessor, to spiral alarmingly. When, as in the case of Olivares, they were coupled with indifferent success in the prosecution of war, these, and the growth in arbitrary royal power which they implied, became too much for the ruling orders of French society to stomach. In this way, the issue of war or peace with Spain became, more than ever before, the central issue of French politics.

Nevertheless, as stated above, Spain, too, had failed in missing the opportunity to press home her military advantage, at least to the point where it might produce a favourable settlement. Above all, she was unable to repair the rupture of her military communications, which had occurred largely before 1640. Without these essential corridors, the Spanish system was by definition doomed, whatever its short-term political situation. This ineluctable fact did not become apparent immediately. Though Mazarin gradually re-established his position, supported by a king who had now achieved his majority, this was not the signal for a new phase of French victory abroad. Indeed, although the cardinal's policies were now more cautious, it did not protect him from further humiliations, when French armies were soundly beaten both in Flanders (Valenciennes, 1656) and in Italy (Pavia, 1655). It may be understood that by this time, Mazarin was preparing to revert to his predecessor's famous formula of 'war by proxy'. In 1656 he made an extremely reasonable *démarche* at Madrid in an attempt to extract France from the war, whilst at the same time casting about for a suitable new partner to share the burden of the anti-Habsburg crusade. Since 1648, and the withdrawal of Sweden and the United Provinces, France had been without a major ally, and Portugal seemed to offer only limited prospects. It was precisely at this moment that a saviour appeared, a man who had extraordinary resources at his command, and who was obsessed with abasing the power of Spain. The cardinal was renowned for his addiction to the gaming table, but a gambler is rarely granted a stroke of fortune like that offered to Mazarin by the peculiar ambitions of Oliver Cromwell.

When Cromwell launched his unexpected but carefully planned attack on Spain and its Caribbean colonies in 1655, it was an entirely unilateral act, made without reference to the main Franco-Spanish conflict. Indeed, the world picture of the Protectoral government placed the Italian cardinal of France in a hardly less desperate circle of the inferno than the Spanish inquisitor-general. However, the English quickly discovered that dismantling the universal empire of Satan was not as simple as it appeared from the council chambers of Whitehall. Their audacious assault upon the main centre of Spanish administration in the West Indies, the island of Hispaniola, was nothing less than a débâcle, worthy of Buckingham. And whilst Blake's great fleet sailed abroad in search of the silver galleons, the privateers of Dunkirk and Ostend swarmed around the English coasts, cutting domestic and foreign trade to ribbons, and causing a severe economic depression. This maritime onslaught, along with the immense cost of his geopolitical policy, confronted Oliver with loss of prestige and internal rumblings against the Protectorate. He needed subsidies; above all, perhaps, he needed to 'take out' Dunkirk, a veritable dagger in his side. Only France was in a position to assist in both particulars. Once Mazarin, for his part, had become convinced that his negotiations in Madrid had reached deadlock, he bent all his energies to the English alliance.

During 1657, a full and strict programme of combined action and respective profits was hammered out. However cynical the basis of this true *mariage de convenance*, it enjoyed a brilliantly successful honeymoon. The military resistance of the Spanish monarchy – which, be it remembered, had been able to repulse attacks in Flanders, Italy *and* the Indies only a few years earlier – crumbled before this renewed assault. Blake gobbled up one silver fleet, on the last stages of its incoming voyage, in 1657; his lieutenant, Stayner, badly mauled its immediate successor. After a decisive battle on the sand dunes outside the harbour, Dunkirk fell in September 1658, the month of Cromwell's death. The last links of imperial communications were shattered, and the 'precarious equilibrium' between the powers, which had effectively preserved the hegemony of Spain since 1635, was at last upset.

Resources

> Only great need drives me to the war,
> I'ld never go had I money in store. (Calderón de la Barca)

Though the complaint of Calderón's ragged recruit is in many ways symptomatic, in one aspect at least he was a fortunate soul. For by the late 1630s, the monarchy had ceased to rely on volunteer levies, and was making much use of conscription, on the one hand, and overseas mercenaries, on the other. The strictly military aspect of Castile's long demographic stagnation had now become of pressing concern for the first time. It coincided, in the mid-1640s, with another financial crisis, the first for twenty years. This 'conjuncture' contributed towards Spain's failure to exploit its opportunities for recovery to an extent which would assure the survival of Spanish hegemony.

Battlefront casualty lists began to assume a wholly new and grave dimension in 1638–43. Though we cannot be exact, the unprecedented series of defeats from Guetaria to Rocroi probably involved the outright loss of some 30,000 military personnel, not accounting for the effects of desertion, disease and wounds. These *gotas de sangre* (or bloodlettings) were all the more damaging since the Castilian population had lost its last reserves of buoyancy. What might be called the 'demographic vacuum' resulting from the great plague of 1599–1602, the decline in births which adult mortality and delayed marriages had then caused, occasioned a kind of missing generation of men of military age in the period 1630–50. Things were (apparently) exacerbated by the resumption of substantial emigration to America after 1620, when employment prospects and taxation pressures in the peninsula both took a turn for the worse, and which largely comprised mature males (B15/I). This military shortfall reduced Spain's ability to plug the gaps through which the French poured into imperial territory in the early 1640s. Nor was this all; by 1647, after the familiar prelude of harvest failures and subsistence crisis, a renewed bout of epidemic began. Valencia and Andalusia, prime areas of recruitment during the peninsular wars against Catalonia and Portugal, were soon in the grip of bubonic plague. On this occasion the central areas of Old and New Castile escaped serious mortality – perhaps through genetic immunity – but the infection travelled quickly north into Catalonia. From the tragic principality it transferred itself, probably via the western Mediterranean islands, to Italy. Genoa and Milan had succumbed by 1650, Rome fell to its attack in 1654, and in the following year the plague reached Naples. In the densely populated capital and impoverished villages of the Regno the mortality was appalling, and one of the monarchy's most productive areas of military recruitment was blighted. The disruption caused by this calamity upon the war systems of Madrid can perhaps more easily be imagined than the kind of privation and horror that it meant for the ordinary citizen, particularly in Naples, where the exploitations of war had been virtually uncontrolled for a decade, and in Catalonia, actual scene of the most bitter and ruinous fighting. As in other cases, at the beginning and the end of this century, pestilential holocaust occurred after a generation of continuous warfare. It seems certain that in both Italy and Spain population density reached its lowest point of modern times in these awful years (B14). My chapter title is rather a misnomer as far as Philip IV's subjects are concerned, for this pandemic probably swept away over half a million of them. The king himself, however, did not escape his share of misery; nearly all of his close relations and contemporaries of the Habsburg dynasty, among them his only legitimate son and his queen, died in this decade. These, too, represented an irreplaceable loss to the monarchy's cause. It is hardly surprising that the Spanish system remained essentially a passive organism in the last phase of its existence.

In 1648, when the moment for dynamism arrived, the Archduke Leopold-William reported from Brussels that his available forces amounted to only 14,000 men – a reduction of some 40 per cent on Don Fernando's strength a decade earlier, and certainly not sufficient to take the offensive. As we have seen, the Flanders army was continually weakened by the demands of Madrid. During the 1640s perhaps 1,000 Walloons a year made the sea passage to Spain for service on the Aragonese front. More recruits came to Spain from Naples (as usual) and from Ireland. Indeed, apart from German professional soldiers released on to the market by the peace settlements of 1648, the trouble-torn celtic kingdom was Spain's main hope of making up the quantitative shortfall. Beginning with the decade, boatloads of raw Irish peasants began to arrive regularly at the ports of northern Spain. A considerable business sprang up, based on shoddy *asientos* made by consortia of merchants, shipowners and freelance officers, paid on a per capita basis. The traffic fully resembled the Atlantic slave trade in its details. At first, an integral source of supply existed in the Irish army raised by Strafford – that infamous body which was at the centre of the English constitutional crisis. But long after this was exhausted, Irishmen defeated in the prolonged wars of their own island, escaped into the scarcely less horrifying conditions of Spanish service. Thousands of them arrived in so deplorable a state as to be more a liability than an asset. One local official in 1644 demanded aid from Madrid for the hospital treatment of four companies (400 men) recently arrived. Others were less fortunate. An eyewitness of 1652 in Galicia described violent local resistance to the landing of the Irish, so that disease broke out on board the overcrowded ferries, and the shores became littered with corpses being fed upon by dogs.[3] Even when such gangs could be transported into the interior, they often saw little in the way of active service. In droves they deserted to become vagrants, or to join the bands of *pícaros* (themselves often refugees from conscription) who infested provincial Spain and the Castilian sierras. In 1656, the newsmonger Barrionuevo reported 'the 1,500 Irishmen recently brought over have plundered everything and scattered themselves all over Castile. Most of them are in Madrid, where they spend their time scavenging and begging, whilst in Segovia they live with the pigs'.[4]

Fit, therefore, for alms rather than arms, foreign levies served more to aggravate the growing domestic instability of the Spanish localities then to help with the reduction of rebellion against Castile. Certainly they failed to relieve pressure on indigenous sources, which built up to a new crescendo during the siege of Barcelona in 1650–2. So anxious was the crown to finish off the Catalan episode, that even the island of Majorca, and the semi-autonomous kingdom of Navarre, were compelled, against stout local protest, to contribute *tercios* of 500 men. When Caraçena captured Casale in 1652, it had to be abandoned immediately, since he had not the men to spare for a garrison.[5] Five years later Condé's achievement in relieving the siege of Cambrai caused acute embarrassment in Madrid because of the cost of reinforcing and maintaining the occupying force! ('All we can now ask of the army of Flanders', the Council noted, almost by way of reproof, 'is to harass and delay the designs of the enemy.')[6] Yet amidst all this exhaustion and despair, Philip still clung to the traditions of his line and his higher heritage as defender of the faith. In 1646 – at the critical point of the Catalan war – when Venice approached him for aid against the Turks, he promptly fitted out ten galleys, and even allowed the unfriendly republic to raise troops in the Neapolitan countryside.

About this time, the king received a memorial from the Council of Castile. 'Complaints are being made', it reported, 'that the number of tax-collectors who eat up Your Majesty's kingdoms now exceeds 20,000; surely these are people who, by their youth and idleness, would be better employed in the armed forces?'[7] Unfortunately, tax-men enjoyed the luxury of a reserved occupation, especially when (as now) there was an impending fiscal emergency. Unlike the earlier 'bankruptcy' of the reign, twenty years before, that of 1647 was precipitated by a dramatic loss of revenue rather than overexpenditure. During the whole of the Thirty Years' War, silver receipts had been maintained at a peculiarly consistent level, the royal share always falling at between 5 and 6 million ducats per quinquennium. (This is a fact often forgotten or ignored in conventional 'explanations' of Spain's European decline.) In 1646–50, however, they dropped by some 60 per cent, making *Hacienda*'s task in the raising of war-credits next to impossible. The crown was committed to providing 13 million ducats for the crucial campaign of 1647. Only a quarter of this sum could be offered in securities to the bankers, and this fraction itself involved a five-year anticipation of revenues. The result was the swingeing financial decree of 1647, which netted the Treasury the outstanding 10 million ducats, at the cost (*inter alia*) of destroying some creditors and driving others out of the market. The main victims were the Portuguese-Jewish families, who may have been singled out for political reasons, but in any case felt the loss of Olivares's protection. These partnerships had between 7 and 8 million ducats of royal credit wiped out, and their ascendancy in the monarchy's finances came to a sudden end.

All the same, this vicious measure helped Madrid over the military hump of 1647. Another spate of coinage manipulation also contributed to victory against Condé in Catalonia. Indeed, it was perversely fortunate for Madrid that during this silver deficiency, the main area of expenditure was within the peninsula, where copper (*vellón*) coinage could be used to pay for wages and supplies, rather than northern Europe, where Spanish armies traditionally demanded payment in specie. In fact, the final reduction of Barcelona was made possible only by a special issue of *vellón* in 1651, which brought in a profit of 2 million ducats. Although the crown's budget had now reached (on paper at least) nearly 20 million, hardly any of this was liquid. Quite apart from the cost of servicing the debt (perhaps a third of total revenue, though often defaulted upon), the conversion of taxes collected in *vellón* into silver caused a loss of $5\frac{1}{2}$ million annually. 'It would have been better for me to have been the poorest *hidalgo* of my home town than to occupy my present position', wailed Don José González, President of the Treasury, in 1650 (G5). It is surprising that the inevitable programme of new and increased taxation was delayed for some years – possibly as a consequence of the new government's desire for popularity, connected with the pressing fear of further rebellion and disorder. The former motive was doubtless present when, shortly after the count-duke's disgrace, the still unfinished palace of the Buen Retiro, sensational 'evidence' of his prodigality and megalomania, was stripped of its silver ornaments and rich furnishings to provide ready cash for the wars.

These were some of the reasons why Philip IV was able to claim, at a session of the Cortes of Castile in 1655, that he had laid out 66 million in the defence of the monarchy in the previous six years, without imposing a single new tax on the kingdom. As with the depressingly familiar ministerial broadcasts of our own day, the statement was not only tendentious in itself, but formed the prelude to a series of fresh imposts more savage than Castile had ever experienced. In this year, the silver fleet was late in arriving ('surrounded with enemies as honey is with flies') and there were fears that it had been taken.[8] Philips's favourite dwarf, Manuellilo, taunted him at court, saying that if he could bring the *flota* home safely, and provide the monarchy with an heir into the bargain, he would deserve canonisation. As it happened, the silver did arrive unmolested and two years later, the queen gave birth to a son!

Only a proportion of the vast sums disbursed on defence actually reached the paymasters of the crown's armies and (rapidly disappearing) fleets. Service charges of all kinds were enormous, and hundreds of parasitical middlemen nibbled away at the precious plant meant to feed the military organism. Moreover, following peace with the United Provinces in 1648, the official subsidy to Flanders was reduced, whilst receipt of the bills of exchange was subject to repeated and prolonged interruption. Though some of the stronger Italian banks were exempted from the suspension of 1647, their combined resources were insufficient to support the offensive strategy needed in these years. 'It would be possible to profit from the internal troubles of the enemy, and begin the coming campaign with an early attack', stated Leopold-William in 1650, 'but we simply lack the funds to do it.'[9] For almost the length of the previous year, no subsidies had come through, and (as in 1644) the Antwerp bourse refused to extend credit facilities beyond already unreasonable limits. In consequence, a scheme to support the Ormée rebellion in Bordeaux, and to mount a double-pronged offensive against France had to be shelved. By the mid-1650s these serious mechanical failures in the transfer system were aggravated by political disputes between Madrid and its main agent in this respect, the republic of Genoa, coming as near outright rupture as the two partners had ever done in the century-old history of their relationship. To some extent, however, the Dutch were beginning to act as substitutes, in a more formal manner than before Munster, if still improvised. The financial impasse in Flanders referred to above, for example, was broken with their aid, six months' supply of silver being sent to Amsterdam in Dutch vessels and transported overland to Antwerp. Overall, however, the plight of the obedient provinces accurately reflected the shift of priorities at Madrid towards the affairs of metropolitan Spain, another tendency of great future importance. Not until Catalonia was firmly back under control could the government feel able to respond elsewhere, by which time it was too late. In these circumstances the actual degree of success achieved outside the peninsula in 1648–52 is all the more remarkable.

Policy

For some time after the fall of the count-duke, Philip IV conducted the affairs of the monarchy through the *antiolivaristas*, the cabal of eminent nobles who had overthrown the *valido*. The three leaders thereof, the counts of Castrillo and Peñaranda, and Don Luis de Haro, were all members of Olivares's family, if only by marriage. In this way the House of Guzmán, which had exercised a dominant influence on government since 1618, remained at the centre of power. It is a fact which seems more than coincidental that the ascendancy of this dynasty was exactly coterminous with the fifty years of continuous war which are the core of our subject. During this period, several key factors in domestic politics and external attitudes can be illuminated by reference to the role of the Guzmanes, their ambitions, preconceptions, and (especially) their internal feuds. These observations are particularly relevant to the years immediately under discussion.

Just as Baltasar de Zúñiga, the founder of Guzmán political fortunes, had played the role of precursor of Olivares in 1618–22, so now Castrillo was instrumental in the propulsion of *his* nephew, Haro, to a position of great influence. The exact nature of that influence, at any stage of Haro's political career, is difficult to establish; but many factors lead me to believe that he never achieved that monopoly of power which Lerma and Olivares had established as the prerogative of the *valimiento* (E16). For one thing, Castrillo, instead of dying obligingly (as did Zúñiga), survived and remained active in high office, actually outliving Haro himself. This and other indications suggest that Haro was, perhaps principally, the representative of a particular oligarchy (within the context of a general aristocratic interest) upon which the king was now dependent. Haro advanced to prominence on a platform of moral and political arguments which were inimical to the whole concept of the *valimiento*. Moreover, his own temperament, mild-mannered and amenable as it was – Domínguez Ortiz refers to him as ' a diffident *valido*' (G5) – precluded the autocratic mien. He had something to be diffident about, for until 1643 he was unknown and inexperienced even at an intermediate level of affairs. Though he does seem to have 'grown into' the high office thus thrust upon him, we know little of his direction of policy, and nothing of his own special contribution to it (if any). Certainly, the circumstances of his administration and the monarchy's weak position in the war, severely restricted his opportunities as a statesman, and limited the sanction of prestige won by glorious victories. These things were enough to reduce his freedom of action, so that Philip's own description of his function as that of 'first and principal minister' seems perfectly appropriate (G4).

Such judgements must remain provisional whilst we lack a biography of Haro (in any language) or respectable studies of his government. None the less, other elements in the rather obscure scene tend, if anything, to support them. In particular, the king's own participation in affairs increased markedly after 1643, and (*pace* many commentators) did not subsequently fall away to any significant extent, except during his recurrent bouts of illness. During 1643, he informed his viceroys and ambassadors that 'I have resolved to take upon my own person responsibility for the direction of policy in my kingdoms'.[10] Sure enough, his attendance at committees became more assiduous, his reading of documents more considered. Of course, the management of such a vast undertaking was a burden too great for Philip to bear alone, hence his decision to share it with Don Luis in 1647. But both the physical fatigue and spiritual agony of his renewed attention to a plethora of duties took a severe toll, as can be observed through the unique conjunction of Velázquez's series of portraits with the king's long exchange of correspondence with the nun, Sister María de Ágreda. The latter (nearly always described as 'enigmatic' for reasons which escape the present writer) had an influence on the king which was political in an elemental way, intuitive in inspiration and simplistically expressed. She reminded Philip, in and out of season, of the necessity for personal exercise of his kingly duties. She constantly deplored the state of war between France and Spain, those two daughters of the Church who ought to be fighting, shoulder to shoulder, against heresy and Islam. She was convinced of the necessity to reconquer Portugal. Sister María was the king's ambassador at the Supreme Court from which he held all his kingdoms in trust, explaining his aspirations and weaknesses to *Nuestro Señor*, and passing on the consequent judgements. In the last analysis, the implications of her unique position for that of Haro hardly calls for exact delineation. When Philip excused his promotion of Don Luis to Sister María in 1647 as an arrangement which did not herald a resuscitation of the *valimiento*, it was both an honest statement and an accurate prediction.

Though Don Luis did not accrete major offices in the same way as his predecessor, like him he operated through juntas of picked men in preference to the traditional councils. These, and in particular the *Junta de Estado*, met at Haro's own Madrid residence, and since their records have been largely destroyed, we are never likely to discover the mainsprings of his government. We do know, however, that the main aristocratic adherents of the Olivares regime retained a residual influence. There was no wholesale proscription of the losing faction such as the count-duke himself had supervised at the outset of his rule. The king's feelings were decisive here; perhaps he had learnt from the earlier experience that a witch-hunt would only store up far more serious trouble in the long run; probably he personally liked the people concerned, and was no more inclined to punish them than their chief for outstanding services to the monarchy. At any rate, the wisdom and knowledge of such men as Monterrey, Leganés, and especially Medina de las Torres (each of them a Guzmán) was, as it proved, indispensable. The period of transition and immense administrative strain in the 1640s cruelly exposed the inexperience of the Castrillo faction, as their incompetent handling of the bankruptcy of 1647 illustrates. According to one observer, the *olivaristas* attempted a counter-coup in 1646, which proved abortive, but in any case by 1649 at the latest they were firmly reinstalled in *Estado* (where they reclaimed the senior positions) and even figured in Haro's juntas. As Haro grew in competence and confidence in the 1650s so the emergence of Medina – the immensely rich and much-titled son-in-law of Olivares – as the leader of an 'opposition' group is equally evident. Medina was certainly closer to the king, in a social sense, than his rival. Perhaps for that very reason (and recalling the nature of Olivares's ascendancy), Philip consistently discouraged his larger ambitions, and an overt challenge to Haro's position in the late 1650s failed dismally.

The existence of political factions (or, more accurately, clan vendettas) at the higher levels of policy-making does not imply any necessary divergence on the broad lines of policy themselves. In essence, though for different reasons, all the interests described above agreed on the necessity of a negotiated settlement with Spain's enemies. Philip wished to free his hands in order to crush rebellion. Sister María wished for the 'peace of Christendom' and a crusade against the Ottoman. The politicians, whatever their tribal loyalties, had in many cases accepted the need for peace, as the essential prelude to demographic and material recovery. In general terms, therefore, it would not be misleading to state that the period witnessed a more sincere desire for *una paz honesta* than was apparent during Olivares's government. Though it is true that representatives had been sent to Germany for the Congress of Westphalia even before Don Gaspar's dismissal, the intensified diplomatic activity which succeeded that event is certainly evidence of a more flexible attitude. The lessons of 1640 had, apparently, been learned. Unfortunately, closer inspection reveals a less simple picture. At even the lowest point of his fortunes Philip was far from ready to accept peace at any price, obstinately refusing to budge from conditions which (in his view) guaranteed the preservation of prestige. Furthermore, when matters improved – as after 1647 – he stepped up his demands proportionately, simultaneously attempting military pressure which might produce the time-honoured circumstance of 'negotiation from strength'. The terms offered to the Dutch just a few weeks after Olivares's fall, for example, were in most respects identical with those of 1619. In the same period, the deaths of both Richelieu and Louis XIII, opening up all the potential of a weak regency government in France, convinced Philip that Spain could recover the position enjoyed during the rule of Marie de Medici a generation earlier.[11] Even the doyen statesman Oñate, who again voted in principle for peace, undermined the idea by the observation that 'since France is so subject to faction and unrest, it is very probable that future events will considerably improve our prospects, and persuade the enemy to accept a peace on more equal conditions' (E14/11). Naturally, by the time that Oñate's prophecy had come to pass, 'equal conditions' had changed somewhat from Madrid's point of view. For Philip in 1650, they meant that France must abandon Catalonia and Portugal, and restore everything she had taken in Flanders and Italy – in other words, the *status quo ante bellum*.

From the start of their relationship, Sister María had prevailed upon the king 'to leave no stone unturned in the search for peace', assuring him in her oracular way that 'whatever interests you may be forced to sacrifice in its making, God will restore to you by other means'. Philip indeed accepted the nun's broad hint about the need for compromise: 'Every effort is being made to proceed along the road to peace', he replied, 'or at least to an armistice which might precede a settlement. My ministers and I are conscious that some concessions might have to be made.'[12]

In practice, however, his response to the directives of his divine master (as mediated through Sister María) was strikingly similar to that often attributed – perhaps apocryphally – to his own viceroys in receipt of orders from Madrid: 'I obey, but do not carry out.' It took Haro and his colleagues five years to wear down the king's opposition to the formal recognition of the Dutch republic in the Munster negotiations. Philip's soul was a fierce battlefield of conflicting principles, his princely duty to give peace and blessed relief to his subjects from a struggle which could not be won, versus his spiritual (as well as material) responsibility for the absolute *conservación* of his territorial inheritance. Little wonder that he underwent in these years a debilitation of his physical strength which was at once pathetic and heroic.

The reader may deduce from his words which form a key quote for this chapter, where the king's ultimate sympathies lay. He did, nevertheless, accept the bitter cup of Dutch sovereignty by the Treaty of Munster. This step was made possible mainly by the unilateral Austrian withdrawal from all war commitments at the Westphalia Congress; Philip could rationalise his decision on the grounds that, if the emperor (still, by what now was only a legal-technical fiction, overlord of the Netherlands) could thus renege on his responsibility, his own was much diminished. The still unsolved question of Catalonia also loomed large, and Munster was in line with the important decision, taken in 1644, to allocate the new rebellions priority over the old.[13] Policy in these years, however, does show the lack of a controlling intelligence, having an uncertain cast caused by the king's vacillation and basic self-doubt, and the inexperience of the new regime. The opening of so many diplomatic contacts to some extent hampered decisive action in the field, and renewed campaigning was often hurriedly improvised after an unexpected hitch or breakdown in (sometimes secret) negotiations. At any rate, talks proceeded continuously, becoming more concentrated in the winter months, easing off during the summer fighting, for the last twenty years of the Franco-Spanish conflict. The late Professor John Cooper neatly encapsulated the issues involved in this process: in the later stages of the Thirty Years' War, he says,

The actions of governments seemed to become identified with the interests of tax-farmers, financiers, and armies, and alien to those of their subjects. The war became not so much one of attrition, but a gamble as to which tottering conglomeration of alienated local interests and exhausted taxpayers could avoid collapsing for longer than its enemies . . . The longer war lasted, the more it seemed that there was little to be lost by gambling on a change of fortune . . . as the stakes spent on war grew higher, the more necessary it seemed for the temporarily stronger party in the negotiations to secure some real gains, hence the difficulty of reaching any real settlement. (C1)

Things reached the critical stage in the summer of 1656, and it should be noted that it was Mazarin who made the strongest attempt to break the vicious circle. His new initiative took the form of a mission to Madrid headed by his closest aide, Hugues de Lionne. In the broiling temperatures of August and September, Lionne's team and that of Don Luis de Haro crawled painfully towards agreement. Philip himself took a full part in the discussions, spending 'three or four hours a day behind closed doors' with delegates.[14] *Estado* held twice-daily sessions to consider proposals as they emanated from the conference room. The Spaniards held many strong cards, and Lionne was driven to a hard bargain, having to exchange (captured Spanish) territory for a set of commercial concessions. An index of the balance of power at this late point in the war was that the French agreed not only to abandon their support of Portugal, but actually to assist Castile in its reconquest. Eventually, only one or two matters of form, even of protocol, were left to be finalised. Philip's honour demanded that his ally, the Prince of Condé, should be restored to all his offices and estates within France. To Mazarin and his young master, the reinstatement of a traitor of this magnitude, the leading *Frondeur* who had inflicted defeat upon his own countrymen (at Valenciennes) only a matter of weeks earlier, was inadmissable. All the same, a deal was yet possible, if only Philip would reciprocate on a point where Louis XIV's prestige was deeply involved. The latter wished for the hand of the elder infanta, María Teresa, a suggestion which Philip regarded with distaste. As things stood, his daughter was heir to the monarchy, and (with the prospects of male issue gradually diminishing), the probable transfer of the Habsburg inheritance to the Bourbon line was something which offended Philip's most deep-seated dynastic prejudices. The infanta must be betrothed to her cousin in Vienna; the issue was non-negotiable. The king swept all the protests of his ministers aside, and with them the agreed clauses which represented the arguments of material logic and reason. Lionne went back to Paris, and war continued, with the consequences already described.

Attitudes

Having seen how the force of 'European opinion' had been moving against the monarchy during the years of Olivares's imperial strategy, it is possible to observe a partial interruption of this process once the military pendulum itself swung against Spain. The Dutch, for example, quickly took alarm at the progress of the French in the Low Countries, an, as yet, embryonic fear which nevertheless influenced their decision to detach themselves at last from the French alliance and seek peace with Spain at Munster. Following this milestone, the regents of The Hague seem to have been concerned to protect the integrity of the Spanish Netherlands. Soon after the treaty, commercial links with the southern provinces were re-established, and (as we have seen) other more directly strategic services were proffered to the Spanish administration. In the internal struggle which ensued between the Estates General and the Orange interest, the shade of Oldenbarnevelt was finally justified. It was the idea of the young stadtholder William II, and one crudely characteristic of dynastic thinking, that the Spanish Netherlands be divided between the victors in a new Franco-Dutch alliance which would settle the question of Flanders once and for all. When opposed by The Hague, William attempted a coup, which was easily frustrated, and promptly died. These events inaugurated the classic period of Dutch civilian government under the de Witts, a period which witnessed a slow but consistent process of *rapprochement* between the Dutch and Spanish systems.

Similar signs can be detected elsewhere, though not perhaps equal in long-term significance. Such was the potential threat of a united and victorious France that in 1652, the aggressively Protestant English republic actually helped the Spaniards to recapture Dunkirk, by Blake's action (later to be bitterly regretted) against a French relieving fleet. The growth of French influence in Germany, hardening into the first Rhineland League under Bourbon patronage, was of some interest to the Swedes. Under the crypto-Catholic Queen Christina, Sweden moved firmly away from the French *ambience*. (After her abdication in 1654, Christina devoted time to canvassing assistance for the Spanish war effort in the European capitals.) Even those who had actually invited the assistance of the French soon had second thoughts. As early as 1644, the Catalan agents present (as part of the French team) at the Westphalia Congress secretly confessed to the Spanish representative that 'under Castile we still enjoyed our liberties but today we have lost them. The French commit all kinds of outrages, and even dishonour our women. It will be necessary one day to take up arms and throw them out of Catalonia.'[15] Of course, Mazarin's ambitions were most deeply resented within France herself. Though there was no revival of the earlier, more 'ideological' opposition to the anti-Habsburg policies of the government, as the chorus of complaint against the cardinal swelled to a crescendo in 1648, the necessity for peace with Spain was constantly reiterated. The *Mazarinades*, that unique series of pamphlets designed to blast the reputation of the chief minister, frequently harped upon the self-interested nature of his foreign policy, and its position at the root of all the grievances of the nation. During the prolonged *Fronde des Princes* the issue was an *idée fixe* of rebel broadsheets, its leading protagonists like Conti and Condé pretending to the leadership of government on this main basis. By 1651, they, as representatives of a fair proportion of the political nation, had offered Spain a compromise peace, which (according to the code of honour) they proceeded to prove upon their swords in the van of Spain's armies.

Such exiled, and increasingly isolated, soldiers of fortune, were joined in 1655 by an even more eminent recruit. The displaced Charles Stuart, King of England since the execution of his father in 1649, ended his wanderings as a client of the Spanish system, not by any free choice of his own but as a result of the calculated manoeuverings of Oliver Cromwell. Two years earlier, the latter had assumed the title of 'Protector', and with it the effective attributes of kingship. The circumstances in which he began his war of conquest against Spain in 1655 are still the subject of considerable debate. Though he had his supporters, the decision was an acutely personal one, and thus will always remain inscrutable in the last analysis. It seems to me that Cromwell's motivation was political. By this I mean that it (of course) incorporated the fanatical emotions of religious extremism and the pragmatic reasoning of commercial ambition both of which have, in the past, been identified as its essential dynamic, but mediated them through a prism of thought which was cool and tactical. It is imperative that 'Cromwell's war' be seen in the context of the history of Anglo-Spanish relations (in the widest sense) in the pre-civil war years, and the effect that this had on the revolutionary cause which the Protector believed himself to be protecting (A2). As in the cases of most other parliamentary leaders, his association of Stuart modes of government with the Spanish Habsburg interest was a profound one, which had always evoked a current of reaction amongst English radicals. Once these men (after many vicissitudes), had taken the ultimate step in abolishing the English monarchy, along with its peculiar institutions, in 1649, their own security became synonymous with that of the revolution and the security of the revolution meant that of England. Given the nature of the government, the question of national defence was enhanced rather above the norm; particularly because of the survival of the Stuart court and claimant on the Continent. Cromwell attacked Spain as a natural enemy of the good old cause, and as a way of perpetuating or renewing its political impetus. As John Thurloe, Oliver's closest assistant, later admitted (or rather, boasted) such a course seemed to him the one certain way of uniting opinion behind the Protectorate; of reactivating and refocusing the fervour of revolution; and, above all, of driving Charles Stuart into the arms of Spain, achieving that union of his enemies which was a beautifully complete object of the hatreds, fears and aspirations of the ordinary Englishman.

This last development was carefully managed. Oliver, in supervising diplomatic agreements with the United Provinces and France, had ensured the expulsion from their territories of the itinerant Stuart court. Although by no means as convinced of the collapse of Spanish hegemony as his immediate predecessors in the Commonwealth government (his rise to supreme power, after all, coincided with the period of Spanish recovery already described) he believed that Madrid was less likely to effect a Stuart restoration by force of arms than either of the other main continental powers. In the war against Spain, he offered his subjects territory, trade and plunder. He expected an access of crusading prestige to the Protectorate which had formerly – to England's shame – belonged to the Dutch and the Swedes. But such desires were, as John Milton put it, 'more inflamed by this change in the state of our affairs, and of the form of our republic'. In a famous speech to Parliament, Oliver epitomised both policy and propaganda: 'Truly your great enemy is the Spaniard. He is. He is naturally so . . . Having thus engaged with Spain, that is the party that brings all your enemies before you . . . [for] Spain hath espoused that interest which you have all along been conflicting with – Charles Stuart's interest.'[16]

No protest or concession that the Spanish monarchy's representatives made was enough to deflect the Protector from his purpose. Philip's London ambassador, Alonso de Cárdenas, was an able and experienced diplomat. He was well known and well connected in Whitehall, having been a member of several missions from as far back as 1640. He was respected amongst the 'moderate' or Presbyterian section of politics, rooted as it was in the City's commercial community, not least for his master's prompt and exemplary recognition of the republic in 1650. Through him, Madrid was well acquainted with the desires of English capitalists with regard to the material resources of the Spanish empire, in Europe and the Atlantic. Indeed, in the circumstances of 1654, the Spaniards were prepared to meet these demands, at least to some extent. The significant package of trading concessions offered by Cárdenas (though perhaps elicited by the impressive performance of the English navy against their rivals in the first Anglo-Dutch war) recognised the desperate English need for markets in the Mediterranean world, and access to supplies of specie. Appropriate concern, however, was shown for Cromwell's own position. According to Thurloe, at least, Philip IV officially congratulated Oliver on his elevation to the Protectorate and undertook, 'if he should wish to go further, and take upon himself the crown, he would venture the crown of Spain to defend him in it'.[17]

For more than a year, Cromwell successfully dissembled his true and 'inalterable' intent. Soon after peace was agreed with the Dutch, his Council of State was discussing plans for an attack on Spain, whilst

English demands from Cárdenas were set at an impossibly high level; aimed, as the envoy put it in a celebrated metaphor, 'at putting out my master's two eyes'. For Madrid to concede 'liberty of trade' to the English in the American empire would be not only to abandon the legal basis of Castile's monopoly (still strenuously defended against all comers), but also to jeopardise its continued existence. Over the years, the Spaniards had come (rightly) to realise that the Dutch onslaught against their colonies was a limited one, aimed neither at outright conquest, nor at massive religious proselytisation. Conversely, both these strongly associated motives were present in the English drive to empire; and what the monarchy had successfully denied the Dutch for so many generations was not to be thrown into Cromwell's lap. Moreover, to permit 'free exercise of religion' by English merchants operating in Spanish ports was clearly out of the question. Catholic uniformity in Spain was a fundamental maxim of state – and one which, recalling the dilemma of all her European enemies, was considerably to her advantage to maintain. This issue had been thrown into relief by the peninsular rebellions of the 1640s. Furthermore, the potential dissemination of heresy by English traders was concentrated precisely in those areas where problems of order and authority had recently been experienced, namely the Basque country and Andalusia. At any rate, the preparations for war went on in the harbours of southern England even while the diplomatic protagonists contested these points in Whitehall. By the spring of 1655, two powerful fleets were on the move against Spain in an operation which anticipated Pearl Harbour, or (more appropriately?) the surprise American attack on Spain's colonies in 1898.

The belief – once current in studies of the Protector – that he wished to avoid a war with Spain *in Europe*, by sheltering behind the legal fiction of 'no peace beyond the line', will not bear a moment's examination. The sailing orders of Admiral Blake were to intercept and appropriate the silver fleet in European waters, and in any case to stand by for other offensive action. In their ignorance and fear, the Spanish port authorities provided Blake with the usual courtesies and services of a neutral during his first sojourn on their coasts. Every effort was made to delay or deflect the blow from the new English military machine. On the other hand, once news of the capture of Jamaica arrived, late in 1655, Madrid did not hesitate to recognise a state of war. They quickly utilised the stratagem of a commercial embargo on all English goods and nationals, which proved as effective and damaging as on earlier occasions against the Dutch. The following spring, the Flemish privateers were loosed against English commerce, to devastating effect. Indeed, the first two years of the war were, from the English point of view, a failure, and an immensely costly failure at that. Once again an enemy of Spain discovered the residual strengths of her system; it became obvious that, as in the late sixteenth century, only a kind of power coalition could achieve the desired results. With Portugal now playing the role of the rebel Hollanders, such a combination existed by 1657, with a carefully orchestrated military programme and cohered strategy.

Conclusions

Though the revolt of Catalonia had a significance which fully justifies the space it occupies in all studies of seventeenth-century Spain, it does tend to subsume other considerations to the point of distortion. When linked with the nearly coincidental coup in Lisbon, it becomes a powerful monopoly combine of the textbooks, focusing our attention rigidly upon the Iberian peninsula, with the great date of '1640' written across it, as it were, in letters of fire. Such a strong classical form and plot, observing the unities of time, place and action, is very seductive – especially when dealing with the age of Corneille and Calderón! Even the dramatic attraction of conjuncture must, however, be seen in context, for history, unlike the play, is not an enclosed entity. The monarchy as a whole, that unique and bizarre phenomenon which offends against every canon of political taste and reason, was at last displaying signs of organic dissolution, a process which begins in the early 1630s and is not really halted for twenty years.

Two earlier and simultaneous incidents deserve our attention. In 1631–3, when the Spanish system was recovering from defeat in Italy, and attempting to improve communications so as to restore the military situation in Flanders, threats to stability became apparent both in Bilbao and Brussels. The home end of the vital seaward link, the Basque country, rose in rebellion in the former year. The motive was the new salt tax, the kind of *gabelle* which caused so much trouble in regional France, imposed by Olivares to pay for the Mantuan war. The standard of living of a province so dependent on fishing and its ancillary trades, and where salt-fish (*bacalao*) was a staple food, was seriously affected. The insurrection was not a particularly serious affair, and was dealt with locally, but it perfectly illustrated the tight-rope which the monarchy was walking after a decade of war. Whilst the Basque provinces quickly settled down (even accepting incorporation into the Union of Arms) the same was not true of dissidence in Flanders. Here the Mantuan war caused a moratorium on supplies which coincided with successful Dutch offensives and with the increasing incapacity of the Archduchess Isabel (d. 1633). A conspiracy amongst a group of nobles, involving military betrayal by the field commander, was discovered thanks to information provided by an agent of Charles I. But there were fears that this was only the tip of the iceberg, especially when the loyal Estates took the alarming step of convening themselves, and threatened to take a 'sovereign' hand in negotiations with their Dutch cousins. The list of grievances of the obedient provinces was long, and its political import pressing. The government of Don Fernando (1634–41) succeeded in palliating rather than solving the problem. In the years following his death, his successors regularly referred to a political section which was inclined to terms with the United Provinces. A generation of war, culminating in the extra fiscal burden of the 1640s, had sapped the loyalty and resolution of the Belgians. In 1644, Philip hoped that the presence of yet another king-substitute (in this case his adolescent bastard Don Juan José) as governor in Brussels, would again act as a soporific. In an unprecedented move, which left a strong impression on its victim, this suggestion was indignantly rejected by spokesmen for local interests, who rightly regarded it as a symbol of Madrid's diminishing concern. Ultimately, the rule of a legitimate (if tangential) Habsburg, in Leopold-William of Austria, was accepted, and the future quiescence of Flanders assured, if only in the last analysis by default of realistic alternatives. But the factor played its part in the decision to settle with the Dutch at Munster (1648); and it remained in evidence to persuade the new regent that a peace with France also was advisable, since 'even those men in Flanders most well-intentioned to Your Majesty, are convinced that it would now be opportune to conclude a treaty with France, for fear of a violent reaction on the part of the populace'.[18]

Leopold-William's choice of phrase may have been affected by the extremely violent reaction then taking place in southern Italy. (Indeed, nearly two centuries later, the stirring chorus to their leader Masaniello, given to the revolutionary mob by the French composer Auber in an opera based upon the Neapolitan events of 1647, was to be the cause of a Brussels riot which led to the establishment of an independent Belgium.) The Italian uprisings were triggered off by new taxation, imposed on staple foodstuffs in order to satisfy the demands of the crown's local creditors. To add to consecutive years of harvest failure, and the endemic corruption of civic life in the Italian provinces, the masses began to suspect collusion between local landowners, bankers, tax-farmers and grain merchants to invent taxes and inflate prices. The explosions which resulted were essentially urban insurrections, centred in the hugely overpopulated cities of Naples and Palermo, both (at 200,000 and 130,000 respectively) larger than any city in Spain itself. The popular and bloody outburst led by Masaniello in Naples came after almost twenty years of fiscal and material exaction pursued by the crown to meet the escalating costs of war

(G10). They were unhindered by local custom and privilege of the kind which elsewhere outside Castile (even in Sicily) provided a more or less effective cushion against exploitation by the central government. As we have seen, Naples was squeezed in these years at least commensurately with Castile, the strain falling with even greater emphasis upon the lower orders. Not surprisingly, the insurrection was shot through with ideas of republicanism and independence and marked in practice by socially discriminate violence against the local nobility and the Spanish administration. Though little danger of actual secession existed in Sicily – where the time-honoured slogan of the mob, 'Long live the king but death to his evil advisers' was general even at the height of success – one cannot help feeling that the integrity of the monarchy was endangered, here as elsewhere, by a tendency of the crown to abandon its duty (some historians would say natural role) as protector of the weak and unprivileged. Such moral and legal borderlines were ill-defined, and had every kind of regional variation within Philip's dominions. Observing them was a matter of tact, judgement, information, even intuition. Under the appalling pressure of the Thirty Years' War, and doubtless often unconsciously, it is clear that Madrid overstepped these boundaries in some vital respect in nearly all its dependencies.

In such circumstances, the continuing stability of Castile itself was of fundamental importance to the monarchy's existence. This is an obvious statement, perhaps, but one which highlights the question for which no investigation has ever provided more than a few clues: why was there no rebellion in the home kingdom, where all the 'preconditions' (including by the 1640s growing aristocratic disaffection) existed? Was it perhaps that in Castile, the level of exploitation and privation had long since passed the point at which any hope, even the optimism of desperation, could remain alive? This piece of speculation is offered since when disorder on a scale sufficient to cause anxiety did occur, it did so in the one area of Greater Castile which had retained economic viability and a relatively high standard of living, Andalusia. The prosperity of the Seville–Cadiz hinterland received a body blow with the collapse of American trade in 1640 and resultant depression, circumstances aggravated by plague, subsistence crisis, and the demands of the Catalan war. As early as 1643, the region's most powerful landowner, the Duke of Medina Sidonia (another Guzmán), had conspired to emulate his brother-in-law Braganza by declaring himself king of an independent Andalusia. Then, in the late 1640s, a series of food riots broke out in the major towns of southern Spain.[19] Fears were expressed that Seville, full of foreigners (especially Portuguese) and in the grip of recession, could become another Barcelona. In 1652, with Barcelona still not taken, the citizens of

Seville indeed rose in revolt (*el motín de la feria*) coming in the classic period of late spring, when food stocks were reduced and prices high. For several weeks, anarchy reigned in the second city of the empire. In terms of the local order and complaisance which had marked the life of Castile's municipalities since the revolt of the *Comuneros* (1520), these events do represent a watershed, for Spain was now passing into an era of popular protest. But no more than in France or England were such calamities, either individually or collectively, of a strength sufficient to destroy the fabric of the state, even one so peculiar and precarious as the Spanish monarchy.

CHAPTER 4

Years of Defeat
1656–78

A great power can maintain itself only by means of its prestige, and the greater part of that prestige resides in the fear which it is capable of inspiring amongst other nations. (Cardinal de Retz to Louis XIV, 1660)[1]

The true reputation of states does not consist of mere appearances, but in the constant security and conservation of their territories, in the protection of their subjects and the wellbeing thereof, and in the respect which other princes have for their authority. (Medina de las Torres to Regent Mariana, 1666) (E16)

Introduction

The generation following the Treaty of the Pyrenees was that in which the Spanish monarchy finally lost its active aspiration for European and Atlantic hegemony. The will to maintain the struggle was slowly suffocated by constant disappointment and humiliation. For the monarchy as a whole this was an almost indescribably miserable period, with few glimpses of hope granted to any of its undertakings. It begins with the petering out, in Naples, of the devastating plague which had begun ten years earlier. It had traversed the whole littoral of the western Mediterranean, leaving perhaps a million victims in its wake. It ends with the opening of another decade of desperate socio-economic crisis within the peninsula, the 'last crisis' of Castile.[2] It is little wonder that historical interest in this period has hardly increased since Rodríguez Villa, over a century ago, attributed the lack of research to 'the melancholy and distaste which the narration of such misfortunes produces in one's spirit'.[3]

Nevertheless, it would be going too far to write as if Spain vanished overnight from the map of Europe as a consequence of the Treaty of the Pyrenees – a disappearing act performed figuratively in the pages of textbooks, and literally in a recent study of the age of Louis XIV.[4] Indeed the whole reign of that king attests to the fact that the Spanish monarchy was, in the widest sense, still a force to be reckoned with. Although the fundamental duty to protect its integrity was by no means abandoned, the circumstances of the time brought about important changes in policy attitudes. Its advocates were not defeatist, indeed in their ultimate objectives quite the reverse. But after the death of Philip IV, during the minority of his successor (1665-75), Spain moved part of the way towards a more rational basis for policy, searching for a suitably reduced (and thus securer) role in the altered European context of 'French ascendancy'. Above all, the monarchy of Carlos II needed (as its historian, Maura, has put it) 'a complete and profound revision of national methods and purposes . . . abandoning the simple and primary insistence on defending and conserving *all* its possessions' (E20). Here speaks, once more, a man of the 'generation of 1898', to whom the obstinate commitment of the Habsburgs to an imperial destiny went far to explain the arrest of Spain's economic and intellectual development. Naturally, since the old certainties and rigid maxims of policy were being eroded, and the nature of a substitute poorly grasped and rarely articulated, ministers were often lost in an unfamiliar maze of pragmatism. The rearguard actions of many influential diehard imperialists, and the precarious political situation of regency government, added to the prevailing confusion.

Yet even in the 1660s, in the twilight of its European supremacy, Spanish government was not devoid of men of intelligence, perceptive of the need for constructive adjustment. Maura's reappraisal was, indeed, attempted in the second half of the decade, following the death of Philip IV – a period similar in some ways to that which ensued after that of Philip II. An attempt to withdraw from commitment, founded on a spirit which may be termed one of 'appeasement', led to some concrete results. Despite the fact – not often appreciated – that Spain remained at war in defence of dynastic interests for much of these twenty years, between 1668 and 1672 a peculiar hiatus supervened during which a radically different course seemed about to be taken. This tendency was not of course either original or simple; in a sense it was almost as 'traditional', as the policy it sought to replace. For, as we have seen, the struggle between the views of 'moderates' or 'realists' and those of a different persuasion is a continuous strain in the politics of Castile almost from the beginning of its involvement in a pan-European strategy.

Narrative of Events

Once Lionne's negotiations in Madrid had broken down in the autumn of 1656, Spain was doomed to another decade of full-scale war.

Indeed, in this penultimate phase of his reign, Philip IV seemed to accumulate commitments as promiscuously (if not as consciously) as his grandfather had done at a similar stage. Like Philip II, he now had on his hands wars with France, England and a major rebel state (in this case the kingdom of Portugal). The last of these three had been dormant for many years; it now was deliberately reactivated by Madrid in a last despairing effort to regain Portuguese allegiance. Substantial invasions were launched every year from 1657-9, again in 1663, and finally in 1665. Bolstered by French and English aid, Portugal's defences took the strain with comparative ease. Terrible defeats were meted out to the motley and ill-equipped Spanish armies, those at Ameixial in 1663 (which saw the humiliation of the king's bastard, Don Juan José), and Villaviçiosa in 1665, being particularly bloody and comprehensive. News of Villaviçiosa was commonly held to have hastened the old king's death, so closely was he personally identified with the Portuguese issue. Though there is little point in setting out its military details, this long, hopeless and debilitating campaign was a potent factor in reducing the Spanish system to the state, bordering on helplessness, which it had reached by the end of the decade.

Prince Juan José had also been involved in another decisive setback, the Battle of the Dunes (or, better, of Dunkirk) in 1658 which constituted the single necessary triumph of the Anglo-French alliance made between Cromwell and Mazarin the previous year. Loss of Dunkirk's facilities seriously reduced the logistical viability of continuing the war in Flanders. Domínguez Ortiz agrees with Cromwell's celebrated contemporary critic, Slingsby Bethel, in regarding the Protector's actions as ending the stalemate which had held French and Spanish power in an equilibrium of attrition since Rocroi, or even since 1635. There seems little reason to challenge this verdict. In 1659, concerned above all to free his hands for Portugal, Philip called a halt to the conflict in the north. It must have been difficult for government and people in Flanders in 1660 not to undertake the seemingly eternal routine of preparation for a new campaign which they had done as naturally as breathing every spring for forty years. The Treaty of the Pyrenees was a relatively even-handed settlement, in which both sides made important concessions. Louis XIV (after all) agreed to reinstate Condé, and to desist from aiding the Portuguese; Philip (after all) surrendered his daughter, along with some territories of more symbolic than material significance, on the Catalan frontier. There is no justification, in my view, for regarding the treaty as the last nail in the coffin of Spanish power, or as the French *diktat* so often implied by historians. Its great weakness, from the point of view of Spain's overall position, was that England had no part in it.

Cromwell's military objective, at the outset of war with Spain in

1655, was to destroy Spanish sea power. The definitive fracture of communications was meant to loosen Castile's hold on its Atlantic empire, which would then fall neatly into England's lap. However, whilst Blake and his subordinates succeeded in the destruction of the enemy navy on the open sea, the Spanish privateering campaign took the war to the coasts and ports of eastern England. The results were so damaging, threatening not only the destruction of England's merchant marine, but also the possibility of a Spanish-supported royalist landing, that they changed the whole nature of the war. Inflated ideas of empire were rapidly set aside in face of more mundane, but immediate, anxieties. After 1657, Cromwell's priority was the capture of Dunkirk, and this (above all) made collaboration with Mazarin necessary, in order to set up a combined assault on the privateering headquarters. With the battle and capture of Dunkirk, the Protector's security and prestige were re-established. After his death, interest in what had become a meaningless conflict declined absolutely; but the chaotic political situation in England during the next eighteen months precluded an Anglo-Spanish settlement. This diplomatic failure (though this time no fault of Philip's) was as important as that of 1656, since England's policy was to determine the outcome of the war with Portugal, just as it had that with France.

In 1660, the restored Charles II, instead of rushing to embrace the Catholic king, his patron and ally (as might reasonably have been expected), found his interests better served by an accommodation with Portugal, which promised whole El Dorados of rewards and profits from her colonial empire. The profound cynicism of this act reduced Philip, for all his experience of affairs, to something akin to stupefaction: 'God will punish this evil alliance', he wailed to Sister María, 'because the one partner is a rebel against his God, and the other against his king.'⁵ As far as England was concerned, Philip was careful enough not to assume the agency of this process, and avoided outright retaliation. In practice this made little difference. In the first half of the decade, overt English military pressure was maintained on many weak points of the monarchy in Flanders, Portugal and the Caribbean (E17). A state of war was therefore, in effect, prolonged (contrary to the statement of so many textbooks of English history) until a series of treaties in 1667–70, including official English mediation of the agreement by which Portugal gained independence. But even in 1670, Henry Morgan was ravaging the Spanish-American mainland, and England and Spain were (if only nominally) at war again by 1672.

All this was much to the satisfaction of the King of France. For Louis, the 1659 treaty was only the beginning of his life's work, the subordination – and, if possible, the incorporation – of the Spanish system. In 1667, following six years of intensive preparation, his armies fell upon the Spanish Netherlands, part of which was held to have 'devolved' to France through the non-payment of the infanta's dowry. Neither Spanish government, confused and divided since the death of Philip IV, nor any part of its physical apparatus, weakened by the Portuguese war, was in a position to organise resistance. The defence system of Flanders, which had previously disputed inches with bloody resolution, now gave up miles. It was the single most disastrous campaign of the Spanish army of Flanders. Such were Louis's conquests that the maritime powers took fright, fearful that the next year the whole of Flanders would disappear into the French maw. The old view, that the so-called Triple Alliance of 1668 compelled Louis by threats to call off his intended programme, is too simplistic. Threats were directed to Madrid, not to Versailles, and Spanish historians are about as grateful for the Treaty of Aix-la-Chapelle as their Czech colleagues are for that of Munich. Moreover, Louis had never intended to ingest the whole of the Spanish Netherlands, a precaution confirmed by his secret agreement with the Emperor Leopold, the first of those treaties of partition of the Spanish monarchy which were the terror of earlier generations of history undergraduates. Louis had made his point, and more, for Flanders was now virtually indefensible by the Spaniards themselves. Spain emerged from the 'war of devolution' shorn of a few towns, but possessed of a 'guarantee', signed by England and the United Provinces, to protect Flanders from further French aggression – again, the fate of modern Czechoslovakia suggests an appropriate analogy.

The death of Philip IV (1665) meant the official succession of his four-year-old son, Carlos II; the 'constitutional' establishment of a regency in the person of his widow, Mariana; and the actual takeover of a junta of ministers which formed the oligarchical centre of power for almost a decade. Neither the queen nor her confessor-cum-*valido*, Everardo Nithard, was able to make any positive impression. The single most significant political fact during the subsequent decade was the existence of the new king's adult half-brother, Don Juan José. Even whilst his father had lived, this prince had made no secret of his claim to share power, and now publicly advanced a cause which amounted to a demand for the regency itself. The politics of this period were dominated by his campaign, and the faction fighting which it encouraged in Madrid. By the late 1660s, Don Juan provided an alternative centre of allegiance for many individuals and sectional interests, like the 'court' of the Prince of Wales in Hanoverian England. His first attempt on power in 1669 was nevertheless abortive. Although his march on the capital forced Mariana to dismiss her favourite, very few of the great nobles were at this stage prepared to tolerate the transfer of authority to a bastard pretender. The queen regent's own behaviour eventually changed their minds, for Nithard's exit from the stage cleared the way for another performer, and one who was as sharp a contrast as any dramatist of the period could have devised. Perhaps Fernando de Valenzuela was conscious of the metaphor, since he was the greatest patron of the theatre that even seventeenth-century Madrid had ever seen. During the early 1670s this upstart *hidalgo* exercised an increasing fascination for Mariana and her son. The nature of this influence, with other matters impinging on policy, may be left aside for the moment. Here it is enough to state that both Nithard and Valenzuela, for all their differences, had a common tinge of illegitimacy in the eyes of the great nobles; Maura (himself an aristocrat) scornfully refers to the latter as a mere *pícaro* (E20/I). In the years of Valenzuela's peculiar ascendancy, Don Juan (who had been 'exiled' to Aragon in 1669) slowly built up the political and material resources for another coup. In 1676, most of the grandees left their posts in Madrid in a 'strike' reminiscent of the early 1640s, or actually deserted to the pretender. In late 1676, Don Juan again marched on Madrid and this time succeeded, not only in ejecting Nithard, but in installing himself in power. By the beginning of 1677, he had captured the authority of kingship, or that of a dictator, depending on your point of view.

In the meantime, the monarchy had become thoroughly involved in another major war. The circumstances in which this arose were surprising and largely unpredictable. Spain had emerged from the 1660s with some apparent residual benefits. The important series of commercial and colonial concessions made to England had settled outstanding differences, and indeed was to provide the basis of good relations until the middle of the next century. On the whole, the makers of English policy had accepted that the arguments for co-operation and peace were potentially the more productive for their economic ambitions. Recognition of Portugal's sovereignty meant the release of a painful incubus on the body politic, and the loss of very little in material terms (*reputación*, of course, was another question). Above all, the complex batch of interconnected negotiations in 1667–70 had represented another step towards co-operation with the United Provinces, which had now become a desired objective for Madrid. For the Dutch, too, a more enlightened attitude towards the Spanish monarchy now seemed the best way in which to exploit its unlimited physical resources, a resolution supported by the precarious situation of Flanders. Once more, however, the caprice and cupidity of an English king undermined European stability. The Anglo-Dutch guarantee of the Spanish Netherlands (supported by Spanish subsidies and Swedish troops) was destroyed by Charles II's defection to France in the notorious intrigues of 1670. Whilst Louis's plans for a war of conquest against the Dutch matured, the partners-in-crime offered a share in the spoils to Madrid. These were indignantly refused; instead, the Spaniards, though in confused manner, were drawn into a military agreement with The Hague for the common defence of the Low Countries. In 1672, only a few weeks after the initial French attack, the main author of this development, the Count of Monterrey (governor of the Spanish Netherlands), duly intervened in the campaign on the side of the United Provinces. By the following spring, France and Spain were again officially at war.

These events marked the second stage in a process whereby the embryo organism of 1668 developed into the mature anti-French coalitions of the 1690s. Nevertheless, for all her initial enthusiasm and persistent effort, the war went badly for Spain. In the Low Countries, the allies (even when joined by Austria) could rarely do more than contain French offensives. The end of every campaign saw Louis counting his territorial gains. In 1674, though the *tercios* under Monterrey saved the main allied army from being cut to pieces by Condé (battle of Seneffe) Turenne took the opportunity to devastate the undefended province of Franche-Comté, effectively acquiring the province for his master in less than a month. Likewise, in the southern theatre of war, while an invasion of Catalonia was parried by the victory of Belgarda (1675) an uprising in Sicily required a diversion of Spanish resources from the peninsula. For the rest of the war, Spain fought a rearguard action in Catalonia and the Mediterranean region generally, a reversion to the precarious situation of the mid-1640s. Remarkably, the monarchy was once again able to extricate itself from a desperate position – and not by the legerdemain of some comic-book hero. In fact, at least in the Mediterranean, the Spanish system remained both tough and resourceful. Partly with Dutch assistance, a huge maritime expedition was mounted for the relief of southern Italy; the French forces were isolated in Messina, centre of the insurrection, and eventually forced to pack their bags. Such successes were, it is true, of limited significance when the France of Louis XIV (unlike that of the cardinals during earlier wars) was able to maintain the initiative and keep up the pressure at all points. Its reward was the Treaty of Nijmegen (1678) in which the Habsburg dynasty surrendered its own homeland, Franche-Comté, the ancient county of Burgundy. Indeed, the war which had begun as a defence of the Dutch republic, ended with territorial losses being incurred by Spain alone.

Don Juan José, who headed the peacemaking government, had played no part in the war. In two sensational incidents, he had refused to serve the regency government, rejecting the call to defend Flanders in 1667, and declining to command the Messina expedition eight years later. Though his motivation was largely (as we have seen) connected with domestic politics, he had also become convinced that the continued integrity of the monarchy could only be guaranteed by a policy of understanding with Versailles. In search of this, and in the hope of establishing his control over the teenage king, he followed up the peace by arranging a royal marriage with a Bourbon princess. Through the mediation of this union, he hoped to work out the future of Spain. Don Juan himself was not yet fifty, but it proved that, each in their different way, both he and his instrument were doomed.

Resources

> In time of war, the Persians used to break up all their musical instruments which conduced to pleasure and delight, listening only to those of a martial sound. This our court should do, leaving aside the viewing of three or four entertainments every day, and putting all its efforts into the defence of Spain.[6]

Thus wrote the professional newsmonger, Jerónimo de Barrionuevo, in early 1657. His stricture on the court and its pleasures was, however, unfair in several respects. Philip IV was certainly attached to the theatre, and great sums continued to be disbursed in the production of *comedias* in the courtyards of the palaces and religious houses of Madrid, despite the stringencies of continuous war. What Barrionuevo neglected to consider was that the diversions of the better-off segment of the capital's population actually helped to provide, through the involvement of charitable foundations, for the needs of the remainder. These needs were never more pressing than in the 1650s; and popular entertainment, too, provided a safety-valve, a soporific which, given the increasing social instability of Madrid and other large towns, was of some political importance. Barrionuevo's sentiments doubtless become more apposite with the continuous round of reckless gaiety compèred by Valenzuela, when such expenditure rocketed to astronomical heights, and it becomes difficult to avoid an impression of mindlessness in the midst of doom. But Philip IV can hardly be accused of fiddling whilst Rome burnt. In fact, despite the considerable extra outlay involved in celebration of two royal births (1657 and 1661) and the huge *fiestas* for the marriage of the infanta to Louis XIV in 1660, the king restrained his own spending to a surprising degree. The court was meagre in the provision of many of its own needs, so that more of the king's liquid revenue could be devoted to defence. In October 1656, Barrionuevo himself had commented on the strict rationing of food within the palace, and that the royal family itself feasted on meat 'which smelt like a dead dog and was full of flies'. So lived the king who was master – on paper at least – of an income of some twenty million ducats a year.

This revenue was, of course, completely pledged in advance, and by the late 1650s the crown had anticipated many of its sources for five years ahead. Philip may have suffered with his subjects, but he did not spare them. Not surprisingly, the last decade of his reign was particularly desperate in the search for augmentation of revenue, resulting in the imposition of several new taxes upon Castile. A kind of road tax on beasts and vehicles of transport was devised in 1655; three years later, an increase in the rate of sales taxes forced Barrionuevo to cry that 'we can only grit our teeth and wait for death'.[7] In 1657, a swingeing 'donation' was imposed on the Indies, to repair the damage caused by Blake. An intense debate took place concerning the morality of a tax on flour. Ultimately – threatened, amongst other things with the displeasure of St Vincent, who (according to popular belief) would withdraw his protection from Spain in such an event – the crown desisted from this awful step. In 1661, however, the slaving contract (*asiento de negros*) estimated to be worth 350,000 ducats a year from the Atlantic run, was revived. Such expedients were eked out by fiscal contributions from the provinces. Naples was still supplying an annual subsidy of 600,000 ducats for the defence of Milan alone in the 1650s; whilst even twenty years later, determined efforts could squeeze large loans from the Neapolitan bankers. A new element in the royal finances was the assistance received from the Catalans, now thoroughly converted to the wisdom of membership of the monarchy. Barcelona alone contributed about 150,000 *escudos* a year, and other Catalan towns in proportion. A hollow laugh may have been heard to issue from the tomb of the great count-duke.

The frantic riot of taxation which marked the last phase of Philip's reign was, moreover, the last of its kind. Between 1646 and 1661, remittances of silver had gradually declined from the plateau on which they had maintained themselves in the first half of the reign. By the late 1650s (because of the English naval exploits) they tapered off almost to infinity; as the gradient on the graph-paper got more precipitate, it created a neat image for the statistically centred analysts of Spain's decline. The Spanish monarchy slithered down this slippery slope of financial insufficiency to the inevitable collapse of its hegemony. There are many ways in which the historian should modify this too-deterministic picture. But in any case, it now appears likely that the data of silver imports themselves tend to expose the danger of overreliance thereon in the interpretation of wider issues. It has long been the assumption – correctly derived from the work of Hamilton and Chaunu – that the crown's American revenues remained more or less at the low ebb of the 1650s for the rest of the century. A more recent estimate of bullion returns, however, suggests that already in the last quinquennium of Philip's reign (1661–5) a dramatic improvement had begun.[8] By the late 1660s, figures similar to those current in the 1620s were recorded, and – an almost incredible revelation, this – little over a decade later they exceeded the record levels established in the 1590s. Though the crown's share did not increase proportionately, it may be that the attempt to alleviate the tax burden on Castile following the treaties of 1668 was a result of this unexpected relief for *Hacienda*. In 1669 the governing junta set up a 'committee of amelioration' which actually succeeded in making some minor reforms, particularly with respect to Madrid. This effort may have been influenced by Don Juan's demands for tax reform during his march on Madrid, and as a way of reducing the prince's popularity in the capital. Whatever the reasons, it began a process of reconsideration of the fiscal system which suggests that some room for manoeuvre was now present in the crown's revenue situation.

Certainly the government remained able to arrange military contracts with its bankers during the Portuguese war. Most of the great firms had been driven out of business by the savage bankruptcies of 1647 and 1652. Replacements were found, however, and despite further suspensions in 1660 and 1662, Genoese partnerships provided financial backing for successive invasions of Portugal (G5). In 1661, Don Juan, who commanded the Castilian forces, declared that the king had ignored his advice to come to terms with Lisbon: 'I therefore begin this campaign in the hope that God in his mercy will supply all that is lacking in the condition of my army.'[9] In fact, the prince was reasonably well supplied and equipped, and (as so often) complaint to the contrary can be seen as an insurance against the loss of honour involved in possible defeat. Again, in 1664, the Council of State reported that the financiers had absolutely refused to negotiate new contracts for defence spending. Yet only two years later, the huge amount of $4\frac{1}{2}$ million *escudos* was expended on the Portuguese war, larger than any annual subsidy which Flanders received in the whole course of the previous reign. The fact should be noted that even this profligate spending did not provide an army large or efficient enough to mount a further invasion of Portugal, and reverse the verdict of Villaviçiosa.

Concentration on Portugal naturally involved a concomitant decrease in the subsidies available for Flanders, at least down to the 1670s. Of course, in this theatre, the crown was far more dependent on the financiers and their international contacts than it was in respect of those nearer home. But in any case, comparative neglect of Brussels was implicit in the policy-decision of 1656 (see below pp. 158), a

situation only confirmed by the coincidental rupture of communications caused by the war with England. Flanders was compelled
to rely on its own meagre resources, and this remained more or less the
case in the tranquil period of 1660–7. The relative surprise of Louis
XIV's onslaught in 1667 left Madrid little time in which to organise the
material basis of resistance, and this certainly played its part in the
swift and comprehensive defeat registered at Aix-la-Chapelle.
Brussels was not much better prepared, however, for the events of
1672. The settlement in Portugal, four years of peace, and the
restoration of bullion imports, enabled Madrid to fix a subsidy of 3
million ducats a year – the traditional figure of war contributions to the
Spanish Netherlands. But by now, problems of the actual transfer and
honouring of bills of exchange (not to mention the transport of specie)
were becoming insuperable, in a world dominated by French military
and political influence. No more than in the 1590s did great supplies of
silver guarantee the smooth working of the credit system or the
automatic success of military effort. In the spring of 1675, the Count of
Monterrey, recently relieved of his post of Brussels, wrote to his
successor that

> . . . the orders issued for your subsidies will come to nothing unless
> the President of *Hacienda* can provide sufficient security for the
> bankers, here and in Antwerp. If you feel assured that the bills for
> 1,200,000 *escudos* being despatched currently will be honoured,
> you are deceived, for personally I am certain that most of it is
> unreliable.[10]

Though such cynicism was amply justified, large sums did get through
if on a more sporadic basis than ever before. From 1669, however, the
crown was increasingly committed to the maintenance not so much of
its own armies as those of its allies and confederates. The two-power
Guarantee of Flanders involved Madrid's financial support of a
Swedish army as a kind of police-force of the Triple Alliance. Even
before the renewal of war in 1672, Spain was providing 50,000 *reales* a
month for the emperor's army on the Rhine. By the end of this
particular episode in resistance to Versailles, subsidies to the Dutch
and German forces were running at the rate of a million *escudos* a year,
at least as much as could actually be supplied to Brussels. Problems in
the *asiento* system apart, there is small reason to suppose that the
monarchy's spending on its overall defence commitments in this period
fell much below the levels established in the previous generation.
  As these developments suggest, the reign of the last Habsburg king
was one in which the Spanish system played a somewhat changed role
in European wars. Madrid had always subsidised its allies (Vienna

itself, the minor German and Italian princes); likewise an increasing complement of foreign mercenaries had come to be relied on to make up the numbers of Spanish armies. This had given Spain the leading voice in the making of policy and strategic planning, whilst even the regiments of 'nations' had always remained – if on occasions indirectly – under her control. By the 1670s, neither was any longer the case, and the defence (such as it was) of Spain's northern interests was now entirely the responsibility of her allies. Repeatedly the monarchy was dragged into wars against France, during which she had little influence on political or military decisions, and was therefore a subsidiary partner in the confederation. An important factor here was the continued reduction in the numbers of men the monarchy could raise from its own resources. The rapidity of decline should not be exaggerated, and the dearth never became total, for Castile and Naples regularly provided quotas of men until the 1690s. But from the reopening of the Portuguese war, the quantitative problem became of vital significance.

Originally, a campaigning army of 40,000 was envisaged; but even in 1661 (when exclusive concentration of the military establishment upon the Portuguese problem at last became possible) it proved well beyond capacity. Don Juan's army of 24,000 was (to begin with) by no means a despicable force. It was certainly larger than any he had commanded in the Low Countries, stiffened as it was by many Flemish veterans and containing a reasonable proportion of cavalry. Lack of success brought degeneration and desertion, and after the disaster of Ameixial, the army simply disintegrated. In 1664–5 another force was constituted, and five fresh *tercios* (some 9,000 men) were raised in the central meseta of Castile. A pathetic and hopeless attempt was made to support the invasion of 1665 by preparing an armada which could blockade Lisbon. The army which crossed the frontier towards Villaviçiosa again mustered 20,000, but was a dreadfully feeble and dispirited instrument, constituted by the old, the crippled, the sick and the scourings of prisons. Furthermore, the armies quartered for a decade along the frontier in Extremadura, 'do so much oppression, it seems that they come rather to destroy the king's own subjects than to make a conquest of Portugal'.[11] Indiscipline and lack of morale naturally resulted from chronic supply deficiencies. Faced with a mounting chorus of complaint, the crown could only repeat the old, weary exhortations. In 1666, a royal decretal maintained that 'the principal means to be adopted in preserving discipline and obtaining recruits is the punctual observance of military regulations. I order in particular that the rules laid down by Don Gonsalvo de Córdoba be strictly adhered to at all times . . .'[12] The inspiration of the *gran capitán* was no longer sufficient, even where it was to be detected. The peace with Portugal in 1668 was truly one of exhaustion, material and kinetic if not financial. All the same, it is unlikely to have been made without the panic of the spring and summer of 1667, during which it seemed that the whole of Flanders was to be irretrievably lost.

As we have seen, Flanders had been stripped of its best men in 1660, and by the time of Louis's attack, only 2,000 Spaniards remained mustered. Including garrison troops, the defending force still comprised over 30,000 men, but this represented a 50 per cent drop in the figure for 1647, whilst the concentrated French army had increased in inverse proportion, leaving aside its tremendous improvement in quality. More notable still was the absence of Italians from the army of Flanders, less than 1,000 being present in 1667. If by now it was virtually impossible to transport men from Naples to the Netherlands, the kind of shuffling and shuttling previously routine on the widest plane could still be managed in the restricted and less vulnerable area of the south. In the late 1650s, and again during the campaigns of 1674–8, Neapolitan levies regularly arrived at Barcelona to assist the Catalans in their tenacious resistance to France. Indeed, just as the reconquest of Portugal had superseded the needs of Flanders so the security of Catalonia came before that of Italy – even of Milan. In 1672, when France threatened both areas, the Council of State replied to the pleas of the Duke of Osuna, governor of Milan, that 'the principality of Catalonia is so unprotected that the reinforcements from Naples cannot possibly be spared for any other defences'.[13] Milan was clearly under strength, Osuna having a field army of only 11,000 at his disposal, but (as it happened) the expected blow on northern Italy did not materialise. As we have seen, the monarchy was able to defend itself stoutly in the Mediterranean theatre, and the Sicilian operation illustrates a residual capacity for large-scale military activity. Reserves of cannon fodder in the villages of Naples, like those of Castile, were nevertheless running out. During the whole of 1672, for example, the viceroy could not raise half the numbers demanded by Madrid. Moreover, areas like Switzerland and Germany, previously relied on to make up such shortfalls now sent their wild geese to the Dutch or imperial armies, where better pay and conditions were assured.

Given the demographic impoverishment of the monarchy, the inability to staff its defence systems is hardly surprising. Though we cannot be certain, it is likely that the population of the Mediterranean provinces (including Castile) reached its lowest point in the period covered by the present chapter. By the last quarter of the century, a tendency to recovery had begun, but this was too late and too gradual to have any bearing on the greater affairs of Europe. It is also worth remarking in this context that the inhabitants of Castile, who experienced the dreadful sacrifices of the Portuguese war only to survive into the almost apocalyptic period of natural calamities which afflicted the peninsula in the following decade, were not quite so complaisant about things as their forefathers had been. Popular disorder, resistance to recruiting-sergeant, tax-collector, and *corregidor*, began in the 1640s and became endemic, affecting Madrid seriously for the first time by the end of Philip's reign. This certainly impeded war efficiency in a number of ways, whilst it is true also (speaking 'impressionistically') that the monarchy's commitment to war did not rest on the solid popular base which earlier generations had provided – indeed, it would be astonishing were this not the case. By the 1660s, the conviction was widespread that war was the single greatest engine of administrative, social and economic dislocation. To do something about it was another matter.

Even had things been different in these respects, a 'forward' policy in Europe was no longer feasible. The monarchy, its economy and monetary system in ruins, its communications networks definitively shattered, now had little access to sources of *matériel de guerre*. In 1675, for example, the general of artillery could not lay his hands on any guns or gunpowder with which to supply the army in Catalonia. Three years later, the governor of Milan stated that, in the remote eventuality of his army being brought up to scratch, he would still be unable to defend the duchy, since he needed 10,000 boxes of shot, 12,000 of musket balls, 15,000 arquebuses and 12,000 pikes![14] These cases underline the fact that the material supports of the Spanish system gave way *before* the capacity to pay for them. But the spiritual basis was crumbling, too; as Maura puts it 'The greatest evil which brought about the frustration of our historical destiny was the constant failure of individual attitudes . . . the lack of a collective spirit, whose disappearance coincided with the collapse of the nation, since the one could not subsist without the other.' (E20/I). A wealth of evidence exists through the whole spectrum of affairs to support this apparently metaphysical and rhetorical observation. In just one letter of Barrionuevo, we read that 'Don Fernando de Tejado has refused appointment as governor of the Canary Islands, where it is said the English are going to attack this year'; and 'Caraçena does not wish to go to Flanders, unless he is offered the *grandeza*'.[15] By the 1670s, the aristocracy had to be cajoled and threatened to discharge responsibilities for which, in earlier days, they had competed and canvassed ruthlessly. The constable of Castile, Iñigo de Velasco, is singled out by Maura as a rare exception, a man who represented the old military virtues. But even Velasco, after a short stint as governor of Flanders, refused to accept the much less onerous post at Naples without a huge bribe, whereas previously the offer was both a signal mark of honour and a guarantee of riches. The outstanding case, which set an example to all, was that of Don Juan. In late 1667, when Madrid had decided to fight on against France in the Low Countries, Don Juan was asked to take command. No one could pretend that the task was likely to add lustre to his name. But energetic preparations were made; a small but well-supplied army of 5,000 was collected in north Spain for transport to Ostend, suitable *asientos* were arranged, and 100,000 ducats in silver bars were earmarked for the prince's use. But he obstinately refused to go, thus setting an evil precedent, and with it the tone for his generation. The nobility 'now declined to exchange the frivolity of life at court for the field of battle, and were no longer disposed to empty their purses to contribute to the growing necessities of national defence'.[16] This was not the same as the flight of the aristocracy from court under Olivares; on the contrary they flocked to Madrid, afraid to leave the centre of patronage to the exploitation of rivals, a tendency exacerbated by the chronic political instability of the reign. The palaces of the capital – those of king, prince, queen regent and the great grandees, were decorated with these gorgeous parasites. Court offices, which rapidly expanded in number, were held in profusion, and often in plurality, whilst the more important posts in the diplomatic service and provincial administration were deserted.

Once in power, Don Juan José of Austria himself felt the pinch of the attitude he had done so much to foster. Even the greatest nobles for the most part relied financially on the immense patronage of the royal household. Yet when in 1678, Carlos II attempted to raise a *donativo* from his own Council of State (50,000 *reales* each was suggested), only two of them responded, though the council members 'did not deny that their persons, riches, and estates, all lay at Your Majesty's feet'.[17]

Policy

After the death of Philip IV, the government of the Spanish monarchy, from being the most stable and ordered in Europe, degenerated into perhaps the most chaotic and vacillating. In little over a decade, Spain slipped from the control of a king, to that of an oligarchy, and even to that of a military 'protector', a process punctuated by the rise and fall of two pseudo-*validos*, and more characteristic of a country in the throes of intense and violent revolution. These changes were mainly (though not entirely) on the surface. The effective removal of a unitary figure of arbitration and co-ordination (which Philip's passing involved) put a strain on the system of government designed for the needs of a mature monarch. In 'normal' circumstances, as we have seen, its complexity did not necessarily lead to inflexibility or confusion; after 1665 however, these characteristics became predominant. It is true that the king's own posthumous attempt to cater for the situation was not entirely in vain. His last testament decreed the establishment of a 'governing junta' (*Junta de Gobierno*) with whose advice and consent his widow was to exercise the regency, derived, mainly on an *ex-officio* basis, from the main councils (E22). In essence, this was a transmogrified Council of State, but one with a new kind of 'constitutional' authority, to be held until Carlos II attained his majority. Though on two occasions their rule was suspended, this group continued in practice to manage the affairs of state until Don Juan's takeover in 1676. Of course, the effective absence of a sovereign encouraged the rise of pure politics in Madrid. This phenomenon, to which the activities of Don Juan also contributed, was, on the whole, novel. Nevertheless, in the junta's survival, and particularly in that of its outstanding personality, the Count of Peñaranda (d. 1676), a kind of continuity can be detected.

The old king himself continued to rule until the last weeks of his life, if anything becoming more arbitrary and obstinate in his direction of policy. Philip's prejudices played the key role in Madrid's rejection of the French overture in 1656, and in the subsequent decision to open the offensive against Portugal – involving what was tantamount to the abandonment of Flanders.[18] It was typical of the king to interpret Lionne's mission as a sign of weakness, reckoning that a last opportunity to reconquer Portugal could not be ignored. In both attitudes it seems probable that he overrode the objections of Don Luis de Haro (not to mention those of the Council of State) whilst in the latter virtually his only active supporter was Sister María. Convinced that the security of Castile, like that of his immortal soul, was bound up in the question, Philip was obsessed with the defeat of the Braganzas at almost any cost. In 1657, accordingly, resources began to be redeployed, in the teeth of opposition from Don Juan José, governor of the Spanish Netherlands. In a struggle of wills which was a pale reflection of an earlier division between a Philip and a Don Juan over Low Countries' policy, the Council of State was inclined to support the prince. In the event, the matter was settled by the war with England which cut Flanders off from further assistance. The invasion of Portugal was launched in 1657; its failure (repeated in two consecutive campaigns) was at least as important as the defeats against France and England in persuading Philip reluctantly to accept the (almost unanimous) advice of his ministers. Madrid's favourable response to the further French initiative, which led to the negotiations at the Pyrenees, was thus largely a result of the feeling that Portugal's resistance could only be broken by the concentration of Spain's remaining resources. As in every other case of major diplomatic settlement in the whole course of the reign, Spain made peace in order to make war. Indeed, the kind of calculation which led to the Treaty of the Pyrenees survived the king, and was present over the peace with Portugal in 1668.

The affair of Portugal was also central to the development of another important line of policy. Despite his contrary undertaking (made in the Pyrenees treaty) Louis XIV continued surreptitiously to supply the Braganza defences, and helped promote the Anglo-Portuguese alliance into the bargain. This, added to a lack of maritime power which was now virtually complete, increasingly inclined Madrid to closer relations with the United Provinces. Partly impelled by the logic of their economic interdependence, the process of conversion of natural enemies into natural allies had begun (as we have seen) in the years following the Treaty of Munster. In 1656, Don Juan was ordered to reach a specific agreement with The Hague, in conjunction with the Spanish ambassador, Gamarra, a man who devoted twenty years in the republic to the achievement of this objective. In 1657, one of Cromwell's agents in the Netherlands reported

> . . . news from Holland of the great preparation they are making for sea . . . It is thought they have an intention to hold with Spain. The Spanish ambassador was bravely received in Amsterdam, in such a manner as the Prince of Orange was never received by them . . . they gave him command [i.e., the freedom] of the city [and] at his return to The Hague he made a ballet for the ladies and nobles there which cost him much.[19]

The diplomatic revolution suggested here was no longer chimerical. The late 1650s saw the growth of Dutch fears regarding the expansion of French military and English naval power. Although the regents cautiously continued to eschew explicit commitments, these factors (along with their established colonial struggle with Portugal) initiated a change in attitude to Spain. In 1659-60, the Dutch took over the transport of Spanish soldiery from Flanders and Italy to the Portuguese front, and in the following year, Ruyter's fleet protected the incoming silver *flota* following rumours of a surprise attack by the English. In Rotterdam, new warships were being built on order from Spain, in an attempt to revive the Armada. In return, Madrid expanded the commercial concessions of the Munster treaty, awarding Dutch ships and merchants favoured treatment in all their Atlantic, Iberian and Mediterranean undertakings. During the second Anglo-Dutch war of 1664-7, Spain's bias towards the republic, clearly observed by the English ambassador in Madrid, was of material assistance. Little wonder that at one stage, 'all Europe was predicting war between England and the undeclared Dutch-Spanish alliance against Portugal'.[20]

Such an outright confrontation was certainly not intended in Madrid. On the contrary, during the 1660s the trauma of the war in Portugal helped to produce a reaction against the traditional assumptions of defence policy. In 1667, Don Juan told the queen regent that 'barring miracles, two things have made the loss of all our dominions inevitable. One is the complete exhaustion of resources caused by the war with Portugal; and the other is the monstrous government of Nithard' (E20/I). The Duke of Medina de las Torres, effective chief minister in Philip IV's last years, agreed entirely with these sentiments. Medina had long been the most consistent advocate of a phased withdrawal from commitments, and after the defeat of Ameixial (1663) he pushed strongly for a settlement with the Anglo-Portuguese alliance. For this statesman, the monarchy's survival depended on peace, and peace was only to be obtained through appeasement. Medina was no pacifist, and saw recuperation as the key to any long-term resistance to the aspirations of Versailles; but he accepted the need for a swallowing of Spain's pride, an idea repugnant to its dynasty and ruling class. Partly for this reason, Philip at his death excluded him from the 'governing junta'. His views slowly gained ground nevertheless. In the politics of this period, the regency government has been characterised by some Spanish historians as 'in the Austrian interest', that is to say, committed to the anti-French line. Though it is true that Mariana and Nithard were both of 'Austrian' origin, in practice their determination (in accordance with Philip's wishes) to prosecute the Portuguese war à l'outrance played directly into the hands of Louis XIV. A typical faction struggle developed in which Vienna supported Medina whilst Versailles encouraged the regency government and its outstanding champion, Peñaranda, in one of the most interesting and significant episodes in the eternal conflict of attitudes over defence policy (E16). The French invasion of Flanders of 1667 brought matters to a head, and Medina piloted through the negotiations of 1667–8 (see above, p. 148), which provided the basis for the respite and reorientation which the monarchy so badly needed.

After Medina's death in 1668, his rival Peñaranda, in a move typical of faction politics, was converted to his reasoning. In 1670, a colonial treaty with England represented Spain's first official abandonment of the principles of monopoly in the Atlantic. At the same time, Peñaranda floated the even more radical suggestion that Flanders be given up to Louis XIV, in exchange for the 'Spanish' territory made over to France in 1659. The relegation of the Netherlands was implicit in many emergency decisions over priorities made since 1640. It was, perhaps, to be detected in the offer of complete sovereignty in Brussels made to Don Juan in 1667, which strangely echoed the

ambitions of his earlier namesake. Certainly there were indications
that (for the first time since the 1590s) many Spaniards felt that
Flanders was little more than a liability to the monarchy. At last it
seemed that Spain was prepared to face reality, and to lop off the dead
branches of empire. Such factors could only have come to prominence
in a context created by the absence of a Habsburg king, a fact which
again (if only negatively) illustrates the central importance of the
dynasty. But in any case, this phase of policy-making (1667–72) was
perhaps one in which the mentality of the *Kleinspanien*, always present
beneath the surface of Spanish politics, emerged for a time to dominate
its deliberations. Its presence there was not a straightforward
phenomenon and was bitterly disputed by many traditionalists.
Though an analogy may be made with the period of reappraisal which
followed Philip II's death (see above, pp. 32–3), these events were the
more prophetic of later developments.

'Despite everything', comments the Belgian historian Lonchay
about the Spanish entry into the war of 1672, 'Spain stubbornly
returned to the battlefield.'[21] For, after apparently grasping the
opportunity for retrenchment, Spain allowed herself to slide back into
the morass of war. At the first real challenge, it seems, 'realism' failed,
and the old automatic responses resumed control of policy. This,
perhaps, is putting the case too crudely, but it is very difficult to give a
clear and consistent interpretation of the events of 1672–3. Madrid
was certainly informed, by the end of 1671, of the main trends of
Anglo-French policy, and that (in the first instance at least) the United
Provinces, and not the Spanish Netherlands, was its target. In early
1672, an English *démarche* should have left little doubt in ministers'
minds. Yet it was difficult, given their own long and bitter experience
of precisely such an undertaking, for the Spanish government to
register the astonishing fact that Louis XIV intended to attack and
subdue the Dutch republic. Naturally, they suspected a ploy somehow
to subvert Flanders. This apprehension prompted the junta to conduct
their own 'secret diplomacy', in practice left to the initiative of
Monterrey and of Manuel de Lira, ambassador at The Hague. The full
consequences of the move were not anticipated. The English envoy
wrote home that 'here they all desire extremely to assist the Dutch, and
would do it without any hesitation [even] though the French were yet
more powerful than they are'.[22] Peñaranda, longstanding advocate of
close ties with the United Provinces, seemed to bear this out, despite
his opinions about Flanders: 'The Council [of State] has always
reckoned such a business as vital to our interests, recognising that it
brings with it the security of dealing with a people of such good faith as
the Hollanders.'[23] Certain aspects of the Monterrey–Lira agreement
with the Dutch, however, caused disquiet all along. Madrid later

pretended that the monarchy had gone gallantly (and almost gratuitously) to war with France in 1672, thus saving the Dutch republic from certain extinction. But perhaps an element of bluff was present in the contemptuous treatment of English approaches and references to the path of honour. To put it mildly, the prospect of another war with France in the Low Countries (not to mention the English aspect) was not faced with equanimity. The likely truth is that Spain, in 1672 (as in 1621), drifted into war, partly through the lack of an alternative, partly through the energy of its diplomatic representatives, and partly, too, because of the lack of a firm general base to policy. When Monterrey consummated the decision by sending troops to the assistance of the beleaguered Dutch, Madrid promised to send reinforcements. The old adversaries who had for eighty years contested its destiny were thus engaged at last in an alliance for the common defence of the Low Countries.

Naturally, the war was unpopular in Flanders itself, especially when an angry and frustrated Louis XIV sent his army to devastate and terrorise the province in the spring of 1673. Spain's resolution wavered, and she hesitated to take the final step of declaring war, or to negotiate a full-scale military agreement with the Dutch to meet the new situation. Madrid's uncertainty was not reflected in Flanders, where Monterrey conducted his campaigns with energy and determination – so much so that he was recalled in 1674. Of course the diplomatic *persona* differed from the gnawing doubts beneath. When France at last made the war official, Louis XIV was condemned as an international criminal, and Spain declared its war objectives to be the restoration of all territorial losses incurred since 1659. 'It is remarkable', as one observer commented, 'to what a pitch they raise their hopes of prevailing over France, and reducing that crown to render up all its conquests.'[24] The real ambition of Spain was to obtain a quick peace, but it proved politically impossible to extricate herself from her predicament. The government could do little as the war wore on except struggle (often hopelessly) with its military demands, and apply pressure (usually in vain) for a reasonable settlement.

In all this, policy was debated and decided by the junta, acting on advice from the traditional Council of State. The influence of Fernando de Valenzuela, the queen's *privado*, was virtually nil, as far as can be judged. Maura affirmed that he had never seen the upstart's signature on any document of importance (E20/I), whilst an English ambassador was five years in Madrid before he regarded his position to be worthy of report (in 1674). In the present state of knowledge, he can only be regarded, at best as a kind of Lerma-*manqué*, at worst as a mere impresario of the huge Habsburg court (including gradually, and maybe significantly, its wealth of patronage). Whilst for a time his popularity was maintained by an endless series of fabulous and spectacular entertainments, eventually the volatile population of Madrid turned from the *circenses* of Valenzuela to the promised *panem* of Don Juan José.

When (in 1677) the ersatz king succeeded the ersatz *valido*, much was expected of the change. It took only a few weeks for disillusionment to creep in: 'The prince rode into Madrid, took out his sword, and performed – nothing', as a popular epigram put it. This is certainly true as regards the expectations of the masses, but Don Juan's influence on what used to be called 'higher affairs' was more marked. At virtually his first session in the Council of State, he supported the faction which reacted favourably towards Louis XIV's peace offers. He was disinclined to continue the defence of Flanders, and deeply suspicious that Spain's allies might – as in 1668 – force upon her a completely humiliating peace.[25] During the war, according to one school of opinion in the council, the Dutch had reverted to type; certainly by 1677 little confidence existed between the allies, and William of Orange was no more popular in Madrid than the founder of his line had been a century earlier. The Hague (it was felt) had merely exploited Spanish resources to concentrate on their own defence, and was blamed (*inter alia*) for the conquest of Franche-Comté. This conveniently ignored, for example, the essential Dutch contribution to the retention of Sicily, an affair in which Ruyter had lost his life.

Another, apparently trivial, consideration, which much exercised the minds of the council perfectly illustrates the dogged survival of the ancient preconceptions. One of Louis XIV's declared objectives in making war had been to compel the Dutch to admit the free practice of Catholicism within the republic. This had been one of Spain's basic principles during its own wars in Flanders. The irony (not to say mortification) of Spanish troops resisting such a triumph of the faith was painful to royal confessors and political prelates, types which had (if anything) gained in influence since 1665. Equally, as the Vatican never tired of pointing out, the continual presence of so many Dutch and German soldiery in the Spanish Netherlands endangered the souls of the king's own subjects. On both these points, Carlos himself, who had now achieved both his majority and (relative) sentience, was extremely vulnerable. They thus played a part, and perhaps a greater one than any calculations to do with material insufficiency (or the truly horrendous plight of the population of Castile) in Spain's acceptance of the disastrous Peace of Nijmegen in 1678. When the opinions of ministers and councils were canvassed over this settlement, Iñigo de Velasco, one of the few opponents of Don Juan to have preserved his position, morosely observed: 'It depresses me beyond measure to see that all these documents express only the fear of whether the Christian king will honour the treaty. Though all admit the peace is a bad one for us, none has considered whether our master should not be satisfied with it.'[26] Spain's tragedy was now to be trapped in the typical dilemma of the appeasing power. If absolute security could have been guaranteed by the surrender of Portugal, Jamaica, Burgundy, even Flanders itself, then the process of withdrawal would have been embraced as viable and worthwhile. But since Spain's enemies, and even (as was sometimes pointed out) her friends, nurtured insatiable territorial and economic appetites, war remained the only mechanism of control. In this way, despite the virtual disappearance of her genuine ideals and positive commitments, Spain was still a slave to the 'domino theory' of empire which had always dictated an existence of struggle and sacrifice.

Attitudes

Speaking very broadly, the characteristic attitude to the monarchy amongst the European states in the third quarter of the century was one of undisguised acquisitiveness. Of course, the desire to probe its weaknesses, and profit from them, had always been present in the counsels of Spain's major rivals. But this ambition was normally moderated by a necessary caution based on the empirical fact of Spanish power; a fact which even the United Provinces had come to recognise and respect. The 'conjuncture' of the 1640s worked a notable change in this approach, for it witnessed the definitive loss of Spain's *reputación* and a consequent boost to the confidence of other powers. None of them, whatever its traditional relationship with Madrid, could hereafter afford to ignore the opportunities for aggrandisement offered by the military decline of the Spanish system. This axiom was present in the calculations of the commercial city-state, like Hamburg, or a territorial-dynastic one, like Brandenburg, as much as in those of Versailles. The new rationale can still be expressed (though preferably with a more comprehensive range of meaning) by the old historical formula of 'the problem of the Spanish succession'.

Although, therefore, it must now be interpreted almost entirely in a negative sense, the material resources and policy of the Spanish monarchy remained central to the affairs of Europe. The atavism of Spain's 'successors' brought about the epic continental–colonial struggles of the period, and consequently the state-system of *ancien régime* Europe. Whether it was advanced by war or diplomacy made little difference. The huge, untapped potential of the Spanish empire, when placed alongside its military breakdown, provided palpable proof of the validity of mercantilist theory. To the intellectual disciples of Thomas Mun, as much as to the practical followers of Colbert, the principles of profit and power were epitomised in the Hispanic world as perfectly as, to the scientist, God was abstracted in the clockwork machine.

For the businessmen of Europe, the monarchy remained an important client, so long as it was in defence of its possessions through war; perhaps – given its now-absolute need for all kinds of support services – more so than before. For the diplomats, increasingly concerned with economic matters, the Spanish court was still the supreme dispensatrix of commercial favour and personal patronage. They were now, however, aware of holding the initiative; their tone changed from the supplicatory to the peremptory, even minatory. In 1664, for example, the English secretary of state felt able to instruct his ambassador to address the Spaniards in terms which would have been distinctly unwise even a decade earlier.

> You must always . . . represent to them that the monarchy of Spain is fallen into a great declination . . . and that the monarchy of England is proportionately elevated and raised to a strength . . . infinitely superior to what it ever was, and consequently *in a state of demanding* . . . the advantages to the fullest extent which are granted the French and Hollanders.[27]

Threatened as she was with the power of her French neighbour, Spain needed the goodwill of every petty princeling. In 1677, when the ministers of three minor German states made joint representations to the Council of State to complain about the delay in payment of various subsidies and pensions, the response of this once-omnipotent body was apologetic and conciliatory to the point of obsequiousness.[28] The politicians of Europe gathered in Madrid to hear the will of Spain in a sense entirely different to that which had before obtained.

England, which had neither the influence of the Dutch nor the French on the thinking of Madrid, was in many ways the touchstone of these attitudes.[29] As we have seen, Cromwell's war rapidly lost popularity, and by 1660 the restored Charles II was bombarded with requests from the mercantile community to bring it to an end. In choosing to ignore these in favour of a deal with Portugal, he made a major error. Whilst Spain's financial situation began to improve, and she was able to cause severe harassment to English trade in the Mediterranean, England's commercial and financial arrangements with the Portuguese ran into enormous difficulties. In 1664, a committee of trade estimated that £1,500,000 had been lost by English merchants through fines, extra impositions and embargoes alone since 1660, whilst the loss of contract opportunities in the Spanish world could hardly be estimated. Sections of English business life wished not only to recapture the healthy position in peninsular trade established before 1655, but also to exploit more thoroughly the trade in Spanish raw materials (especially wool) and in the agrarian produce of Andalusia. In addition, commerce with the extra-European world depended to a large extent on access to supplies of silver, and this was particularly important for the business of the East India Company because of the endemically unfavourable 'balance' of trade east of the Cape. Finally, the new Royal African Company (in which the Stuarts and all their prominent courtiers had an interest) could succeed only by obtaining a dominating position in the slave trade. The notorious *asiento de negros*, grant of which was in the purlieu of Madrid, was valued not only for itself, but for the lucrative (if still illicit) opportunities it offered for deriving other business in the Caribbean and the Spanish Main.

Not only were all these things denied English capitalism, but (more galling still) were increasingly coming into the hands of its closest competitors, the Dutch. The United Provinces benefited enormously from Anglo-Spanish hostility in the years after 1655, improving their position in almost every area of the economy of the Hispanic world, a process which (as we have seen) was smiled on by Madrid. Ruyter's action in defence of the silver fleet of 1661 (in which the direct Dutch interest was considerable) was symbolic; by the 1660s, the English had to confront the Dutch, the established power in Spain's markets, in order to achieve the economic breakthrough. This fact lay behind England's provocation of a second maritime-colonial war with the republic in 1664. The main issues of this conflict were all tangibly connected with the material resources of the Spanish empire – the 'Spanish succession' with a vengeance. And it was no accident that the English failure in this war was followed by the conclusion of a series of treaties with Spain by which the policy of physical intimidation was abandoned. Though, at first dash, England did not achieve the range of concessions necessary to put its merchants on the same footing as the Dutch (in fact little advance was made on the deal offered to Cromwell by Cárdenas) in the 1670s began that significant expansion of her commerce which formed a prelude to the appearance of 'the first industrial nation'. There were, of course, other factors at work in this latter phenomenon. But the recovery of the whole European economy which seems to have taken place in this generation was (surely) intimately associated with the crumbling of Spanish hegemony, and the different approaches to the exploitation of its resources which the process involved.

'We do naturally all love the Spaniards and hate the French' recorded Samuel Pepys, diarist of London, in the summer of 1661. The observation was at this stage perhaps more prescient than accurate. Indeed, his own master, the Earl of Sandwich, commanding the fleet on which so much of Pepys's work was centred, was on the high seas at that very moment with intentions rather removed from such sentiments. It was true all the same that changes in the regard for the Spanish monarchy, in London as in other European cities, were closely linked to the rapid development of French power. In the 1650s, the hatred reflected (for example) in the thundering propaganda of John Milton, was fully reciprocated in Spain. To Barrionuevo, Cromwell was 'that great beast aborted from the mouth of hell', who murdered Irish priests and tortured babies. Fanciful tales of persecution of Catholics still found a ready reading public in 'the nest of wolves' – as an English pamphlet of 1660 referred to Spain. Even in 1667, the (clerical) vice-chancellor of Aragon condemned the commercial treaty with England as 'a scandal which redounds to the shame of the whole monarchy'; whilst ten years later, at the height of the Popish Plot, a London mob invaded the house of a Spanish envoy in search of Jesuits. English 'pirates', captured in the Caribbean, still sweated in the gaols of Seville in the 1660s, and religious ceremonies in the towns of southern Spain could still be interrupted by the blasphemy of some fanatical (or drunken ?) English sailor. Generally, nevertheless, the passions of religion were a dying force, so far as influence on the ruling maxims of state were concerned. Whilst it would be foolish to deny the residual influence of the 'Black Legend' on English prejudice (even down to our own times) the active element in confessional fear now transferred its forebodings to France.

Although the 'golden age' of Spanish art was drawing to a close, there was still a cultural aspect to English attitudes. Many of the courtiers who returned with Charles II from the Continent in 1660 were influenced by the Habsburg magnificence which had its last, dazzling expression (organized by Velázquez) at the Franco-Spanish marriage festivities of that year. Men like Clarendon and Arlington, key figures in English policy-making down to the 1670s, had been in Spain, and were conversant in some degree with Spanish language and thought. The English ambassador in Madrid in the 1660s, Sir Richard Fanshawe, was one of the founding fathers of Hispanic scholarship in England; and his successor (the same Earl of Sandwich who earlier threatened the silver fleet) was seduced by Madrid society, learning to play guitar duets with Don Juan José, under the tutorship of Gaspar Sanz, first *maestro* of the instrument. The decline of religious fervour enabled Englishmen to travel in Spain with greater freedom of mind, and (for example) the dramatists Congreve and Wycherley brought back dozens of plots from the bounteous heritage of the Spanish stage, which so-called 'Restoration dramatists' were to make full use of in succeeding years. As the libraries of both John Evelyn and Pepys himself attest, English books on Iberian themes continued to appear in some quantity down to the end of the century at least.

Religious considerations had also ceased to exercise any real influence on the attitudes of Dutchmen towards the inveterate adversary of earlier generations. Moreover, it may be suggested that the republic was, if anything, the least acquisitive of Spain's 'successors'. The dynamic phase of Dutch commercial and colonial expansion was in fact already over, and in many respects the aspirations of its capitalist grandees were now sated. The businessmen of Amsterdam had established predominance in Mediterranean and Atlantic markets, apart from providing a whole range of services for the public and private sectors in the Spanish monarchy. The relative decline of the city's active trading interests after about 1650 must be set against its huge and growing 'invisible' earnings in fields such as this. In 1662, the republic even settled its colonial differences with Portugal, ending a struggle which had lasted for some seventy years. Above all, the fear of French designs, fast becoming the dominant strain in European politics, was (for obvious reasons) of much earlier birth in the United Provinces than elsewhere. The ancient grievance of the 'separation' of the Catholic (Spanish) south of the fatherland – though its deposit can still be found in the writings of Dutch historians like Pieter Geyl (G8) – had in any case ebbed away. But it was now totally eradicated as a principle of policy by the determination on no account to have Louis XIV as a neighbour on the frontier of the republic. After 1648, commercial contacts between the two halves of the Netherlands began to flourish. In the 1660s, Versailles as much as London became painfully aware of the kind of benefit derived by the Dutch from their position as the 'favoured nation' of Spanish economic policy, and the resentment this occasioned, given its rationale by Colbert, played its part in the thinking of Louis XIV. For some time the French persisted in their schemes for a joint 'cantonment' of the Spanish Netherlands, but the regents of The Hague could not be shifted from their belief in the *Scheidingszone* (or buffer state), the role in European politics to which Flanders was now reduced. The last occasion on which Madrid suspected a Dutch threat to the integrity of Flanders was during the convoluted diplomacy of 1668. In fact, despite its original ambiguity, the Triple Alliance effectively proclaimed that Holland's interest was now, in a pejorative as well as a real sense, the 'protection' of the Spanish empire. In general terms, the survival of that empire (and, of course, the origins of 'Belgium') owed a good deal to this development.

The fundamentals of French policy could hardly have stood in greater contrast. For the present writer, at least, there is no escaping the impression that from the earliest days of his personal rule, Louis XIV consciously sought to capture for himself, whole and intact, the European role of the Spanish monarchy and its physical and 'moral' basis. Louis was, after all, himself half a Habsburg, with a Habsburg queen, and his attitude to 'the Spanish succession' took full account of these facts. As the full nature and extent of the physical condition of the last of 'las Austrias' emerged in the 1660s, Louis came to regard himself as the divinely chosen heir of the monarchy ruled by such a stricken and feeble creature. Though one must recognise the Sun King's original contribution to the craft of kingship, nevertheless, in so many of his actions and policies he seemed deliberately to take over the principles of Spanish supremacy. A concern for prestige (or *reputación*) elevated into a monolithic spiritual sanction; a sensational loathing for heresy and republicanism; a frantic search for immediate cultural triumphs based on lavish artistic patronage; a desire to dominate the Vatican, much more crudely articulated than that of any king of Castile. Of course, Louis had to act with relative moderation and within certain ever-present limitations to encompass his full programme. In any case, also present (in the first phase at least) was a profound apprehension concerning the actual degree of Spanish weakness, and the possibility of a recovery in her affairs. In 1660, Louis had been mortified by the grand spectacle made by the Habsburg court at the marriage festivities at Bidassoa on the Franco-Spanish border – a kind of 'Field of the Cloth of Gold' of the seventeenth century, at which the Bourbon performance had been completely eclipsed by the taste and splendour behind which lay two centuries of Burgundian tradition. To Louis, this represented a military defeat, and a major one at that; it resulted in the symbolic general directive to his ambassadors, to assert 'precedence' over their Spanish counterparts on every possible occasion.

Louis's creation of a new absolutism in France must not be exaggerated, nor should we assume that it sprang into existence overnight. The building of Versailles, the imposition of the *intendants*, the construction of a new, standing army (all of them having obvious Spanish precedents) occupied the best part of a decade. Religious circumstances certainly favoured Louis's aims. The old *dévot* zeal for the interests of Counter-Reformation Spain had by now disappeared, and the energies of France's ultra-Catholic lobby were drawn off into the prolonged struggle against Jansenism. The fact that the passions of this rogue element in French politics were now subsumed into the dominant orthodoxy of the court and its great clerical propagandists was a great relief. Nevertheless, other problems, especially in the fiscal and economic spheres, inhibited Louis for many years. During them, he followed what was basically Richelieu's old tactic of 'war by proxy' against Spain via the subsidy of England and Portugal – an interesting reversion, intended to husband French resources, assist her preparations, and weaken the enemy indirectly. Somewhat in contrast to its previous use, this policy proved immensely successful in the 1660s. When Louis began his campaign in 1667, despite all previous indications and 'trends', it changed the political context of Europe radically and suddenly. The phrase the 'War of Devolution', like the wider movement of 'Spanish succession' of which it forms part, is capable of an interpretation far beyond its immediate frame of reference.

Conclusions

Part of the discussions between England and France in 1670, from which emerged the notorious 'secret treaty' of Dover, centred on the question of the Spanish-American colonies. According to Charles II's ministers, England was the natural inheritor of this legacy, and was, indeed, prepared to take it over, lock, stock and barrel, should the Anglo-French schemes result in an all-out war against Spain. At the moment when these plans were on the point of being launched (in the spring of 1672) what concerned the caretaker of this massive empire, the regent Mariana, more than anything else was the issue of the Immaculate Conception. She compiled what was (for her) an effusive comment of more than a hundred words, recording her pleasure at the fact that the clergy of Milan had declared its support for this proposition to be recognised by Rome as an article of faith.[30] Of course, the English crown had long been interested in acquiring an imperial dimension, and Spanish kings – especially Philip IV – had for years been campaigning in the cause of the BVM; and the juxtaposition of these two aspirations in the foregoing manner is, doubtless, somewhat artificial. None the less, it may be held to illustrate, even to epitomise, a certain qualitative divergence of approach between the monarchy and its main European neighbours which becomes sharply apparent after the 'conjuncture' of the late 1660s.

The crisis of the years immediately surrounding 1668 seems profoundly significant and symbolic in the history of the Spanish monarchy. Following the humiliating and unprecedented military failure in Portugal, Spain's attempt to defend Flanders against Louis XIV's army was a fiasco. By 1669, the principle that Flanders could only be protected by foreign powers was accepted by Madrid. The following year, Spain effectively abjured its immemorial rights to exclusive presence in the New World by a treaty with England in which (*inter alia*) Cromwell's conquest of Jamaica was formally recognised. Louis XIV, meanwhile, negotiated the first partition treaty of the

Spanish empire with the Viennese Habsburgs. Above all, and exactly simultaneously with this last event, the monarchy accepted the secession and sovereignty of the kingdom of Portugal (1668), along with its colonial possessions in Africa and Asia. Not only, therefore, was the era of Spain's European hegemony at an end, but also that of the classic Philippine empire, the global agglomeration which had come into existence in 1580. The nature and preconceptions of the Spain of the 1670s were thus radically different from those of the 1650s. It betokened nothing less than a change of identity.

The narrowing of vision concerning the monarchy's European role, to which many references have been made in this chapter, was accompanied and influenced by political changes within Castile. Even before the death of Philip IV (which naturally increased the tendency), the local and sporadic disorder which had begun in the late 1640s had spread to the capital. Serious riots in Madrid broke out – for the first time in its history – upon the news of the disaster of Villaviçiosa, a popular protest against the suffering engendered by endless war. (A broadsheet, suitably illustrated, described Castile's fortunes as being suspended 'between two suckling babies', a reference to the dying king's diet of milk [E22].) This development was as significant as the protests of 1640 and 1647 in Catalonia and Italy. From now onwards, mounting social instability in Castile's major cities was a constant consideration of policy. We have already noted how Valenzuela coped with it (above pp. 162–3); even more ominous was the formation, after Don Juan's *coup* of 1669, of a regular regimental palace guard in Madrid, a crack outfit of 4,000, nicknamed the 'Chambergos' after Schomberg, Louis XIV's general in Portugal. Apart from the token presence of a few 'Switzers', this was the first concession by the dynasty to the need for civil protection against its own subjects. Although there were no great peasant uprisings until later in the century, the danger of urban insurrection illustrates that the problem of popular unrest was growing in Spain just as it was beginning to diminish in France. A very similar observation may be made about comparative political conditions generally between the two states. Following the steady impoverishment of its physical and legal foundations, caused by the various exigencies of war, the effective exercise of royal absolutism became impracticable upon the succession of a (largely incapacitated) minor in 1665. The untended growth of regional autonomy and aristocratic oligarchy in Spain during the reign of Carlos II stands in clean contrast to contemporary developments across the Pyrenees. The exchange of roles between the Catholic and Christian kings was thus a phenomenon of considerable verisimilitude.

Meanwhile, the government of Spain, managed as it was by men who existed in a political context which had suddenly become precarious and unpredictable, moved into a phase which can only be called introverted. The later career of Don Juan José illustrates many aspects of this trend to perfection. It was he who most intimately experienced the military disasters in Flanders and Portugal during his father's last decade; who set the example of a different code of conduct, or scale of values, to the nobility; and who helped create the unusual (but prophetic) political realities of later seventeenth-century Spain. And although the exhaustion of material resources, and the ubiquity of military failure, clearly play central parts in the process of 'withdrawal', analysis of it should not end, and perhaps should not even begin, with such components. All the same, it is interesting to observe the appearance of a widely commented cartoon in the 1660s, which portrayed Spain as a great cow, feeding the nations of Europe from her enormous udders. Dutch and French merchants now infiltrated and controlled every important aspect of the Spanish economy. Madrid could only protest impotently when Henry Morgan pillaged Panama City in 1670. Meanwhile, the ill-fated invasion of Portugal in 1665 was the last offensive operation which Habsburg Spain proved capable of mounting from its own resources. When, in 1674, Monterrey reported the French occupation of Franche-Comté, the appendix of the Burgundian empire, Mariana pathetically noted that 'the loss of such good vassals has caused me great distress, and the council should consider how the province can be returned to the allegiance of the king my son'.[31] Perhaps aptly, the official Spanish acceptance of the loss was made by a bastard of the once-glorious dynasty, when Don Juan accepted Louis XIV's terms for peace in 1678.

CHAPTER 5

Pathology of a Power System
1678–1700

I am touched by your expressions of esteem, and do not doubt that
co-operation between France and Spain can more and more
advance the public peace of Europe which we have now re-
established through treaty . . . (Louis XIV to the governor of the
Spanish Netherlands, 1679)[1]

None of the treaties made with the Christian king has been
successful, because he has immediately broken them all . . .
(Carlos II to the pope, 1692)[2]

Introduction

Sometime in the opening years of this period, one of the anonymous
lampoonists in which Madrid abounded, circulated a 'Parallel of the
Courts of France and Spain':

France:	she sounds the trumpets of her men-at-arms
	and in her shipyards builds up navies
Spain:	makes majordomos of her men of charms,
	mature, discreet, of sagest qualities.
France:	invades the homeland of her enemy
	and from the Austrian eagle strips the feathers.
Spain:	orders with care her ranks of hierarchy
	preserving protocol, in whatever weather.[3]

The author of these sentiments presumably knew nothing of the
baroque and intense structure of court life (much of its detail blatantly
imitated from Spain) which Louis XIV created at Versailles. But this
hardly detracts from the relevance and point of his argument. The
procrustean image of the court of Madrid, moribund, gloomy, fatefully
ritualistic, seemed to many Europeans out of joint with the times, yet
also an appropriate comment on Spain's lack of dynamism and
purpose. Published accounts by many French and English visitors,
marked with faint amusement and contempt, and garnished by

exaggeration and gossip, had a ready sale throughout the Continent. Reports of this kind identified the Spanish sickness and provided contemporaries with a pathology, an 'anatomy lesson' on a cadaverous empire, which (like incipient science itself) was instinct with moral nostrums in which malady and error inhabited cognate worlds. The rediscovery, many generations later, of the writings of the Castilian *arbitristas*, provided an apparently firm intellectual base to the observations of foreign dilettantes.

As early as 1630, an English envoy to Madrid had commented on the serried ranks of court ladies, white-faced and still as in a tapestry; and sneered at the dubious honour of being allowed to 'kiss the king's hand, or rather his foot, that other being seldom granted to strangers'.[4] Even at this stage, the actual poverty of the royal circumstances stood in almost farcical contrast to the godlike arrogance of palace demeanour. Indeed (as our poet suggests) the Habsburgs continued to protect these elaborate rites with an insistent and jealous fervour. Every infanta who left at marriage to join a strange court was enjoined to maintain the unique distinction of her caste by guarding them as closely as she would her immortal soul. They had a shaping effect on the character of princes which (as in the case of the illegitimate Don Juan José) could easily become obsessive. The interface between the ceremonial of the court and the liturgy of its religion is illustrated by the best-known Spanish painting of the period, Coello's picture of Carlos II attending mass. It provides an image which is somehow eternal, and its context was the butt of satire from Quevedo's era to that of the novelist Pérez Galdos more than 200 years later. But the fact is that the maintenance of these procedures was quite as important as the dynasty, in common with that of France, believed. Prolonged and repeated ceremony centred upon the figure of the king himself, *was* the identity of the monarchy, the self-affirmation of its being – and, indeed, of its purpose. Recent experts in Renaissance politics have stressed the vital significance of such matters in the maintenance of authority and credibility. The Burgundian heritage nurtured in the palaces of Castile, and reproduced in those of viceroys over much of western Europe, was no more a mere sterile routine than the traditions of our own monarchy, the popularity and meaning of which have recently been effectively demonstrated. It was, in itself, an appropriate synthesis of all the late-mediaeval courts of Christendom – Italian, German and French, as well as Spanish – and it epitomised the dynasty's unchanging commitment to the ideals of its founder, Charles V. It is true, of course, that the Universal Emperor's sorrowful descendant and namesake (in the words of a memorial to which he appended his personal agreement in 1691) believed 'that all our misfortunes proceed from our sins alone'.[5] But it would be a mistake to conclude that the solutions of the *arbitristas* put forward in more sensible documents, were not ceaselessly discussed and even attempted. Habsburg Spain, like the ritual of its court, was a symbiosis of the spiritual and the material.

Narrative of Events

Under the leadership of Don Juan, the Madrid government hoped that the general pacification of 1678 (Peace of Nijmegen) would inaugurate a process of Franco-Spanish understanding. This basis of recovery was cemented by the betrothal of the king (now 17 years old) to the French princess María Luisa of Orleans. Expectation of issue from such a union was perhaps not as fantastic as it now seems in more knowledgeable retrospect. The new queen herself was, after all, the daughter of a homosexual father and his fragile Stuart wife, whilst Carlos was born when his father was 56 – an old man of whom all hope had been surrendered! In dynastic affairs, miracles were not only possible but confidently expected. Some of these hopes were not justified by events, but others proved not entirely in vain. The 1680s was the most peaceful decade that Spain had experienced for a long time, arguably for more than a century. It was not completely devoid of economic and administrative achievement. And it was certainly the happiest in Carlos II's benighted existence.

All the same few shared the sanguine hopes of the king and his dictator-premier. As far as Brussels was concerned, France was merely waiting for an opportunity to pounce, for the right moment when international support for Spain would either be tardy or altogether unforthcoming. Indeed, Louis XIV was determined to punish the monarchy for its 'betrayal' of 1672, just as he had in that year punished the United Provinces for their action of 1668. Louis, the Emperor of the West, had put Spain under ban. His forces continued to terrorise the frontier populations of the Spanish Netherlands, several garrisons refusing to withdraw for long after the formal ratification of the treaty. In early 1680, the Brussels privy council recorded its conviction that French ambition made further war inevitable. Where would the blow fall? The answer was delayed only as long as the usual meticulous period of preparation by the Bourbon technocrats, military, legal, diplomatic. The ingenious policy of 'reunion' was crowned by the unresisted occupation of Strasbourg and Casale in 1681; then, in the late summer of 1683, the main (and massive) French army moved into Luxembourg, besieging the Spanish-manned fortress of the ducal capital. Louis's concentration on the Rhineland was proof of his determination to push French borders away from vulnerable Paris, but an essential part of this reasoning was the memory of the 'Spanish road' and the bitter 'year of Corbie' (1636).

None of Spain's ex-allies was prepared to undertake a war with France to save Luxembourg, since none was directly threatened by its loss. When the Spaniards resisted and declared war nevertheless, Louis invaded Catalonia and Flanders to bring Madrid to its senses. Once again the Walloon towns crumbled at his assault; the French armies also pushed deep into eastern Spain. Genoa offended Versailles by assisting Spain's war effort in the Mediterranean, and the French fleet bombarded the republican city for twelve successive days. The actual conduct of war by the French was becoming more destructive than ever before, a development based on the Swedish methods of the Thirty Years' War and involving the systematic employment of devastation and terror in the lands of an invaded enemy. From now on, many areas of the monarchy were to suffer from the direct ravages of war in increasingly terrible aspects and prolonged phases. Despite this, Catalonia (at least) resisted stoutly, and the troops of the town of Gerona salvaged some pride by the rout of a besieging army. Luxembourg, however, capitulated late in the campaign of 1684, and with this, Louis's objective was achieved. At the Ratisbon negotiations, he traded off his gains in other theatres in return for the formal Spanish cession of Luxembourg. This war, which punctuated the decade of peace referred to above, therefore lasted barely a year. But its events illustrate the steady development of the 'French system' since Mazarin's failures in the 1640s. The French now commanded both the resources and the techniques necessary to attack her traditional adversary on several fronts simultaneously, bringing the whole weight of its physical superiority to bear in an earlier version of blitzkrieg. Conversely, Spain's loss of her last toehold in the Rhineland was indicative of the final breakdown of the Spanish system, as previously understood. Flanders, northern Italy, even Catalonia, had now achieved (in a sense) the independence which earlier historians imagined was the constant aspiration of their indigenous politics. They were isolated outposts of empire (as much if not more so than the smaller Caribbean islands) utterly dependent on their own resources, or on the self-interest of powerful neighbours, for salvation.

Louis XIV's timing in the war of 1683 had also been expert. His move coincided with that of the Turks towards Vienna, culmination of the last great Ottoman offensive in eastern Europe. The inability of the Habsburg states to help each other in this dual crisis seemed to confirm the estrangement of the two dynastic-territorial spheres. This, so far as Versailles was concerned, was a consummation devoutly to be wished and too long delayed; and Marshal Vauban proceeded to build a physical barrier between the Habsburg cousins by the fortification of all France's gains in the Rhineland. These appearances, however, proved in part deceptive. To be sure, when the second general war of Louis's policy began in 1688, Madrid for some time resisted the appeals both of the Dutch and the Austrians, in her turn holding aloof from a conflict in which the monarchy's own territories were not affected. Within a short time events conspired to change Spain's mind. The utterly unpredictable ease of William III's accession to the English throne, succeeded as it was by the recruitment of that country to the ranks of the allies, enormously enhanced the prospects of success against France. The temptation to share in this was too great, and in 1690 Spain duly joined the coalition, aiming at the total restitution of her losses to Louis since 1659. France immediately turned upon the weakest partner in an attempt to knock it out of the ring. The so-called 'Nine Years' War' (1688–97) saw renewed French invasions of Flanders, Italy and Catalonia, in which huge territorial losses were only staved off by a strong Anglo-Dutch commitment, both by land and sea, to assisting their defence. Inevitably, Flanders was cauterised during the campaigns of the 1690s, and despite the continued brave showing of the Spanish infantry, the military record was dismal. In 1692, Namur fell to the French engineers, and the following year at Neerwinden the allied army was emphatically crushed. Meanwhile, in Italy, Savoy (which had reverted to the anti-French camp) struggled to prevent complete French domination of the north of the peninsula; and in Catalonia, Gerona was at length lost in 1694. Perhaps the most galling defeat was that at Fleurus a few weeks after Spain's declaration of war, for this was the site of a great triumph over a Dutch–German army in 1622.

Notwithstanding the reverses of the field, hope continued to subsist. Louis's victories, individual or collective, had not been enough to remove a major opponent from the ranks of the alliance. The Habsburg family compact was far from defunct, though its impulse and inspiration now came from Vienna and not Madrid. The growing material sufficiency and war experience of the Austrians, gained in the terrific campaigns against the Turks which virtually created a new Danubian empire, was beginning to checkmate the ambitions of Versailles on all sides. Before Louis loomed the dread possibility of the revived – if differently directed – universal strategy of the Habsburgs. Moreover, the maritime powers had stuck to their main priority of reversing French naval predominance, and in spite of appalling losses to the enemy privateers (based largely on the old Spanish centre of Dunkirk) had achieved this by the mid-1690s. The campaign of Louis XIV against the encirclement of France – the so-called 'Habsburg ring' – had therefore been, in the last analysis, counter-productive. The

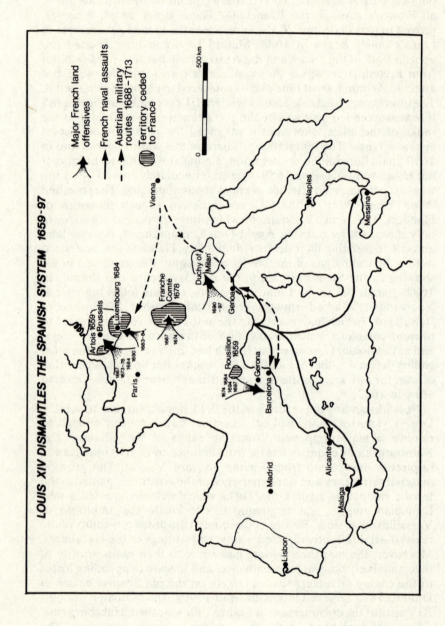

LOUIS XIV DISMANTLES THE SPANISH SYSTEM 1659-97

Major French land offensives

French naval assaults

Austrian military routes 1688-1713

Territory ceded to France

Vienna

Naples

Messina

Duchy of Milan

Genoa

1690-97

Brussels

Artois 1659

Luxembourg 1684

Franche-Comté 1678

1667

1674

1683-84

1673-78

1684

1690

Paris

Roussillon 1659

Gerona

Barcelona

1674

1684

1694

1697

1667

1674

Madrid

Alicante

Malaga

Lisbon

0   500 km

coalition powers had managed, despite their divergent interests and constant squabbles, to pool their resources, to co-operate in strategy and logistics, and to share responsibilities. In effect, this created a new system which surrounded France with a network of military defence and communications. Though it would be wildly inaccurate to suggest that this was a new lease of life for 'the Spanish system' – the nature of political control, spiritual mores and basic resources had changed too much – it still had a strong Habsburg component which was linked to the preconceptions of Spanish hegemony. This element was, moreover, stronger in one crucial respect than ever before; for the Austrian Habsburgs now seemed to have solved the major problems of a two-front war, proving able in the 1690s to discharge huge commitments in eastern and western Europe simultaneously. In direct contrast, the France of Louis XIV, was proved after all (like that of Mazarin), to be fallible when it came to 'total war' with a geopolitical dimension. The strain on her socio-economic structures developed into one of the most catastrophic of all her seventeenth-century crises. The superficiality of much of Louis's commercial and industrial policies was exposed by widespread dearth and unrest, though the weight of his administrative apparatus was enough to prevent a serious political expression to his subjects' grievances.

The angle of interpretation utilised above must not be made too acute. In the negotiations which led to the Peace of Rijswick (1697) France managed to preserve its prestige and its basic gains, the core of Louis's foreign achievement. The Grand Monarch was obliged to restore to Spain the plundered cities of Barcelona and Luxembourg, and expert opinion differs as to whether this move was one of constraint, without which France would not have obtained much-needed peace, or a deliberate ploy to convince the Spaniards of French generosity. Certainly a contemporary Spaniard remarked that 'he only returned some stolen sheaves in order to reap the whole harvest',[6] that is to say, Louis's action was a public-relations one aimed at strengthening his dynastic claim to the Spanish monarchy. By now he had recognised that legal and peaceful succession was the only practical avenue to the achievement of his fundamental aspiration. Not only had military pressure failed, but the momentous point of decision was fast approaching in Madrid. It remains true that in 1697, Louis accepted something less than a peace of victory; for the first time since 1656, France had been fought to a standstill. In this the stubborn military resistance of Spain was perhaps less important than the sponge-like ability of its dependencies to absorb violence and soak up the energies of its enemy.

Resources

Most modern authorities agree that, in the provinces of metropolitan Spain at least, population levels began to rise after the middle decades of the century. The general epidemic of 1647–52 was the last to be caused by a single plague virus, though in the late 1670s heavy mortality was caused by localised outbreaks of various killer diseases (ranging from smallpox to typhus), in the wake of a series of natural disasters. Along with demographic recovery, it is claimed, went a notable improvement in indices of economic activity – particularly in the maritime regions of the peninsula. Certainly, evidence is available for an increase in commercial investment across a limited range of trades involving the businessmen of Barcelona; there was an augmentation of manufacture both in Catalonia and the Basque country; furthermore, some diversification of both trade and agriculture impacted a new (if not dramatic) element of resilience to Spanish economic structures. There was a partial resurgence of native capitalism, which may have been stimulated by access to government contracts and funds, and even (though this is conjecture) to specie (C2).

These changes encouraged, and were in turn further stimulated by, a greater initiative in central government. From the 1670s on – a period when the European economy as a whole was moving out of depression – we can see the rise of a bureaucratic group in Madrid which took an interest in improved economic administration. Various juntas were set up which were overtly 'departmental' and vocational in nature, and were only loosely related to the traditional conciliar system. There were energetic attempts to ameliorate the burden of taxation upon the non-privileged sectors of society, and to rationalise the regional trade regulations which impeded the creation of a unitary home market. The massive deflation of 1680 was actually planned (and successfully), to create the conditions for a permanent reform of the coinage. The coming of political leaders who were more prime ministers (at least in the contemporary English sense) than royal *validos*, though it proved an ephemeral phase, was also helpful. There was even – and this might be blasphemously regarded as the greatest miracle of all – a more critical attitude towards the Church. It was significant that most of these reforms were not conceived nor attempted purely in order to increase the efficiency of the war effort. In this sense, they were different in nature from earlier projects. Some historians have detected in all this a distinct anticipation of Bourbon reforms in political economy, and even a whiff of the enlightened Spain of the late eighteenth century (D2/II).

Such opinions are perhaps rather extreme. The developments of this period fell far short of a true revival, and to speak of a take-off or boom in the economy would be clearly absurd. To some extent, its scattered and sporadic statistical evidence can even be offset by figures which give contrary indications. Doubtless we ought to consider its potential significance in terms of previous trends, of slightly better living standards, even of different mental attitudes. But it is also the case that the process was sporadic (at best) and susceptible to reversal. The demographic recovery of the crown of Aragon was real and important, but the case for a similar movement in Castile is weak and depends upon the interpretation of figures for urban population, never a reliable guide to overall trends (B2). Whatever conclusions are eventually reached as a result of future research, the economic condition of the peninsula – as opposed to its fundamental structures – made little difference to the international destiny of the monarchy. As I have tried to suggest, the relationship between economic viability and power politics (or, if you like, war performance) was not as definitive as modern writers automatically assume. Just as Spain's economic failures and insufficiencies did not, except by an immensely long process of attrition, affect her ability to defend her hegemony, so the delayed and partial recovery of the period after 1670 could not help her to regain it.

This can be observed at the most basic level in the continuing problems of recruitment for the armed forces: 'What they may do in the provinces I know not, but I have seen in Madrid that in four months they have not, with all their diligence, been able to get 1,000 men, though they are beating the drums every day; for as fast as new ones come in, the former run away.'[7] Thus the gloomy report of Alexander Stanhope, ambassador of Spain's ally William III of England, concerning attempts to raise levies for the campaign of 1694. In raising (or rather failing to raise) an army for the defence of Catalonia, the government had threatened to *quintear el reyno*, that is forcibly to conscript every fifth man of military age – an operation which was in fact quite beyond its powers. If anything, things *were*, as the ambassador hoped, slightly better in the provinces. During the war of 1683–4 (for example) five complete *tercios* were raised in Galicia, Vizcaya and Andalusia, and at least 2,500 men were safely ferried to Flanders. The Catalans, whose lands were invaded repeatedly, responded by raising men on a scale which surprised both Paris and Madrid. In Flanders itself, the military administration at last abandoned the policy of trying to defend every inch of ground and every fortified town. By the stripping of garrisons (including some still in position on the frontier with the United Provinces) a field army of some 30,000 became available during the war of 1688–97. In an effort to augment this further, continuous negotiations proceeded with various German princes for the hire of small mercenary armies at exorbitant rates. In *Estado* (early 1684) it was noted that 'we have paid over 150,000 *reales* to German sources in the past few months, on the understanding that they would put 12,000 men on to the Rhine, which still has not been done. These persons are so unreliable that the Marquis of Grana [governor in Brussels] will have to look elsewhere even if it is more expensive'.[8]

In Milan, the Count of Fuensalida faced a similar predicament, finding himself with a force of 10,000 men – an indication, this, that the recruiting grounds of Naples were at last exhausted. Nevertheless, it was the relative rather than the absolute aspects of the manpower crisis which were crucial in the wars against Louis XIV. Even had Spain been able to maintain her traditional levels of recruitment, the enormous development of the French war-machine would still have overtaken her. Men like Le Tellier and Louvois had vastly increased, not only the average size of operational armies (to some 60,000, thrice the numbers of the Thirty Years' War) but also their quantity of equipment and firepower. It was the atomised dispersal of Spain's armed forces which now crucially counted against her. In terms of artillery and small arms, as well as men, Spain could only compete in the northern European theatre, where her allies made up the shortfall. Elsewhere, the ubiquitous lack of *matériel de guerre* was pitiful; Madrid could never find suitable sources of guns and powder, horses and uniforms to supply her Mediterranean defences against an enemy whose prosecution of war was becoming ever more sophisticated, technological and destructive. The tools of campaign still manufactured in one or two places in Spain were obsolescent by the time of the Nine Years' War. The deployment of artillery and the introduction of the bayonet rendered the pike archaic. In the rapidly developing field of ballistics, Spain's capacity (never great) had ceased to exist altogether. It is notable, too, that the development of fortification- and siege-techniques by Vauban literally undermined one of Spain's few remaining areas of military expertise. In 1692, a survey of peninsular defences revealed that although half a million men were officially listed as of military age in Castile, less then 60,000 'muskets and arquebuses' were available to arm them. In Olmedo, a typical 'Home Guard' dilemma existed, with only eleven weapons in the arsenal to be shared between a militia force of 300! Spain had become, in the words of a Genoese envoy, 'an open field, with hardly a gate or fence to prevent the intrusion of the enemy'.[9]

It is not surprising, therefore, that the Spanish infantry of this period was usually pushed off the field of battle by the sheer weight of numbers and guns. All the same, the fighting qualities of the *tercios* were still recognised, by the allocation of the place of honour on the right wing of the allied armies, where they invariably proved (as, for example, at Fleurus, Steenkirke and also Marsala in Italy) the last regiments to crack. In 1684, the constable of Castile, the irascible old warhorse Velasco, fulminated to the Council of State, 'only one thing can restore the discipline and reputation of our arms, and that is to punish any lapse from them with the greatest rigour. The French infantry used to be the worst in Europe, and has become the best mainly by the improvement in their officer material'.[10] The implied slur against the quality of command and comportment was, in fact, less justified than it had been in the 1660s, during the hopeless campaigns against Portugal. Moreover, when it came to the immemorial enemy of the Spanish Christian kingdoms, all the old zeal and courage came flooding back. During the lull of campaigning in western Europe following the Treaty of Ratisbon, the Count of Oropesa raised an army of 12,000 in Spain to be sent to the aid of the Empire against the Turks – purely by voluntary enlistment. The mortal danger posed to the Catholic states of eastern Europe by the Ottoman assault had an amazing effect on Spaniards; two dukes and seven marquises 'took the cross', in Hungary, along with (for example) sixty artisans from Barcelona. In 1688 they bore the brunt of the attack on the key Turkish citadel of Buda, and, according to the imperial commander 'distinguished themselves so much above all the other nations that I cannot find words sufficient to congratulate Your Majesty on their courage, quality, and spirit. Without their contribution, Buda would still be in the hands of the infidel.'[11]

The overall financial position of the crown in this period is virtually a closed book. In the current pitiable state of work on later Habsburg Spain, it is unwise even to guess at the size of revenue and the budget for defence. On the basis of recent investigations of silver returns from America, we may tentatively assume that (on paper) the former was even higher than in the closing years of Philip IV's reign. The dichotomy between the figures for silver imports and the continued desperation of the crown's financial officials is more apparent than real. Even during the 1590s – the previous highest decade for silver imports, and when the royal share was almost certainly much greater – the Treasury had protested its indigence *ad nauseam*. Most of the *donativos* sought (usually in vain) by the king from his noble subjects were intended to defray his own domestic expenses, for which budget provision was always improvised. Such costs escalated considerably after the death of Philip IV, partly through the duplication of establishments to cater for the needs of the queen dowager, partly through the uncontrolled multiplication and peculation of court officials. Even had the king commanded the authority to do so, he could hardly justify forced loans or expropriations for this purpose, as earlier governments had done to surmount crises in defence expenditure. Carlos was occasionally advised that, instead of begging assistance from the conciliar aristocracy, he should simply reclaim the debts which these families owed the crown – 7 million ducats in capital since the start of the reign, according to an estimate of 1691.

One may conjecture that part of the problem of war financing was that despite the increase in totals, the royal proportion of specie remittances from the Indies was contracting. An increasing amount of royal credit was being reclaimed at source in the colonies, whilst the large-scale alienation of revenue, regalian and territorial rights in the Americas which marked the middle decades of the century was now having its effect. The notable revival of commercial activity in Europe, in which Mediterranean entrepôts shared if only in a secondary capacity, may also have attracted potential investment away from the crown's debt into more profitable fields. Whatever the reason, the problem of raising *asientos de dinero* was more intense, and the conditions more onerous, than ever before. The state no longer enjoyed the virtual monopoly of large-scale credit facilities which it had during the long phase of general depression. In 1691, the Genoese bankers achieved a tawdry apotheosis as financial agents of the crown when the head of the Grillo House, almost the last survivor of his species, was elevated to the *grandeza* for a consideration of 300,000 silver *reales*, needed for the emergency defence of Milan. The outcry at court was so great that only two years later the family was crushed by the arbitrary confiscation of all its reserves. The Genoese epoch thus came to an end after 150 years, and for the time being much of the crown's credit machinery reverted to Spanish (especially Catalan) hands. But in any case, Madrid could no longer manage, or even perhaps afford, the regular transfer of major sums in exchange bills from Seville to Antwerp. About this time Stanhope observed: 'The present exigencies of this monarchy are inconceivable. Most of the bills they have sent for Flanders have been lately sent back protested . . . I am assured . . . that upon no branch [of revenue] can be found a credit for 100,000 ducats, be the occasion ever so urgent.'[12]

Continual attempts were made to overhaul the cumbrous financial machinery. Under Don Juan, a reform of the military budget was suggested in which liquid revenue estimates were arranged under categories, ranging from the 'certain' to the 'doubtful', and eliminating all bad (that is, already mortgaged) areas of income. When *Hacienda* objected, it was firmly reminded that policy was the concern of *Estado* and that it should stick to its job of 'making provision for the money supplies which are necessary for our operations by land and sea, ambassadorial expenses, and subsidies to our allies'.[13] But in the event, little was done to alter the time-honoured situation in which no rational planning of expenditure was possible. Both revenue and outlay priorities and methods were merely tinkered with under Medinaceli and Oropesa. The latter did manage a pruning of royal commitments in favours to its dependants – an unimaginably vast deadweight – but this was mainly at the expense of the smaller and less well-connected beneficiaries of the crown's welfare system. In general, financial administration remained a sticky morass, by which even the energies and vision of the Bourbon experts were to be dragged down in the next century.

Policy

The period enjoyed by Don Juan José at the head of Spanish government was quickly prorogued. Less than a year after his triumphant entry into Madrid, his control of affairs was weakened by serious illness. By the winter of 1678–9, direction had reverted to the councils, whilst the prince who had waited and schemed so long for his reward entered a prolonged death agony. During his effective twelve months of power, he devoted great energy to revindicating his personal reputation (down to the most trivial issue of wounded pride) and to revenging himself on his enemies. As well as the preparation of proscription lists and the accumulation of titles and offices, it seems nevertheless possible that he also gave a new impetus to policy. These years certainly saw a positive attempt at constructing a basis of progressive relations with France, a desire which now became respectable in court and government. If such speculation is justified, then the prince's rule was not entirely the non-event pictured by most historians of the period. John Dunlop, a writer admittedly of the romantic age, saw Don Juan as 'the bravest, the most accomplished, and most learned of his race', bewailing his early death as a great blow to the monarchy.[14] But according to Maura, when he died in the autumn of 1679, 'the man who shortly before had been idolised, disappeared amongst indifference' (E20/I).

Long before this event, the beaten party of 1676, men like the Count of Monterrey and the constable of Castile, had regrouped around the queen mother to plan for the new situation. In the early months of 1680, this group of conciliar grandees produced the first candidate for political leadership who was, in any meaningful sense, appointed by consultation and consensus. It was supremely ironic that this 'prime minister', the Duke of Medinaceli, should have followed on the heels of Spain's first 'military dictator' who came to power through a violent coup. Medinaceli was a rich Andalusian nobleman, chosen in competition with Velasco. Very aptly as the representative of the higher aristocracy, his character more closely resembled that of Don Luis de Haro, where his rival was considered as temperamentally similar to

Olivares. In the present state of knowledge on the politics of the reign, estimating his influence on policy is no more than a lottery, though he certainly made little impression (for what it was by now worth) on the Council of State. Moreover, his period in office coincided with the rise of three other luminaries who emerged by more traditional methods. Jerónimo de Eguía had been a prominent bureaucratic functionary even during the Valenzuela period, but he seems to have come to dominate the administration after 1678. As *Secretario del Despacho Universal* – a kind of permanent under-secretary of state – Eguía managed to inject dynamism into the new juntas, acting as co-ordinator and liaison officer between committees and ministers. By the time of his death in 1684, he had significantly resuscitated the power of the secretariat, and himself was perhaps the most influential civil servant since the time of Francisco los Cobos under Charles V. He was succeeded by two equally dynamic men, who, at least until the ending of the prime ministerial 'experiment' in 1690, supervised a series of successful reforms. Given the moribund condition of the conciliar system, staffed as it was by a collection of somnolent geriatrics like the Duke of Alba (aged 78) and the Count of Povar (80), this revival of professional expertise in government was a significant, even if ephemeral, development. Of the old councils, one historian remarks that 'it would be difficult to imagine another group of state governors who were more decrepit or more divided' (E22). Alongside this anachronistic shadow now existed an embryonic new system. The fact that its reforms were undertaken for their own sake and not, as in previous periods, under the pressure of war, seems a significant novelty. For the first time the mainstream of Spanish history lay elsewhere than in the prosecution of war.

For the other new influences referred to above, we must turn from the inherent promise of these administrative changes to the more sterile and operatic world of palace intrigue. The queen mother had found a new adviser to replace the two *privados* sequestered by Don Juan José. This time she reverted to the cloth, in the person of the ambitious and energetic Archbishop of Toledo, Cardinal Portocarrero. The faction politics of the succession question were now beginning to crystallise. The imperialist cause (for which these two formed a nucleus) was for the time being eclipsed by that of the Francophiles. Don Juan's initiative in diplomacy, and particularly the influence of the new queen, gave the latter party a position approximate to that of a ruling interest. To Mariana's intense chagrin, María Luisa quickly displaced her from the affections of the weak-minded Carlos, and political ascendancy over the king was reinforced wherever necessary by the bottomless purse of Versailles. In the early 1680s, this group ensured that Spain would not seek new alliances in

Europe in a sense inimical to French interests; in addition, favourable economic concessions were made to the French. Both could be easily justified as being in line with the policy of reform and retrenchment at home. Nevertheless, elsewhere at court the degradation of bending to Versailles was keenly felt.

In the event, the progress made by Louis XIV's supporters in Madrid was vitiated by his own precipitate action against Luxembourg in 1683. At first the Spaniards, in view of their diplomatic isolation, hesitated to declare war. Carlos himself was against a violent response in this, the first crisis in which we can detect his personal participation. In charge at Brussels, however, was a governor (the Marquis of Grana) who had previously been the imperial ambassador to Madrid. Grana, not unlike Monterrey in 1672, began military action on his own initiative and before orders from Madrid could forestall him. The move can be interpreted as in the interests of his Austrian master rather than in those of Spain. Rhineland security was Vienna's problem, but resistance to Louis from that quarter was precluded by the Ottoman attack. Be this as it may, the monarchy was once more plunged into war as a result of the possession of Flanders. The *damnosa hereditas* still afflicted the fortunes of Spain as strongly as ever, if in a sense different from that which had before obtained. The events of 1683 perhaps illustrate the passing of Belgium into the ambit of Vienna, a generation before this was made official at the Treaty of Utrecht. Indeed, the hiving-off of the obedient provinces in a way which would both save the crippling expenses of their maintenance and immunise Madrid from the strategic liability they represented (first suggested twenty years early by Peñaranda) was often discussed, but no satisfactory arrangement could be arrived at. Grana's initiative was sternly criticised in the Council of State, but little could prevent a war – the ruthless prosecution of which by Louis XIV also helped the Austrian cause by discrediting the Madrid Francophiles. The queen desperately attempted to control Carlos's feelings by a series of pretended pregnancies, acutely satirised in a popular squib:

> Give birth, beautiful fleur-de-lys,
> Since Spain has so many woes,
> That should you deliver, you save us from our foes,
> But if not, you give us to Paris. (E22)

Nevertheless, the Austrian faction revived, so much so that it retained its hold on power until almost the end of the reign. The war, and the humiliating Treaty of Ratisbon, played a part in the removal of Medinaceli from the premiership in 1685–6, and his replacement by the Count of Oropesa. In practice, neither man seems to have been instrumental in the making of the monarchy's defence policy – such as it had now become – though the latter did help to rebuild the bridges with Vienna, a move consequent upon the reversion to traditional attitudes in Madrid, in the second half of the decade.

The traditional stance was again enunciated by Velasco at the outset of the 1680s: 'I do not disagree with the drift of our negotiations and alliances; but we must not be misled by them into believing that our security depends upon our allies alone. Such an unreliable maxim would cause us to abandon our own military commitments in Flanders, a move which we should certainly regret in the future.'[15] Despite many vicissitudes, the Habsburgs never really betrayed this apparently unrealistic counsel. The king's conscience, and the deeply rooted prejudices of his ministers, demanded the maintenance of Flanders, so long as it remained the moral responsibility of the dynasty. On the other hand, it seemed that the best manner of satisfying the prescription was to steer clear of entangling alliances altogether, a policy upon which both sides in the faction context could passively agree. It was in this spirit that the decision to remain on the sidelines was taken in 1688, when Madrid resisted the pressure of The Hague and Vienna to join the new anti-French coalition. Not for the last time, however, events turned on dynastic conjuncture – that of the death of María Luisa, depriving the French party of its sheet-anchor, with the accession of William III in England, bringing that country into the war against Louis. The former was acclaimed by the Austrian ambassador as 'an amazing miracle for the house of Habsburg' (E22) – so much so (indeed) that accusations of foul play were prolific. The latter provided the hope (as a Spanish envoy in London observed) 'of the restoration of all France's usurpations, and – if God wills it – a just vengeance for the horrible insults and injustices offered to our crown'.[16]

As we have seen, such optimism was not justified. In both a military and a material sense, the Nine Years' War proved an unmitigated and prolonged torture for the Spanish monarchy. One disastrous campaign was enough to bring about the fall of Oropesa, who was succeeded by a commission, a new *Junta de Gobierno*. This was the end of the prime ministerial experiment. It was true that the junta was dominated by the Duke of Montalto, an outspoken critic of the war; and that, by 1692, ministers were searching for a convenient release from the new commitment. In the autumn of 1693, *Estado* noted that 'it has become not only timely but urgent to finish with a war which had been so fatal to us'.[17] The operation was, however, fraught with difficulty. For a start, neither the council nor the junta was, in reality, in control of affairs. Government had now been effectively usurped by yet another queen, the German harridan Maria Anna of Neuburg, with whom the Austrian interest had replaced María Luisa. With her to Spain she brought a huge retinue of adventurers, who (like many indigenous politicians) were in the allies' pay and charged with keeping Spain in the war at all costs. The locust-like rapaciousness of this gang was ultimately counter-productive, alienating the conciliar aristocracy who discovered a spurious unity in resistance to it. But in the meantime, actual power had moved from 'government' to 'court'. In this sordid series of international matches, it is true that Carlos himself played little more of a role than the football. However, despite his total lack of personal will, he does seem to have occasionally performed his allotted routine, and in the first few years of the war actually attended *Estado* and considered its documentation.[18]

Though men like Montalto occasionally succeeded in persuading the king to support a bid for a unilateral peace with France, he seldom kept to his resolve for long. Furthermore, the intelligence system of the queen and her allies provided them with the ability to monitor and even to sabotage the decisions of the junta. As the decade of disaster wore on Montalto received help from a peculiar and unprecedented source. The scandalous excesses of the German camarilla assisted the rise of a group of Madrid patricians who formed a powerful peace lobby called 'The Company of the Seven Just Men'. It was led by Don Francisco Ronquillo, *corregidor* of Madrid, and seems to have held proto-enlightened views on social policy – indeed, they can, in anticipation of a later age, be called *afrancesados*, men dedicated to administrative reform and the French succession. Ronquillo succeeded in invigorating the government of the capital, curbing the behaviour of the aristocracy, reducing taxes, and struggling to introduce regular and fairly priced food supplies. In the 1690s, he was fast becoming a popular tribune, which, in view of the increased political importance of Madrid and its population, represented a threat to the Austrian-dominated court. Despite the covert support of Montalto, therefore, Ronquillo was removed from his office in 1695.

Carlos's health had now declined to the stage where the difference between life and death became merely a medical (and, of course, theological) statistic. The battle lines were firmly drawn between the factions. The continuing predominance of the imperialists was illustrated by the events of 1696. In that year, three of the five major coalition partners (England, the Dutch republic, and Savoy), suddenly negotiated secret deals with France, leaving the Habsburgs high and dry. The emperor's interest in the Spanish succession kept him in the war but the (official) Madrid government in no way felt bound to stand at his side. 'Since we have no force or authority of our own', commented one member of *Estado*, 'we will have to be content with the terms the English and Dutch obtain for us'. Montalto strongly agreed: 'I have been pointing out for years that the settlement of this war will be that which our allies, not our enemies, will impose upon us. This being so, it is meaningless to lay down conditions in this body, since our hopeless condition makes us unable to fight for them.'[19] Thus the Olympian Council of State, charged by its founder Charles V with managing the general affairs of a universal monarchy, and which had long decided the fate of nations, recognised its own bankruptcy and obsolescence. It seems appropriate therefore that the decision was taken outside the council chamber. The triumvirate of Maria Anna, Portocarrero, and Harrach (the imperial ambassador) persuaded Carlos to support Vienna. Thus the war was continued for another year – as it proved, the last campaign of the Spanish-Habsburg monarchy.

It was during this period, as the French again rolled into Catalonia, capturing Barcelona with contemptuous ease, that Carlos II drew up the first instrument of succession. He bequeathed the monarchy, entire and inviolate, to neither of the main pretenders, but to the Bavarian candidate, the Wittelsbach prince, Joseph, infant son of Duke Maximilian. The main reason for this compromise choice was in order to avoid the major European war (certain to end in the truncation and division of the inheritance) which any other would bring about. In one sense, it was confirmation of the direction indicated when, some years earlier, Maximilian himself had been granted what amounted to sovereign powers in the Spanish Netherlands. Paradoxically, however, it tended to reaffirm the association of Castile and Flanders, to maintain, at this ultimate stage of its existence, the link with northern Europe forged by another south German prince two centuries earlier, and which had always been the basis of the Spanish system. When Portocarrero, main advocate of the Bavarian succession, officially proclaimed it to the people of Madrid it was greeted with demonstrations of popular joy and relief. This was evidence of the anomalous, even contradictory, feelings of most Castilians about the empire which they had done so much to sustain. They may have wished to be free of the Habsburg dynasty – *las Austrias* as they continued to be called, long after they had become thoroughly naturalised – and of the heritage of purposeless suffering which commitment to its cause involved. But, at the same time, they hoped, with almost equal fervour, to protect the monarchy, the so-called 'seamless garment' (a metaphor referring to the robe of Christ at Calvary) from blasphemous division by the centurions. At any rate, the stratagem failed of its object. The premature death of the Bavarian infante early in 1699 faced Spain with simple alternatives, either of which involved the virtually certain dismemberment of the empire.

There is no need to recapitulate the detailed and confused history of its death agony. The key development in the matter of policy – which now had become a question of the best way to wind up the Spanish system – was the defection of Portocarrero to the French side. This was a consequence of the Madrid riots of May 1699, which convinced the cardinal of Castile's alienation from *las Austrias* (see below, pp. 193–4). Like Montalto and Ronquillo, Portocarrero was now persuaded that the power of France, joined with and infused into the monarchy, could save it from ultimate dissolution and maybe revolution, too. Even at the cost of subordination to Versailles, such an option had to be embraced. After a bitter and sordid struggle the cardinal eventually defeated the queen – the eternal sanction of the Church overwhelming that of his earthly partner in the soul of the dying Carlos. The German hangers-on were cleared out of court and kingdom. Government reasserted itself. In September 1700, Portocarrero obtained the required majority for the Bourbon succession (by seven votes to three) in the Council of State. 'Ya no soy nada – now I am as nothing', Carlos is reputed to have said on signing the fateful document. This was not quite so. Though he had at last made Spain over to the great enemy of his House, he did so in conformity with his conscience (that intangible but living organism which was the foundation of policy) and at the same time satisfied the wishes of the Castilians. These facts were rightly recognised by Louis XIV, the new master of Castile's destiny, in the declaration by which he accepted the testament of Carlos II shortly after the latter's death in November 1700.[20]

Attitudes

'The King of France stands in a good window' was how one Spanish minister described Louis XIV's position in the matter of the succession, shortly after the death of Philip IV in 1665.[21] The image neatly conveyed France's geographical, and thus strategic, advantages in any race for power in Madrid. At that time, the sheer physical potential of Spain's neighbour was not fully appreciated. All the same, more than thirty years later, having forced admittance through windows, doors and skylights – always having to retire in varying states of discomfiture or frustration – Louis, now himself on the brink of old age, still occupied the same vantage point. Stanhope reported home in 1698:

> The French ambassador has officers in his family [i.e. his retinue], brigadiers, colonels, majors, sufficient to command a little army, whose business cannot be curiosity to see this country, but to be ready for the occasion. They seem already to have besieged Spain both by sea and land, with considerable bodies of troops ready on all the frontiers, and galleys and men o' war expected hourly.[22]

For the Grand Monarch, Spain and its empire was, beyond legal or moral question, the inheritance of his House. Over a generation he had done considerably more than nibble (according to a nice tactical plan) at the territorial edges of the monarchy. There was also a gradual economic and demographic penetration of the peninsula from French sources. Throughout our period, immigration on a seasonal and permanent basis had been going on, especially into the kingdoms of Aragon and Navarre. By the last quarter of the century, there may have been as many as 250,000 *gavachos* (as French emigrants were called). From the 1670s, if not before, the French commercial presence in Spain was a notable feature. On balance, the thrust of French business interests was towards the eminently exploitable market represented by old Spain, rather than the Atlantic area. It is true that the enterprise of French traders at Seville increased steadily. Versailles was, of course, entranced by the prospect of mineral and commercial wealth derived from the American colonies, and during Louis's reign France belatedly entered the colonial stakes both in north America and the Caribbean. In these areas, however, they obtained little encouragement from Madrid, and had to compete on the same terms as the other predators. In 'Old Spain', by contrast, various treaty concessions to France whittled away the position of the maritime powers. By 1700, according to some authorities, they had obtained the lion's share of markets and monopolies on raw materials, despite the confiscations and embargoes which war continually visited upon French capital resources. Spain was of vital importance to the nascent manufacturing industries and financial enterprises of the French economy; the presence of constant government encouragement illustrated the importance to Louis of binding the two countries together. Whatever its indigenous recovery, the Spanish economy had itself become 'colonially' dependent on the dynamic centres of capital and production in northern Europe. In 1670, if not in 1620, she was 'the Indies of Europe'.

But if the Sun King already looked upon the Hispanic world as a mere fief of the empire of Versailles, he was much deceived: Spanish culture and religion was totally unaffected by the waves of influence now emanating from Paris. The ruling class of Castile rejected French customs in manners and dress as contemptuously as they had those of the Dutch in an earlier period. For all her material weakness, Spain was no Rhineland principality, a mere satellite of a dominant cultural centre. The proud obstinacy of the peninsula in such respects seemed in France to be an index of her refusal to become part of the ambit of western civilisation. Attitudes sprang up which regarded Spaniards in terms similar to those employed concerning the Muscovite or the Ottoman – a barbarous and obscurantist, if somewhat exotic, people.

Such prejudices began another chapter in the Black Legend which was to flourish in the period of enlightenment, and produced the Spain of Prosper Mérimée and George Borrow.

The opening of a new chapter did not mean the immediate closing of an old one. As late as 1680 in London, a Mr Dugdale could still produce *A Narrative of unheard of Popish cruelties towards Protestants beyond Seas: or, a New Account of the Bloody Spanish Inquisition published as a caveat to Protestants*. Doubtless the author of this revealing intelligence hoped to profit from the aftermath of the Popish Plot, but in fact he rather misread the mood of the times. By the 1680s, the Spanish ambassador was helping to whip up popular feeling against France, himself utilising language familiar to any English radical. Of course, the recognition by English patriots that France now posed a greater danger to their cherished ideals and interests than ever the Don had done, did not of itself liquidate anti-Spanish feeling, as any student of nineteenth-century attitudes would witness. But during the era of Anglo-French conflict (a phenomenon which was to dominate international affairs for a century and a half) prejudice against Spain retired into the background to become part of the general fabric of English self-identification myth rather than its most sensitive strain. Much the same was true of the Dutch republic, perhaps more intimately linked to Spain in the common struggle against Versailles. In 1677, the States General even permitted its great admiral, Michael de Ruyter (killed shortly afterwards defending the Spanish possessions in Italy) to accept a title of nobility from a grateful Carlos II. The fortunes of the House of Orange were once again based upon collaboration with the Habsburgs; to William III's subjects, whether English or Dutch, Spain was, at worst, the lesser of two evils; to those of Carlos II, the massacre of Irish Catholics was almost pardonable when they were in arms to support the Bourbon cause.

Since the Spanish monarchy, whose continuous struggle to survive is the main concern of these pages, was now at last on the eve of dissolution, the attitudes within its peculiar structure are most deserving of comment. For we can already trace the divergences of interest which were shortly to divide it against itself, and to bring about civil war inside the peninsula. Castile, as we have seen, had had enough of the Habsburgs. Another Thirty Years' War had oppressed the kingdom and her people, at last rising above their incredible level of toleration. In the reign of Carlos II, aristocratic rapaciousness, coupled with official incompetence and disinterest, had reached a peak. Blatant pillage of public and royal resources by Spaniards was surpassed, however, by the rapacity of the queen's German retinue which disgusted all Castilians, privileged and unprivileged alike (E20/II). The failure both of war and reform was ubiquitous. In the spring of 1699, during a food crisis which drove up prices according to an almost annual pattern, the Madrid mob took to the streets. What followed was the most serious and significant urban protest in the peninsula since the revolt of Barcelona in 1640. For several days, the town houses of prominent nobles were attacked, public authority collapsed, and a major insurrection was only averted by the king's concession of the Madrileños' main demand, the reappointment of Ronquillo as *corregidor*. Meanwhile disorder had spread to several other Castilian towns, including Valladolid and Salamanca, where it was suppressed only with considerable bloodshed. These events looked forward to the enthusiastic welcome given by Castile to the Bourbons in 1701. However, the sentiments they embodied were by no means common to all the dependencies of the crown.

According to Domínguez Ortiz, the reign of Carlos II was one in which the demands of central government on the provinces were relaxed, both in the fiscal and political domains.[23] Devolution of autonomy was perhaps a passive result of the prevailing political conditions in Madrid rather than an active policy programme; nevertheless both this and the easing of financial pressure brought with them a considerable access of loyalty to the dynasty. This was particularly notable in regions like Flanders and Catalonia, where the crown's deference to local privileges had been (on the whole) stolidly maintained, and was strengthened by the natural hatred of Bourbon France resulting from constant invasion since the 1660s. Both these provinces accepted as governors members of the Austrian royal family and nobility, and (particularly in the last decade of the century) were defended by many imperial regiments. In Catalonia, in a reversal of what had been the normal pattern of Madrid-Vienna relationships (and was, in effect, a dress-rehearsal for the internecine War of Succession), the Austrian Habsburg viceroy brought with him a German army, constantly reinforced via the Italian route. Both Catalonia and the 'obedient provinces' were regularly and systematically devastated by the 'scorched earth' policy of the French generals. From Brussels regular lists of atrocities ('like those which the Turks commit in Hungary')[24] were sent to Madrid. 'I hope to God', wrote Grana in 1684, 'that the enemy will not produce the effect he imagines, and that the loyalty of these subjects to Your Majesty will not be weakened, but rather strengthened, by the horrors with which they are oppressed.'[25] It seems that Grana's prayer was fully answered. In this period, the Belgians made increasing financial contributions to their own defence, and even offered to forego a Spanish subsidy altogether – a suggestion rejected by Madrid more through the influence of vested interest and peculation than by any desire to maintain political control. During the Nine Years' War, the countryside within a twenty-mile radius of

Brussels was the almost continuous scene of military activity and destruction. The turn of the capital itself came in 1695, when (like Genoa, Alicante, Barcelona, and several other towns) it fell victim to massive bombardment by heavy artillery. Marshal Villeroi's guns reduced much of the city to rubble; yet within a few years the Grande Place was rebuilt in the gilded magnificence of the late baroque style to form one of the architectural glories of present-day Europe. The businessmen of Antwerp and Brussels were still denied access to Spanish markets which were open to their Dutch, French and English competitors. Like those of Catalonia, they had never been permitted to derive benefit from the overseas empire of Castile. Such injustices and anomalies, which must have seemed inexplicable to them, did not diminish the loyalty of the burghers of Brussels. A year or so before the death of the last Habsburg (who refused to relinquish the title of 'Duke of Burgundy', despite the loss of Franche-Comté), the new headquarters of the various merchant guilds were completed in the main square of the city. The imposing façades of these buildings incorporate several testaments to the affections of the citizens for the Habsburg House, including, on the north side of the square, the splendid Maison des Boulangers with its central decoration of Carlos II triumphant over the subject peoples of his vast empire: 'Here the baker has set up the symbols of victory, as monument to the glory of Charles the Second.'

The succession crisis therefore witnessed Flanders and Catalonia pulling away from Castile on the central issue. So also did northern Italy. 'Flanders they look upon as being our concern rather than theirs',[26] commented Stanhope of the Madrid government, and his imperial colleague may have made a similar remark about the Duchy of Milan. Now manned by Austrian troops and administered by Vienna's nominees, Milan was slowly reverting to its imperial overlord. The Milanese, too, preferred the effective autonomy of Habsburg rule to the threat of a neutralised autocracy posed by Versailles. The diminution of Madrid's physical presence permitted other Italian princes to afford the long-lost luxury of prestige – backed up, of course, by their switch to French subsidies. In 1697, for example, the Grand Duke of Tuscany demanded that the galleys of Spain should now salute (that is, strike their flags to) his own in Italian waters. Members of the Council of State were stung with shame, since the Florentine galleys were regarded as a despicable gang of pirates. All the same, they felt it unwise to resist.[27] (Spain's naval power was by now non-existent in any case. Ten years earlier, the Elector of Brandenburg sent his squadron into Ostend harbour unopposed to tow away enough merchant ships to satisfy an unpaid debt.) In contrast to Milan, the kingdom of Naples inclined to the Bourbon solution for the monarchy's problems. It was no accident, surely, that Castile and Naples, the two provinces which elected spontaneously for a change of dynasty, were those most materially exploited by the policy of the Habsburgs. Conversely, of course, neither had yet been actually invaded by the French. It seems true that in the later years of the century, some economic recovery took place in the Regno, and certainly the city was becoming a centre of intellectual and artistic endeavour for the first time in half a millennium. Nevertheless, its patricians welcomed the new Bourbon king when he visited the kingdom shortly after his accession, and long refused (eventually with success) to accept the local victory of the Habsburgs imposed upon them by the powers in 1713.

Despite all internal and external degradation, disorder and defeat, the servants of the crown in Madrid ('the city whom all peoples serve, and who serves none', as one writer put it in 1658 [D4]) continued their functions and routines with all the old distant arrogance of natural superiority. We are now (perhaps) better placed to understand this phenomenon; but our contemporary representative, Stanhope, was perpetually irritated and perplexed by it: 'I relate these instances', he reported to his superior, 'only to give your grace a taste of the temper of these people, who, though reduced to the miserable condition they are in, are yet as haughty as in Charles V's days.'[28] In reality, however, this very characteristic was an asset to the cause of the allies. In 1689, as part of a propaganda campaign aimed at cajoling Spain into joining the anti-French coalition, a pamphlet was published in Cologne, which pointed out that

> . . . although France has dominated over Spain since the death of Philip IV, Carlos II is still master of the monarchy. He still holds the Indies, and his ships come and go every year [sic] stuffed with gold and silver as before. And Spain is the same power as in earlier days caused jealousy and fear amongst European princes, forcing them to join together to survive against her.[29]

Conclusions

In 1699 the old and the new in Castile joined forces to reject the House of Austria. The former was represented by the Church, in the person of the primate of Spain, Portocarrero; the latter by 'The Company of the Seven Just Men', the group of public-spirited *hidalgos* of advanced ideas. Both, in their different ways, were closely in touch with the needs and the feelings of the mass of Castilians. It may always remain impossible to conclude whether these attitudes were for a clean and radical departure from the past – a renunciation of the imperial heritage and 'the Spanish system' – or merely a desire to reinvigorate them with the human and material resources of a new dynasty. What is certain is that the supremely symbolic impotence of Carlos II offered them an alternative (if only a nebulous one) at which they eagerly grasped.

The reign of the last Habsburg had seen a rise in the power of princesses and priests such as Spain had not known since before the inception of the dynasty. In terms of political influence this seems to be as central to the period as the strictly aristocratic revival which most authorities consider its primary feature. True, there was a brief secular interlude under Don Juan José – a period of *machismo*, perhaps, though, to be fair, Spanish historians have little time for the bastard *caudillo*. But even during the decade of 'prime ministerial' government, queens and confessors pulled many of the strings of policy and patronage, whilst in the ultimate decade they emerged openly to dominate affairs of state. Their final struggle for supremacy took the form (as we have seen) of a confrontation over the prone and dying king, the kind of scene familiar from mediaeval chronicles, and irresistible to the romantic novelist. Cardinal Portocarrero was disgusted by the behaviour of Maria Anna and her fortune-hunting crew, assumed the effective leadership of the pro-French faction, and became the single main instrument of the Bourbon succession. With him went the whole Church of Castile, and indeed the official sanction of the Vatican, fearful of the renewed 'universal monarchy' implicit in the claim of the Austrians.

Portocarrero was a competent politician, but hardly an intellectual. According to court innuendo, his library was 'one of the three virgins of Madrid' (the others being the queen, and the sword of the Duke of Medina Sidonia, a notorious coward). Nevertheless he was as important in the conjuncture of 1699–1700 as his great and brilliant predecessor, Cardinal Cisneros, had been in that of two centuries earlier, which saw the foundation of Habsburg rule in Spain. In Carlos's testament, Portocarrero was appointed regent, and charged with the task of securing the monarchy for the new dynasty, which he subsequently carried out with some vigour. One Spanish primate was therefore the funeral director of the Habsburgs, as another had been their midwife, and in this apt way the dynasty departed, as it had arrived, under the robes of Holy Mother Church. The difference was that whereas Cisneros had gone against the mainstream of Castilian opinion, imposing on it the rule of a foreign German court, Portocarrero was swimming with the tide. In a sense, therefore, he took up the banner of the *Comuneros* (hidden away since Villalar) finally rejecting the heritage of Burgundy, with all its connotations of north European involvement, continuous war and continuous exploitation. The long, hopeless and transcendentally painful war of 1690–7, accompanied as it was by the abuses of the Austrian faction in Madrid, focused these issues as never before. The Habsburg dynasty, fighting for a German cause and surrendering its offices and its wealth to Germans, had apparently reverted to type. It seemed sensational testament of how elementally alien and unwanted was everything represented by *las Austrias*. Those chauvinistic sentiments which had always smouldered beneath the surface now emerged and triumphed.

Perhaps here I could be accused of simplifying the issues somewhat in order to make a point. However, the point itself is underlined by the career of Ronquillo, a man from the lower (untitled) ranks of the aristocracy, who became – uniquely, if in a limited context – a successful popular leader. Ronquillo and his *Compañía* had resolutely opposed the war, acting as an organised group where previously the revisionist cause had been advanced by isolated individuals. They had continually impressed on the king that war lay at the root of the structural deprivation of the Castilian masses, with whose symptoms they struggled to cope by reforms in the capital. Again, they were not original minds; most if not all their ideas came from the writings of the *arbitristas*, fused with a desire to imitate French examples. But, if only in the microcosm of Madrid, they did something more than merely write about and discuss improvement. Doubtless they were driven by the increasing pressure of popular discontent, which was becoming unmistakable. The revolt of the *segadores*, the peasants of Catalonia (1688) was followed five years later by a new *germanía* (again evoking memories of the early sixteenth century) in Valencia (G9). Neither of these can be interpreted as a *direct* protest against crown or government but they were certainly directed against the regime of the landowning *señors* whose impositions exacerbated the privations of war. During the decade, harvest failures widened from the sporadic and local to the endemic and general, culminating in the subsistence crisis which sparked off the Madrid riots already described. The anti-aristocratic animus of these latter events was also noticeable; the violence of the mob seemed to concentrate on the person and property of the Count of Oropesa, who was held to be responsible for the war policy of the 1690s. The war itself was over, and Oropesa no longer in office; but he had insinuated himself back to court as an adviser to the Austrian faction, the 'war party' and chief oppressors of the *Madrileños*. He defended himself against his accusers on the grounds that *Estado* as a body had decided to enter the war in 1690, and that the peace (of Rijswick) had been surprisingly favourable to the monarchy. 'Your Majesty's ministers', he complained to Carlos 'had to work hard and make great personal sacrifices to gain such ends.'[30] Such pleas were no longer relevant. Portocarrero, Ronquillo and the people of Madrid concurred in Oropesa's banishment (from whence he eventually defected to the Austrians during the civil war).

Oropesa was thus the last scapegoat of the failure of the Spanish system, unwilling epitome of the Castilian nobility's complaisance in the imperial mission of the Habsburgs notwithstanding the genuine interests of the kingdom. When the Bourbon monarch was greeted with effusive demonstrations of loyalty throughout Castile in the early years of the new century, most of the higher aristocracy continued to nurse profound reservations. Many of them took the opportunity, during the vicissitudes of the civil war, to follow Oropesa, more through a proud unwillingness to accept French control than through an inability to break with the old dynasty. In any case, these factors illustrate the paroxysm of weakness and disunity in which the Spanish monarchy ended its lifespan.

Eighteenth-Century Horizons
1700–20

I thought Spain was on our side. I never expected them to call in the French. (Hensius to William III, 1701)[1]

Now, since Spain by a revolution as mysterious as surprising, is wholly at the devotion of France, her ancient enemy, and Madrid seems to be entirely governed by directions from Versailles, perhaps, if due care is not taken to prevent it, a new spirit may arise in their councils, and from thence animate the huge but disjointed members of their government. (Preface to *Hispania Illustrata*, 1703)

Hardly had the new era got under way than the essential paradox of Spain and its European power was made manifest. The country which had dominated the Continent for two centuries, and had in the process exhausted and ruined itself, was now invaded by Europe in return. In an apocalypse worthy of the pen of Gibbon, all Spain's enemies, allies and auxiliaries – regiments of Dutch, French, English, Austrians, Walloons, Portuguese and Italians – met on the battlefields of the peninsula to decide the destiny of the monarchy. The War of Succession, a decade of internal torment, was the last legacy of Habsburg imperialism to the Castile which it had annexed, transfigured and ultimately damned. Louis XIV's acceptance of Carlos II's testament involved the rupture of his formal partition agreements with the European powers. Louis was (after all) a descendant of Charles V; the observation of his higher dynastic obligations was a categorical imperative which overrode the mere functional legality of treaties. Furthermore, it is unlikely that he ever seriously intended to fulfil the crucial caveat in the instrument of succession by which Carlos had made a last feeble attempt to avert such a war. It is hardly necessary to know whether Louis ever made the celebrated statement concerning the disappearance of the Pyrenees. He could not be dictated to by the dead king of a moribund realm that 'this crown and that of France shall ever remain sundered'.[2] Louis may by now have recognised that he personally would never enjoy the apotheosis to which his life's work had been addressed. But the heirs of his body, through the union of France and Spain, would be able to make good a claim to the empire of the west which would eclipse the memory of any earlier pretender, Charles V included.

When Louis's adolescent grandson entered Spain as Philip V, he therefore was accompanied by a multitalented team of soldiers and bureaucrats whose task was to mould the institutions of the kingdom into shapes by which they could neatly fit into those of France. Eve was to be created (or recreated) from the rib of Adam. Doubtless it would have proved difficult to reproduce in every detail the administrative foundations of Bourbon greatness, even had the situation remained stable. In fact, before the first year of Philip's reign was out, Austria and the maritime powers had declared war in defence of their various vital interests in the Hispanic world. French armies were ready in strength on all the key borders of the monarchy. In 1701, they swiftly occupied the Spanish Netherlands, installing in Brussels what was effectively a French puppet government. A similar move was made towards Milan, passage for which was demanded and obtained from the authorities in Turin. Little wonder that the allied powers asserted 'That it is now the case that the fates of the kingdoms of France and Spain are so intimately bound up in each other that it will not be realistic henceforth to think of them save as one and the same, a single, unified, realm.'[3]

The new century thus began as the old had ended, to the familiar strain of international war, in this case soon to become internal rebellion and civil war. Even before the allies intervened in the peninsula, in order to make good the Austrian claim to the succession, Louis's nominees were firmly in the saddle at Madrid. The French ambassador, Marsin, took the role of chief adviser to the government of the young Philip. The Princess des Ursins, governess to the even younger queen, became a formidable arbiter in the hardly less important sphere of the court. Child monarchs, ruled by women and diplomats – in most key respects the conditions of the 1690s were duplicated, only this time in France's interests instead of Austria's. The native nobility, equally usurped, quickly became equally resentful. But the prolonged emergency which developed after 1704 allowed the *Versaillis* steadily to tighten their grip, making themselves indispensable to every aspect of affairs. During the vicissitudes of the prolonged military campaigns, the constant disloyalties and desertions of the Castilian aristocracy enabled the Bourbons to clear them out of the conciliar system. Without the stiffening of noble prestige and obstinacy, the archaic structure at last collapsed, a boon which allowed the creation of a handful of permanent streamlined juntas which took its place. This quiet revolution went some way towards the achievement of a professional and department-based system, and it undoubtedly contributed towards the ultimate victory of the Bourbons in the military struggle. On the other hand, it represented the only solid success of the team of reforming civil servants which Louis had sent to Madrid. Broadly speaking, the prior needs of war and political survival persistently frustrated the worthy schemes of improvement and rationalisation. Even during the interludes of firmer control, the Bourbons had to strive against the intractability of Spanish law and custom – the *fuerza de costumbre* as it had been called in Olivares's day. In any case, Louis XIV was too experienced to ignore reality:

> It is to be wished [he instructed Marsin] that one could carry out a general alteration in all the different states of the Monarchy. But as this idea is too vast, you must try as far as possible to remedy the most pressing evils, and think principally of enabling the King of Spain to contribute in some way to the war that I am preparing to endure. (G6)

Sure enough, plans for reform of government and economy were to assume a low priority until well into the eighteenth century, despite some piecemeal successes. Indeed, in many ways, the period from the late 1670s to the late 1740s has a unity which partly distinguishes it from 'imperial Spain' and the Spain of the Enlightenment; a twilight era of struggle between two incompatible mores.

King Louis's belief that Spanish resources could be a great asset to his war effort was an unconscious (though also, characteristic) tribute to the former of these two Spains. In practice, however, the golden fleece was a leaden chain around his neck. During the decade 1702–12, the Bourbon succession was a fragile and precarious entity. Whilst Italy resisted French occupation and Flanders chafed under it, the allies prepared a series of huge offensives against the new French empire. In 1705, following the recruitment of Portugal to their ranks and the capture of Gibraltar, expeditionary forces landed (almost simultaneously) at Málaga, Valencia and Barcelona. Catalonia, instinctively Francophobe since the experience of the 1640s, declared for the Habsburgs, and the whole of the Levant was in allied hands within a short space. By 1707, all Spain's Mediterranean provinces (including the African *presidios*) acknowledged the rule of Carlos III, younger brother of the Austrian emperor. The year before, Madrid itself had been taken and occupied for several months by allied forces (an event which recurred as late as 1710); at which point Philip V retained control only of Cadiz amongst the major cities of Spain. Hard pressed by Marlborough in the Low Countries and by Eugene in Lombardy, Louis could ill afford the commitment of valuable regiments in the peninsula. Beginning in 1706, a series of allied victories all along the continental frontiers of France, from Flanders to Savoy, reduced him to desperate straights. Instead of France breathing new life into her Spanish partner, it seemed that the reverse had happened, for military defeat was accompanied by a terrible subsistence crisis in both kingdoms. In France herself, internal chaos was exacerbated by the onset, in 1709, of Europe's last great plague epidemic. Louis was forced to withdraw his troops from Spain and to open negotiations with the allies. The extent of his plight can be measured from his offer to assist them with the reduction of Castile, so long as it did not involve actual declaration of war upon his own grandson. At this juncture, the Habsburg return to their ancient inheritance seemed nothing less than inevitable. Castile stood alone in support of a cause which even its progenitor had deserted.

Despite his youth, Philip V had rapidly come (like all his predecessors) to appreciate the primary importance of his Castilian provinces. Though he made early errors, he learnt from them in setting himself quite deliberately to become the Most Catholic King. He succeeded in this task even to the point of acquiring the conservative fatalism of *las Austrias* in his later years. In 1704, he appealed to the profound religious inspiration of the ordinary Castilian in declaring the war to be a crusade against the enemies of the Faith. In subsequent years, Bourbon propaganda constantly harped upon the irreligion of the allies, as a conspiracy to subvert Catholicism in which both Germans and Portuguese joined.[4] By a neat reversal of roles, the Bourbons now became the pristine defenders of orthodoxy and Christendom, the Habsburgs and their heretic supporters its opportunistic adversaries. The occupation of every Castilian village by the Protestant soldiery of the allies was made an occasion for exaggerated report and outrage. 'Our Holy Faith', announced Philip with the news of the victory of Almansa in 1707, 'has been cleansed of those who would attempt to sully her.'[5] The local clergy (encouraged by Rome) stimulated everywhere in Castile a spirit of fanatical resistance to the invader, who as a result was never able to gain a firm foothold within its borders. Castile's desertion of the old dynasty was total. Its inhabitants endured for a decade the constant ravages of war, rural dislocation and privation on a massive scale, culminating in the awful winters and harvest failures of 1708–10. Yet over and again they rallied to the counter-attack, even when Flanders and Italy had been lost, when the capital was in enemy hands, and their coastlines surrounded by hostile fleets. It was as convincing a testament to their qualities as anything in history, yet somehow it remains less evocative to the extra-peninsular imagination than the heroic exploits of Catalans or Basques.

During this ordeal, the people of Castile remained, in their perverse way, as opposed to the French as they were to their enemies in the field. Louis XIV's control of Spanish policy came to an end virtually overnight with his physical abandonment of the struggle in 1709, when French troops and functionaries were pulled out of the peninsula. This, in fact, proved to be a temporary lapse, and before the end of the following year, they had returned in strength. Doubtless the turn of the military tide for the final time in these campaigns (above all at Brihuega in 1710) would have been impossible otherwise. But the effect on Philip V was traumatic and represented the coming-of-age of his independence. He emancipated himself inexorably from Louis's paternalism, strongly reasserting native interests in the administrative and economic life of Spain. Ministers of Philip's choice moved into the key positions of state, whilst the setting up of a new *Junta de Comercio* rapidly reduced the level of French economic exploitation. In the negotiations which settled the War of Succession (beginning in 1711) the French position was as irretrievably lost as that of the Austrians. In the Treaty of Utrecht, Louis was obliged once more to detach himself from his grandson's cause, and his death two years later removed altogether the spectre of the Frenchified Spain. Meanwhile, the interventionist powers also abandoned the conflict. Foreign soldiery on both sides now withdrew, and the army which finally reduced the recalcitrant city of Barcelona, last ironic outpost of Habsburg Spain, was a purely Castilian one. Ten years after Philip V had declared war on the allies, the civil war came to an end.

The peninsular war, however, had been only one theatre (and hardly the most important) of an international struggle of global dimensions. During the continental campaigns, Flanders had been taken from Spain by conquest, whilst an effectively similar result was ordained by northern Italy's successful resistance to the French. Louis had used the Spanish Netherlands as a kind of small-scale proving ground for the radical reform he ultimately intended for the whole monarchy, but the Flemish guinea-pigs reacted strongly, and at length assisted Marlborough to get rid of the French. At Utrecht in 1713, they gratefully exchanged the iron yoke of Versailles for the ermine collar of Vienna. Flanders thus reverted to its Habsburg allegiance, and (like Milan) to the authority which had been its strictly legal overlord all along – the Holy Roman Empire. In this way the northern dimension of Spanish policy was at last eliminated for good and all, and with the disappearance of the Brussels–Milan axis the Spanish system, too, vanished. Neither of the primary parties, however, was prepared inwardly to accept the verdict of the peace treaties, imposed by the congress of European statesmen as the solution to the Spanish problem. The putative Carlos III, emperor since 1711, retained a passionate, if informal, claim to the Spanish kingdoms. During the great Austrian artistic revival which marked his rule in Vienna, this was asserted through the ubiquitous use of the symbol of the pillars of Hercules in painting, printing and architecture. (A vestigial relic of Habsburg Spain can be observed today in the US dollar sign, derived as it is from the Austrian *thaler*.)

Philip V, for his part, was even more active in defying the settlement which put an end to Spain's European empire. By this, Naples and Sicily had been allocated to a cadet Habsburg branch, but it was a development which ran clean counter to local inclination. As early as 1718, Philip, under the influence of his second queen, Elisabetta di Farnese, and her Italian favourite Alberoni, sanctioned a somewhat farcical attempt upon Sicily, only to be forestalled by the British navy. Alberoni was representative of many Italians in the entourage of the Spanish court who kept alive its Mediterranean ambitions. Under him, the old imperialist motions were going through, even to the extent of holding discussions with the Old Pretender in Madrid with the object of planning an invasion of England![6] He also (quite appropriately) fostered a revival of the armada in a programme which was continued successfully beyond Alberoni's fall from power in 1719. By the 1730s, less than a generation after the civil war, Spain's military establishment had made an impressive recovery. The war of the 'first Bourbon family compact' between Madrid and Paris witnessed an attack upon southern Italy which threw out the Habsburgs, and an equally successful expedition (30,000 strong) against Oran, the main African *presidio* which had been lost during the War of Succession. Castile's crusading and imperialist fervour was not dead, but it was only capable of revival in the version of Atlantic and Mediterranean endeavour which had predated the Habsburgs and the Spanish system. All the same, when one considers that Philip V's long reign of forty-five years saw barely a decade of peace, it is clear that the horizons of the new century encompassed very familiar terrain.

The lack of any substantial material improvement during (at least) the first half of the century tends, if anything, to confirm this impression. Stripped of later Bourbon propaganda, this era was one of the great hopes and little achievement, indistinguishable from some phases of seventeenth-century government. Indeed, the demands of war ate into Philip V's revenues more voraciously even than had been the case under Carlos II. At the height of the civil war, expenditure was running at over 10 million *escudos* a year – the defence of Castile alone costing as much as the defence of the empire had cost Philip IV. In these circumstances it is not surprising that no serious reform of *Hacienda* and its tax structure was attempted until the beginning of a new reign, in 1749. Where, after all, was the need? As under the Habsburgs, the

Treasury continued to perform efficiently its essential task of provisioning the war effort. Indeed, it was the reform of the coinage and the drastic deflationary measures of Carlos II's prime ministers, rather than any Bourbon innovation, which enabled Castile to pay her way during the great military crisis of the civil war. The massive contracts with French firms for the supply of her armies were all discharged. Louis XIV's troops in the peninsula were fully maintained by Castile between 1704–9 and again in 1710–13. In 1717, twenty ships, the nucleus of a new armada, were purchased outright from France, and the succeeding decade saw enormous military and naval expenditure, comparable to that of Olivares a century before.

During this period, too, there was little sign of decisive population recovery; indeed, if anything, the expansion which had begun under the last Habsburg actually slowed down under his successor. After the nadir of the 1650s (between 5 and 6 million) the demographic level of Castile and Aragon improved to perhaps 7 million by 1700, mainly because of the performance of Catalonia. Yet estimates for the middle of the eighteenth century suggest a total only some 500,000 higher, indicating that Spain had still not regained the population standards of 1580 (B14). On the other hand, this population was much more evenly and securely distributed, since the centrifugal tendencies evident since 1600 had continued, resulting in a doubling of the figures for Catalonia, Galicia, Asturias and the Basque provinces, and a tripling of that for Valencia. Not surprisingly, demography and economy stagnated during the peninsular war of 1704–14. The rural devastation caused purely by campaign should not be exaggerated. Spain was virtually a sideshow compared to the wars in Flanders and the Rhineland, and the average size of the armies which met in battle was smaller than Marlborough's casualty list at the single engagement of Malplaquet. What seems important was that the main theatres of conflict – the borderlands of Portugal and of Catalonia – were identical to those which had already suffered prolonged debilitation through war in 1640–68 (and, in the later case, 1674–97). The subsistence crisis of 1708–10, moreover, again hit Andalusia particularly hard. Seville, for example, which had lost no less than 60,000 citizens in the plague of 1647, was once more severely reduced. Nevertheless, the era of general famine and epidemic disease was coming to an end, and agricultural changes along with steady economic improvement began to correct the worst features of the structural deficiencies of Spain. The Bourbon government was more inclined to take an active interest in industrial and commercial projects, through financial inducement and direct participation in manufacture – for instance, in textiles and metallurgy. Furthermore, the adoption of more efficient types of trade protection, and a limited number of technological advances, provided greater incentives and employment.

The effect of Gallic administrative nostrums was much more dramatic at the level of central government itself. The actual exercise of royal authority, in abeyance under Carlos II, was now thoroughly resuscitated. It is true that large numbers of the titled aristocracy who had deserted the Bourbon colours (including even some who had taken up residence at the court of Vienna) were in due course pardoned. They repossessed their estates, along with the wealth and local political influence these entailed. But their alleged rights of intervention in the central processes of royal government were now annihilated, in a system which became steadily more meritocratic and technocratic in nature. The emasculation of the Castilian *grandeza* interestingly coincided with the recovery of the political power of the French aristocracy during the French regency, so that, in a sense, Louis XIV's style of absolutism was transferred to Spain. This did not, of course, involve any real change in social conditions for the mass of Spaniards, but it did help to fulfil some of the ideals which such men as Ronquillo had envisaged. Both conciliar administration and official regional distinctions had been swept away during the civil war. The Castilian Cortes, which had not met even during the reign of Carlos II, was called henceforth only to confirm the status of the heir to the throne, or to take the oath of allegiance upon his succession. Castile's taxes which made up the *servicio* traditionally granted by the Cortes were now fixed and levied arbitrarily. The abolition of the estates and *fueros* (privileges) of the crown of Aragon in 1707 had a similar effect for the historic regions of the peninsula. The control of this newly united Spain resided in a privy council, headed by a secretary who effectively exercised the powers of chief minister; though again (as his title of *Secretario del Despacho Universal* indicates) this partly derived from late Habsburg precedents, particularly the work of Eguía. Despite the contribution of energetic Frenchmen on secondment before 1715, as Dr Kamen concludes, 'in policy and personnel, the Bourbon regime in Spain was Spanish and not French' (G6).

The prolonged emergency of the civil war, and the definitive loss of the northern European provinces, thus brought about a salutary simplification and streamlining of government in Madrid. It was a violent (if neither profound nor revolutionary) shock, which created conditions in which many of the basic reforms preached by the *arbitristas* throughout the previous century were established. These, in turn, permitted a gradual retrenchment and reorganisation of Spain's material resources which was to bring a kind of prosperity and stability unknown for two centuries or more. Even from our present standpoint, when the country is witnessing a (periodic) resurgence of regional feeling, it is possible to conclude that the destruction of the

Spanish monarchy helped to create a Spanish nation. Furthermore, as some Spanish statesmen had long realised, the amputation of Flanders and Italy from the monarchy materially benefited its government and economy. It restored to Spain a mastery of its own destinies, by emancipating external policy, and thus (indirectly) internal behaviour, from the onerous demands of *reputación*, the incubus of an impossible empire. If only by default, the inchoate ideals of the *Comuneros* had at last triumphed. The end of the Spanish system was therefore the beginning of Spain's independence.

APPENDIX 1

References

The following acronyms and abbreviations have been used for the documentary sources of the quotations and of some specific citations in the text. Volume and page (or folio) numbers are given in addition to the relevant series. Some ms. unfoliated documents are identified by date. Material in scholarly articles is noted under name of author, periodical title, and date of publication. An asterisk indicates that this reference is also the source of an immediately preceding quotation.

Archival Sources

AGS   Archivo General de Simancas (Spain).
           ES   Estado Series.
AHN   Archivo Histórico Nacional (Madrid).
           ES   Estado Series.
ARB   Archives du Royaume de Belgique (Brussels).
           SE   Sécrétairerie d'Etat et de Guerre Series.
BL   British Library (London).
           EG   Egerton Mss.
           AD   Additional Mss.
           HA   Harleian Mss.
BN   Biblioteca Nacional (Madrid).
           SA   Sucesos de Año Series.
           CO   Colección Osuna.
           PV   Papeles Varios.
PRO   Public Record Office (London).
           SS   State Papers, Spain.
           SF   State Papers, Flanders.
           GT   Gardiner Transcripts.

Printed Sources

CCE   *Correspondance de la Cour de l'Espagne sur les affaires des Pays-Bas*, Vol. 4 (Brussels, 1933).
CDI   *Colección de Documentos Inéditos para la Historia de España*, 112 vols (Madrid, 1854–90).
Díaz-Plaja Fernando Díaz-Plaja (ed.), *La Historia de España en sus Documentos: el Siglo XVII* (Madrid, 1957).
Flores   Xavier Flores (ed.), *Le 'Peso Político de Todo el Mundo' par Antony Sherley* (Paris, 1963).
Hargreaves W. M. Hargreaves-Mawdsley (ed.), *Spain under the Bourbons* (London, 1973).
HI   *Hispania Illustrata, or the Maxims of the Spanish Court fully laid open . . .* (London, 1703).

Melia   A. Paz y Melia (ed.), *Los Avisos de Jerónimo de Barrionuevo*, 2 vols
             (Madrid, 1968–9).
Serrano   C. Seco Serrano (ed.), *Cartas de la venerable Sor María de Ágreda y del
             Señor Rey Don Felipe IV*, 2 vols (Madrid, 1958).
Shaw   D. L. Shaw (ed.), *Historia de los primeros años del reinado de Felipe IV de
             Virgilio Malvezzi* (London, 1968).
Stanhope   *Spain under Charles II; or, Extracts from the Correspondence of the Hon.
             Alexander Stanhope, 1690–99* (London, 1844).

References to General Introduction

1 Díaz-Plaja, 5.
2 See H. Lapeyre, *Las Monarquías Europeas del siglo XVI* (Barcelona, 1975), 257.
3 G. Ungerer (ed.), *A Spaniard in Elizabethan England. The Correspondence of
   Antonio Pérez*, 2 vols (London, 1974–6), I, 48.
4 V. von Klarwill (ed.) *The Fugger Newsletters* (London, 1926), II, 258.
5 C. – P. Clasen, *The Palatinate in European History, 1555–1618* (Oxford, 1963).

References to Chapter 1

1   See A. Domínguez Ortiz, *Anuario de Estudios Americanos* (1956).
2   BN SA/2348/533.
3   Flores, 71.
4   BL EG/543/115.
5   Flores, *passim*.
6   BL EG/335/318v.
7   BL AD/6902/225.
8   BN SA/2360/340.
9   BL EG/335/394v.
10 BL AD/21004/380.
11 ARB SE/183/65v.
12 BL EG/318/216.
13 Shaw, 96.
14 PRO GT/31/12/32.
15 BL EG/318/200.
16 ibid.
17 London, 1624.
18 See G. Davies, *University of Leeds Review* (1977).
19 T. Scot, *Certain Reasons and Arguments of Policy . . .* (London, 1624).
20 T. Scot, *The Second Part of Vox Populi . . .* (London, 1624).
21 ARB SE/183/38.
22 See L. van der Essen, *Revista de la Universidad de Madrid* (1954).
23 BN SA/2348/351.
24 ibid., 463v.
25 Shaw, 46–9.
26 Flores, 157.

References to Chapter 2

1   See L. van der Essen, *Le Cardinal-Infante et la politique Européenne de l'Espagne* (Brussels, 1944), 4.
2   PRO SS/42/148v.
3   *CDI*, 86/183–5.
4   J. Deleito y Piñuela, *El Declinar de la Monarquía Española* (Madrid, 1955 edn), 80–6.
5   Shaw, 163.
6   BL AD/14007/45.
7   ibid., 365.
8   PRO SS/42/32.
9   ARB SE/229/89v.
10 AGS ES/2061/10.
11 Above, n. 8.
12 BN PV/2396/71v.
13 BN PV/1935/74.
14 ARB SE/204/49bis.
15 ARB SE/229/84.
16 ARB SE/230/62.
17 Serrano, I, liv–lv.
18 AGS ES/2042/23 April 1628.
19 ibid., 7 March 1629.
20 ARB SE/201/28.
21 ARB SE/204/232–6.
22 BL AD/25689/395.
23 AHN ES/694/no. 5.
24 See C. Burckhardt, *Richelieu and His Age* (London 1940), I, 126. (I am grateful to Dr Nora Temple for drawing this to my attention.)
25 C. Garcia, *The Antipathy between the French and the Spaniard*, trans. R. Gentylis (London, 1641).
26 *CDI*, 82/26.
27 BL AD/28452/233.
28 Flores, 58 (my emphasis).
29 H. and P. Chaunu, *Annales, ESC* (1954).
30 PRO SS/42/24.
31 BN SA/2361/499.

References to Chapter 3

1   Serrano, I, 35.
2   *CDI*, 82/x.
3   PRO SS/43/205.
4   Melia, I, 243.
5   AHN ES/674/No. 10; ibid., 2815/2 December 1652.
6   AGS ES/2090/27 June 1657.
7   *CDI*, 95/199–200.
8   Melia, I, 202.
9   *CCE*, 179.
10 *CDI*, 59/215.
11 AGS ES/K1420/No. 88.

12   Serrano, I, 30–3.*
13   BL EG/340/108.
14   Melia, I, 311–14.
15   *CDI*, 82/37 and 53.
16   W. Abbott, *Writings and Speeches of Oliver Cromwell* (London, 1944), III, 876–8*.
17   See S. von Bischoffshausen, *Die Politik des Protectors Oliver Cromwell* . . . (Innsbruck, 1899), 190.
18   *CCE*, 98.
19   A. Domínguez Ortiz, *Alteraciones Andaluzas* (Madrid, 1973).

References to Chapter 4

1   See van der Essen, *Le Cardinal-Infante* . . . , 44.
 2   H. Kamen, *Economic History Review* (1964).
 3   A. Rodríguez Villa (ed.), *Misión Secreta del Embajador D. Pedro Ronquillo en Polonia* (1674) (Madrid, ?1874), 5.
 4   R. Hatton (ed.), *Louis XIV and Europe* (London, 1976), xii.
 5   Serrano, II, 170.
 6   Melia, II, 64.
 7   ibid., I, 168 and II, 6.*
 8   M. Morineau, *Annales, ESC* (1968).
 9   BN CO/10838/391v.
10   BN PV/2408/150v.
11   PRO SS/44/127.
12   AHN ES/692/13 June 1666.
13   AGS ES/3383/155v.
14   Díaz-Plaja, 424–9.
15   Melia, I, 251.
16   J. Reglà, *Historia de España y América* (Barcelona, 1971), III, 292.
17   AGS ES/3861/28 April 1678.
18   A. Domínguez Ortiz, *Hispania* (1959).
19   PRO SF/31/444.
20   K. Feiling, *British Foreign Policy, 1660–72* (London, 1930), 41.
21   H. Lonchay, *Le Rivalité de la France et de l'Espagne aux Pays-Bas, 1635–1700* (Brussels, 1896), 294.
22   *HI*, 140–2.
23   AGS ES/3861/17 January 1672.
24   *HI*, 190.
25   AGS ES/2553/14 January 1677.
26   BN CO/10129/556.
27   PRO SS/45/173 (my emphasis).
28   AGS ES/3861/10 January 1677.
29   For the material of the following paragraphs, see my unpublished doctoral thesis, 'Anglo-Spanish Relations, 1660–8' (University of Wales, 1968), Ch. 3, and sources there cited.
30   AGS ES/3383/65.
31   AGS ES/3861/17 July 1674.

References to Chapter 5

1   BN PV/2408/414.
2   Díaz-Plaja, 475.
3   BL AD/8703/141.
4   PRO SS/34/143.
5   BN CO/11034/146.
6   J. Dunlop, *Memoirs of Spain in the Reigns of Philip IV and Charles II* (Edinburgh, 1834), II, 281.
7   Stanhope, 57–8.
8   AGS ES/3874/16 February 1684.
9   Díaz-Plaja, 453.
10 AGS ES/3874/19 February 1684.
11 Díaz-Plaja, 450–1.
12 Stanhope, 42.
13 AGS ES/3861/27 September 1677.
14 Dunlop, op. cit., II, 155.
15 BN CO/10129/500.
16 Duque de Maura (ed.), *Correspondencia entre dos Embajadores, 1689–91* (Madrid, 1951–2), I, 134.
17 AGS ES/3903/13 October 1693.
18 Stanhope, 22 and 61.
19 AGS ES/3903/2 November 1696.*
20 Hargreaves, 6.
21 BL HA/7010/337.
22 PRO SS/74/313–14.
23 A. Domínguez Ortiz, *Homenaje a Jaime Viçens Vives* (Barcelona, 1967), II, 124.
24 AGS ES/3874/19 February 1684.
25 ARB SE/287/38.
26 Stanhope, 55.
27 AHN ES/2815/30 March 1697.
28 PRO SS/74/11.
29 Díaz-Plaja, 461.
30 BN PV/2489/5.

References to General Conclusion

1   See Hatton, op. cit., 39.
2   Hargreaves, 1.
3   ibid., 17.
4   M. Áviles Fernández *et al.*, *La Instauracion Borbónica* (Madrid, 1973), 26–7.
5   Hargreaves, 34.
6   H. Livermore, *A History of Spain* (London, 1958), 327.

APPENDIX 2

Glossary of Spanish Terms

Adehalas	Service charges on the raising and transfer of government loans.
Alfárez	Royal conscription official (army).
Arbitrista	Writer who is analytical (often pertinently) of Spain's social, economic or demographic problems.
Asentista	Businessman having a contractual relationship with the Spanish system; used here normally to describe the large banking houses.
Asiento	Any contract with Spanish administration(s).
Asientos de dinero	The annual short-term loans negotiated for defence purposes and at high rates of interest.
Caudillo	Military chief or (more recently) dictator.
Comuneros	The great revolt of the Castilian towns against Charles V (1520–1), still having a mythic potency in Spain.
Conservación	See p. 27.
Consulta	The formal report of a council or junta to the king, usually containing detailed minutes of discussion and advice on action.
Corregidor	Royal official in the localities.
Cortes	Irregular assembly of Castilian municipal delegates with restricted, even specialised, legal and financial powers.
Cronista	Contemporary observer and chronicler of political events.
Donativo	Money gift to the king (without prejudice), usually not unsolicited, sometimes a compound for legal dues.
Ducado (Ducat)	Unit of financial accounting (not a coin); the contemporary English equivalent was nearly five shillings.
Empresa	Great military (usually 'amphibious') enterprise.
Escudo	Standard gold coin of exchange, worth slightly less than a *ducado*.
Estado, Consejo de	The Council of State, regular – but neither supreme nor exclusive – policy-making committee.
Flota	Annual convoyed trading fleets sailing to and from the American colonies.
Grandeza	The status of 'grandee', traditional pinnacle of the noble caste.
Hacienda, Consejo de	The Royal Council of Finance (Treasury).
Hidalgo	Lesser noble category, encompassing nearly half a million Spaniards, and ranging in economic terms from the wealthy 'squire' to the impoverished 'gentleman'.
Maestro de Campo	The field commander of a company, usually also its raiser, 'owner' and paymaster.
Nobleza	Signifies strictly the nobility as a whole, more often used to represent its higher echelons.

Pagador	Royal official (civilian) who administered army accounts.
Pícaro	Vagrant (often criminal) type, characterised in the 'picaresque' novel of the period.
Presidio	Spanish fortified outpost, usually coastal (North Africa and Italy).
Privado	A close adviser of the king. Usually one of a number, and may or may not have ministerial office or political standing; thus not identical with *valido*.
Real de a ocho	Standard silver coin of exchange, worth four-fifths of an *escudo*.
Reputación	See p. 27.
Señor	Any noble (or ecclesiastical) landowner.
Servicio	Castile's regular tax concession to the crown, the integrated total of which was negotiated with the *Cortes*.
Tercio	Regiment of infantry (Spanish, Italian or Walloon), originally designed to be 3,000 strong, but rarely more than one-third that size in this period.
Vellón	Copper coinage issued (beginning with Philip III) for circulation in Castile, and much debased.
Valido	The king's closest intimate, political mentor and chief minister, a unique status 'institutionalised' in the *Valimiento*. Only roughly approximating to the English 'favourite'.

Index